Screen Saver

Private Stories of Public Hollywood

Screen Saver

Private Stories of Public Hollywood

*For David Kleiler =
You've seen the play;
now read the book.*

BY NAT SEGALOFF

Some of the material in this book originally appeared in different forms in *The Boston Herald, Boston After Dark, The Tab, Backstory 3 & 4* and HollywoodDementia.com. In all cases the copyrights remain with, or have reverted to, the author. Their appearance here should be considered the preferred text. Excerpts from non-auctorial interviews and other material appear under a Fair Use Rights claim of U.S. Copyright Law, Title 17, U.S.C. with copyrights reserved by their respective rights holders.

Photographs from the Nat Segaloff Special Collection are courtesy of the UCLA Performing Arts Library with thanks to Genie Guerard, Julie Graham, Cesar Reyes, and Simon Elliott.

Many of the designations used by manufacturers to distinguish their products are claimed as trademarks or service marks. Where those designations appear in this book and the author and/or BearManor Media was aware of such a claim, the designations contain the symbols ®, ℠, or™. Any omission of these symbols is purely accidental and is not intended as an infringement.

Oscar®, Academy Award®, and AMPAS® are registered trademarks of the Academy of Motion Picture Arts and Sciences ©AMPAS.

Library of Congress Control Number: 2016912451
BearManor Media, Duncan, OK
Segaloff, Nat, 1948 –
Screen Saver: Private Stories of Public Hollywood /

The motion picture stills in this work were provided without restriction at the time of their films' release and the publisher has included them in good faith. Any photographs in question will be removed from future editions upon presentation of proof of ownership.

Published in the USA by:
BearManor Media
P O Box 71426
Albany, Georgia 31708
www.bearmanormedia.com

Printed in the United States of America
ISBN   978-1-59393-958-8 (paperback)

Edited by Robben Barquist
Cover Illustration by Christopher Darling
Book design and layout by Darlene Swanson • www.van-garde.com

For my former colleagues in
the Boston press corps
but especially to
Marjory Adams, Peggy Doyle,
and Donald H. Cragin
who taught me the ropes.

"The tragedy of film history is that it is fabricated, falsified, by the very people who make film history. It is understandable that in the early years of film production, when nobody believed there was going to be any film history, most film magazines and books printed trash . . . But since about 1950 film has been established as an art, and its history recognized as a serious matter. Yet film celebrities continue to cast themselves as stock types—nice or naughty girls, good or bad boys—whom their chroniclers spray with a shower of anecdotes."

~ Louise Brooks, *Lulu in Hollywood*, 1974 & 1982

Contents

Preface

Hollywood was dead; long live Hollywood. The studio system that had flourished for half a century was in mid-crumble when I got my first job promoting it in 1970. Over the next five years I would watch it collapse and be rebuilt by a new generation of filmmakers that took over and began making the changes that would lead—for good or ill—to today's corporate system of homogenized tent pole blockbusters, sequels, franchises, reboots, and do-or-die opening weekends. In essence, they killed the very thing that made them love movies in the first place, and yet they also reenergized a staid medium, expanded its technology, and made it respond to the international market.

This is the world in which I made my modest way. If the stories seem disjointed—I prefer to call them picaresque—it's because I want them to be about other people, not me, even though I'm the one who was there to witness them. In this, I had the best of both worlds. Ordinarily, movie publicists see everything but say nothing while movie journalists see nothing but say everything. When I became a movie journalist, I called upon the contacts and knowledge I'd amassed as a movie publicist to inform my reporting. This made many people nervous. (They're the ones who checked the index of this book for their names before buying it.) First a little background.

Some time after I stopped being afraid of her, I asked Marjory Adams—who had covered movies for fifty-two years for *The Boston Globe*—if she'd kept a scrapbook of her many articles and celebrity interviews. Her answer surprised me: "Of course not! You see, little love, if you're any good, people will remember you, and if you're not, a scrapbook won't help."

Whether I'm any good by Marjory's measure will be revealed in the next pages, but I hedged against fate by saving tearsheets and tapes anyway. Everything that follows is as true as those tapes, tearsheets, and memory permit.

You haven't heard of me because you weren't supposed to. For forty years my job was to keep other people in the spotlight. From 1970 to 1975, I worked as a publicist for major motion picture companies, handling celebrities who would come through town promoting their latest films. You'd think celebrities would be on their best behavior while a guest in someone else's town, but that wasn't always the case.

At the end of 1975, I got fed up with publicity, and vice-versa, so I crossed the professional street and became, for the next thirty-five years and in various combinations, a film critic, author, producer, broadcaster, and teacher. These professions, when practiced properly, share one attribute: in each of them, the story is more important than the person telling it. I have tried to keep myself out of this book as much as possible and report as just an observer. If it's unclear at times whether I'm speaking as a publicist or a journalist, be assured that the two jobs never overlapped, either in my mind or in my bank account.

This was a transitional time for the American film industry. For half a century it had been the domain of established studios that dominated the world movie market. In the middle 1960s, however, Hollywood began to change and become more corporate, less adventurous, and shamefully uninterested in showmanship. The tipping point was two-pronged: first the Baby Boomers emerged as the primary entertainment market, and then film school graduates started working their way into the motion picture industry. The two came together, it's fair to say, with *Easy Rider* in 1969, a film the old moguls couldn't understand and a massive youth audience embraced. I was fortunate to be an onlooker during this era and I paid attention.

But first there are a fair number of people I want to thank for their help along the way, both in writing this book and in the years it took me to have something to write about. Many are mentioned in these pages, and some can be best thanked by not mentioning them at all. Additionally, I offer my sweeping gratitude to (alphabetically) Leslie Agnew, Phil Alcuri, David Austin, Terry Barker, George H. Bentley, Liane Brandon, Robert Brown, David Brudnoy, Raymond J. Carrier, Eileen Cushing, Garen Daly, Kirsten Davis, Bob Ecker, Harlan and Susan Ellison, George Fall, Richard Farkas, Karl Fasick, Gary Fleder, David M. Forbes, Bill Gitt, Carl Goldman, Paul Gonthier, Ellis Gordon, Tom Gray, Gary H. Grossman, Sonny Grosso, Jane Badgers Harris, Linda Harris, Dana Hersey, Ralph and Molly Hoagland, Andy Hoy, Larry Jacobson, John H. Jones, Mike Kaplan (the elder), Mike Kaplan (the younger), Tom Kauycheck, Daniel M. Kimmel, Gayle Kirschenbaum, Don Kopaloff, Barry Krost, Bruce Laing, Frank Lane, Meg LaVigne, Susan Leeds, Malcolm Leo, Leonard and Alice Maltin, Russell Manker, Virginia Meyn, Rochelle O'Gorman, Jane Oakley, Anne Oliver, James Robert Parish, David Permut, Norman R. Poretsly, Arnie Reisman, Bob Rich, Julian Rifkin, Melanie Rose, Tom Ryder, Larry Silverman, Clark Smidt, Donald B. Spragg, Fred Spring, Barry Steelman, Allan Taylor, Maureen Taylor, Joyce Teitz, Chris Telladira, Bill Tunis, Wayne Wadhams, Fran Weil, Robb Weller, Bill Wight, and Ira Yerkes.

Particular thanks to my former Boston colleague and Los Angeles friend Myron Meisel for his intelligent counsel and approbative memory. Thanks as well to Nikki Finke who publishes my showbiz fiction on her website, HollywoodDementia.com.

Agnes Birnbaum of Bleecker Street Associates had faith in me even when every publisher (until Ben Ohmart) did not, and I thank her for her friendship and her efforts.

Finally, as always, I thank Ami, Ivanna, Joseph Benjamin (JB), and Adam Lahmani for the gift of love, which goes in both directions.

A note on quotes: except where cited otherwise, all the quotes in this book are drawn from either my formal recorded interviews with the people at the time I worked with them or from my memory of those encounters. This is a memoir, not a deposition.

— Nat Segaloff, Los Angeles

Screen Saver

C OME OVER for dinner," Barbara O'Kun said in her ever-cheerful way.
"It's Lan's birthday and we've invited a few friends."

I'd met Lan and Barbara O'Kun in 1995 when I was making the A&E
Biography about her older sister, ventriloquist Shari Lewis.[1] Shari had
shaped my childhood with her characters Lamb Chop, Charlie Horse, and
Hush Puppy and, when she and I taped our interviews for the show, I was
as seduced by her puppets as I was by her. Not only did her lips never move,
the illusion was so complete that I spent the hour blissfully talking to a gym
sock in her right hand.

Like Shari, Barbara had begun a show business career that included
modeling and dance, but she ultimately forsook it when she married her
childhood sweetheart, Lan O'Kun. Lan was a magician with keyboards of
both piano and typewriter. For thirty years he wrote Shari's skits and songs
and collaborated with her in the creation of Lamb Chop and Hush Puppy.
Perhaps because he mastered telling stories to children, he became a captivating adult griot.

Unlike Shari and Lan, however, Barbara shunned the spotlight, becoming an in-demand upscale interior designer. When Lan agreed to an interview for my show, Barbara accompanied him cautiously, unsure whether she
wanted to appear on camera. Once we met, however, and she saw that we

---

1   "Shari Lewis & Lamb Chop"

were telling a positive story, she changed her mind and gave a lovely interview that not only graced the show but led to an enduring friendship. Over the years we spent many dinners, movies, and Fourths of July together.

I looked forward to seeing them again and meeting their friends for the birthday party. When I arrived at their Malibu home, however, I was surprised that there were no lines of cars as I'd seen at other showbiz affairs. There was no music coming from the house, not even Lan's piano playing. Was this the wrong night? I rang the doorbell with uncertainty, but almost immediately Barbara answered with a bright, "Oh, good, now everybody's here. Come in and I'll introduce you."

Two steps inside and I understood why there were no valets. Instead of a house full of revelers, the table was set for an intimate seven: Lan and Barbara, Dom and Carol DeLuise, Martin and Janet Sheen. And me.

I was the only person in the room that I didn't recognize.

Of course, I had encountered both Sheen and DeLuise over the years as a reporter, asking questions and taking down their answers, either in hotel room interviews or press junkets in one city or another. Strictly business. Neither remembered me from any of these encounters, nor did I expect him to (some reporters fantasize that they bond with the people they interview, but that's part of the seduction process).[2] Besides, this was a social occasion. And I'm proud to say I had the good sense to shut up and take only mental notes.

The DeLuises and the Sheens were long-time friends of the O'Kuns but— unlike what everybody thinks about Hollywoodites—they had never before spent time with each other. As the evening passed, I watched a miraculous exchange: both Martin and Dom bonded as actors and as men. Each recalled entering his profession and, in particular, the difficulty he'd had earning his father's approval. Dom told how his junior high school teacher made a trip to his Brooklyn home to persuade his parents to allow their son to attend a new school that was just about to open in Manhattan, the High School for the

---

2   I did, however, become friends with Dom subsequent to this, as will be told later.

Performing Arts. Despite the teacher's assurances that their son had talent, it was years before Dom's father, who was a city garbage worker, accepted the fact. "All-a you do is-a da-talk?" Dom repeated in his father's Italian accent, adding that, no matter how successful he became, his father always assured him, "You still got-a your room here" if he ever needed to move back home.

Martin told a similar story. Born Ramon Estevez to an immigrant family, he had to justify both his craft and his masculinity when he announced that he wanted to take up acting. It was such a foreign discipline that he was never sure whether his father understood why he pursued it. Finally, on the night he opened on Broadway in *The Subject was Roses* in 1964, Sheen, then twenty-four, waited in his dressing room after curtain. His father came backstage and entered hesitantly, clearly moved by his son's performance yet unable to make eye contact. He stared at the floor and managed to mumble that his son indeed had talent and that he now understood what the boy had been trying to tell him all along.

The night was more of a revelation for me than it was for either of these world-famous figures. I had been working with celebrities for thirty years, first as a publicist, then as a reporter, but always as a fan. What I took home from this evening was an understanding of the many levels of fame and the conflicts that rage within the heart and soul of those who dwell in the public eye. Neither Sheen nor DeLuise chose his profession desiring celebrity. Both just wanted to act and, because of talent, luck, and timing, both became famous. How each used his notoriety—Sheen to effect social change and Dom to lift the spirits of countless people—is a testament to their character that is seldom seen by outsiders.

Too many people confuse fame with leadership. Leadership has a purpose. Fame does not. I was famous for a split-second in the late 1970s when I was a regular on a Group W TV series called *Evening Magazine* (a franchised version of it was known as *P.M. Magazine*). After two or three months on the air, I began to be recognized in public. For some reason, this happened mostly in Chinese restaurants. But it was an odd kind of recognition: even though my name was spoken and superimposed every time I appeared, people who stopped me on the street only knew me as, "the guy on that TV show." This taught me an important lesson: television is a medium that conveys impressions well and facts less well. (If you think I'm wrong, name two stories and their reporters from the last newscast you saw.)

Fame was awkward. I'm not shy, but it's strange to have complete strangers come up and recognize you. Even before social media made stalking a sport, it was creepy. For four years I covered entertainment and public affairs for WEEI-FM, the CBS radio station in Boston, and time and again I'd be chatting with someone at a party when suddenly he or she would recognize my voice and I could see his or her face change expression, signaling recognition and, with it, an end to our substantive conversation. Where I believe that reporters should cover a story and not be the story, I grew increasingly uncomfortable with even my limited level of notoriety. I began to wonder what sort of person actually *wanted* to be famous, and I began to marvel at the way extraordinarily famous people dealt with it. It took years before I saw the best of the best in action. It was after a play opening in Los Angeles. I was backstage with the friend who had brought me there and was talking to one of the actors. My friend elbowed me to meet the people she was talking to. I ignored her as long as I could and then spun around, prepared to ask her why she was being so rude. Instead, she asked me matter-of-factly, "Nat, you know Brad and Angelina, don't you?"

Yes, it was Brad Pitt and Angelina Jolie, two of the most exquisitely beautiful—not to mention famous—people on the planet. We shook hands and proceeded to chat about world hunger and the importance of getting help to sub-Saharan Africa. Silently, ten feet to one side, someone quietly pulled out a SmartPhone and aimed it at the famous pair. You don't do this backstage. Backstage is off the record. Pitt instantly noticed this breach. But instead of making a scene, he looked directly at the interloper and gently shook his head while mouthing, "No." Then he continued our conversation, disarming the would-be paparazzo without making either a fuss or an enemy. *That* is stardom.

Fame, like Pringles, is artificial. Unlike Pringles, it has no preservatives. Fame carries with it the illusion of achievement. If it's the Pope, the achievement is self-evident. If it's a Kardashian, it's non-existent. This is what makes a celebrity; indeed, the definition of a "celebrity" is someone who is famous for being famous, not for having done anything in particular. This book is not about them.

⚜

Allow me to establish a personal baseline.

I was born in Washington, DC where fame and power are local crops that are harvested every election, but they don't travel well. I moved to Boston for college in the turbulent late 1960s and lived there off and on for the next two decades, moving to Los Angeles in 1993. For five years in Boston and New York I was a movie publicist, and then, in Boston, a reporter covering the film industry as a business. The stories in these pages happened when I was first one and then the other. I was never both at the same time.

While in college, I haunted the local sales offices of the Hollywood studios hoping to make contacts that could pull me to California. This was a time of great uncertainty for them. The old-line studios were crumbling and the film brats were on the cusp of changing movies forever, although word of the revolution hadn't yet seeped out of Los Angeles, where most of it was happening at the University of Southern California (USC) and the University of California at Los Angeles (UCLA). Other schools that offered courses of study, such as Harvard, New York University (NYU), and Boston University (BU), insisted that film was art, not commerce. But USC and UCLA were no fools, and up-and-coming young agents prowled their halls in search of matriculating clients. The American Film Institute had just been chartered, and they looked promising, but one of their first academic moves was banning agents from the premises (craftier students found ways around this).

Then came *Easy Rider* in 1969. The story of "a man who went looking for America but couldn't find it anywhere," it bitch-slapped staid Hollywood into realizing that there was such thing as a youth market. Trouble was, the conglomerates that had bought the studios were afraid of the free sex, drugs, politics, and music that came with it. Emblematic of the dichotomy was a response given by Peter Fonda. Someone challenged him, "If you're such a rebel, how come you make films in Hollywood?" to which the *Easy Rider* star/producer answered, "Because they have all the cameras." This would change as lightweight film and video equipment got cheaper and became more available.

And then YouTube turned every kid's bedroom into a movie studio.

The chasm between art and commerce was ingrained at Boston University's School of Public Communication where I, like others of my privileged generation, had been avoiding the Vietnam War draft while learning about film. (I would later return as an instructor to teach my students what I had failed to be taught ten years earlier.) During the first week of May, 1970, our group of tyro filmmakers was holed up in BU's basement screening room running our final projects when word arrived of the violence at Kent State University in Ohio. Like an expanding number of schools across the country, students at Kent State had been protesting President Nixon's and Secretary of State Henry Kissinger's illegal invasion of Cambodia. On May fourth, Ohio Governor Jim Rhodes called out the National Guard to quell the protests. The young Guardsmen, frightened and poorly commanded but armed to the gills, fired sixty-seven rounds into the unarmed protesters, killing four and wounding nine others. Campuses across America exploded in frustration and outrage.

In response, Boston University's administrators canceled classes, called off final exams, and dismissed the student body, urging everyone to go home to avoid violence. (This was disingenuous; it later came out that some administrators had singled out certain dissidents for police to clobber during demonstrations).

While this was going on, we continued to run our student films until Professor Robert Steele, an aesthete with the soul of a radical, slashed into the darkness of our screening room and challenged us, "Why aren't you out there in the streets? You're filmmakers, you should be with the people!" Like idiots, we responded, "Because our job is to preserve history, not make it." It sounded pretty good at the time. In truth, it was selfish, lazy, and, worse, the most reprehensible thing an artist can be: cautious.

The Kent State killings changed that for us, as it did for my whole generation. The day I left school I lost my student deferment and was reclassified as fit for duty. With thousands of other young men that summer, I reported to the Boston Army Base for my pre-induction physical. The Army had shrewdly staffed the facility with draftees rather than enlistees on the belief that we would feel more sympathetic toward those who also had no choice, but the air still crackled with anti-war energy. Throughout the long day of standing in lines, turning this way and that, coughing, and filling in forms, there were interruptions from guys who were feigning insanity, acting effeminate, overly medicated, or just plain anti-war. Once an hour we would randomly starting chanting, "All we are saying/Is give peace a chance." When that didn't get a rise from the protest-hardened military personnel, we started singing, even louder, "You can get anything you want at Alice's Restaurant," in acknowledgment of Arlo Guthrie's epic song about being rejected by the Army because he had once been arrested for littering.[3]

Alas, there was no littering at the Boston Army Base. But I was surprised when I was discovered to have an accelerated heartbeat. To make sure it was my heart and not drugs or fear (in those days it could have been both), they told me to get a doctor's certificate confirming my condition over a three-day test span. I asked around and was given the name of a physician not far from Boston University. After filling out more papers in his office and handing the receptionist my Selective Service forms, I was turned over to an attractive nurse who took me into an examining room.

---

3   Years later when I wrote the biography of Arthur Penn, who directed the film of *Alice's Restaurant*, I told him this story and he smiled in appreciation.

ave a fast heartbeat," she said, reading the paperwork.

at surprised me. I was hoping for a bad back."

bly nervous," she reasoned. "But 120 beats a minute is

"If it stays there, will they draft me?"

"Never. You'd be too much of a liability, not necessarily on the battle-field, but in the veterans benefits they'd have to pay if you had a coronary."

"What should I do?" I asked.

"You see that door there?" she smiled. "It leads to the stairwell. Run up and down a couple flights and come back here so I can take your pulse."

When I returned, thoroughly winded, I topped at 130 and nearly passed out. I returned the next morning and afternoon, when we did it again. And another day. As I was leaving on the second afternoon, she confided to me that her husband was one of the organizers of the anti-war groups at nearby Brandeis University and that she, herself, had helped arrange medical ex-emptions for draft-eligible men. I went home that night happily anticipating liberation the next morning when she took my final reading. When I got there, however, the receptionist said, "The doctor himself asked to take your pulse rate. Follow me."

She led me down the hall to a private examining room where the doctor was sitting at a desk checking a patient's chart. "Why don't you lie down on the table?" he said, barely looking in my direction. I turned my head to get a look at the chart he was reading. It was mine. Then I looked on the wall across from him. Hanging there was a framed picture of President Nixon.

"Your heart rate is pretty fast for someone your age," the Republican right-wing arch-conservative pro-war John Wayne apple pie motherhood patriotic love-it-or-leave-it screw-Medicare physician declared matter-of-factly. "This is supposed to be a resting heart rate, so why don't you rest for a little while." He kept working.

Fear is the key to adrenaline, but, once you outgrow being afraid of the dark, abstract fear is toothless. I lay on the table, trying to make myself afraid, urging my heart to race. I conjured images of the body counts that the Pentagon issued every Thursday and the television news ritually reported. I thought of seeing the fabled Vietnamese elephant grass in person. I tried to imagine myself unprepared for a final exam, or my car breaking down, or drowning in Boston Harbor. All middle-class, white bread fantasies.

Then I tried yoga. This was presumptuous since I had never done any kind of meditation beyond singing "Ohm" along with a Moody Blues album. Besides, wasn't yoga supposed to calm you down?

Perhaps it was fear of yoga that did the job. Or maybe it was looking at Nixon's puss. When the doctor finally listened to my heart, he made a soft grunt, added up the readings, divided by six, and said, "Well, it looks like you just made it. 120 on the nose." He looked as surprised as I did. But when he asked, "Where can I send the bill?" I knew I was home.

As I left the office, I tried to find the nameless nurse to tell her what her wonderful Democratic left-wing radical anti-war Gene McCarthy activist Amerika-out-of-Vietnam anti-draft boss had done and to thank her for her help. She wasn't there, so I asked if it was her day off.

"No," said the receptionist. "The doctor fired her last night."

There are all kinds of casualties of war.

I was free of my draft obligation but also burdened by the knowledge that, however nobly I had cheated the System, someone else would probably die in my place. Now I needed a job. Fate carried me to Boston's Film Row on a blisteringly hot day in August of 1970. Walking toward me was Carl Goldman, Executive Director of the exhibitors' trade group, T.O.N.E. (Theatre Owners of New England), who smiled and said, "Hi. Do you know Harvey Appell?"

I didn't.

"Harvey is the branch manager for AIP," Carl said. AIP was American-International Pictures, a low-rent company that was famous for beach blanket, motorcycle, and horror films. "He needs somebody quick. They just got some new film or other and he wants someone to do group sales."

AIP. Harvey Appell, then in his mid-forties, wore tinted
curly red hair, and absolutely no pretensions about the

good picture, we wouldn't know what to do with it," he
often said. With such titles in the AIP library as *Wild in the Streets, Scream
and Scream Again, Diary of a High School Bride* and the early Roger Corman
canon, he was as successful as he was honest and direct. His favorite curse
was "I wish you nothing but failure" said with such charm that the recipient
took him seriously, but without offense. I once stood by while he yelled into
the phone, "You owe me film rental and you know what I'm gonna do? I'm
gonna come over to your house, run my car through your front door, pick
up your color television and throw it in the swimming pool that you bought
with the money you owe me, you prick." There was a pause and Harvey said,
"No, I'm not threatening you. Where are we gonna have lunch?"

I was hired to help AIP in general and Harvey in particular. As a part
of the bankruptcy settlement of a company called Commonwealth United
Entertainment, AIP had acquired their slate of completed but unreleased
films, figuring that all they had to do was put up the P&A (prints and advertising) and collect the rental. It seemed like a good deal until they took a
look at the pictures. CUE's roster left little doubt as to why they'd gone belly-
up: *Futz!, Orgasmo, Viva Max, Color Me Dead,* and an early Robert Altman
production, *That Cold Day in the Park.*

The picture they decided upon for their maiden voyage into a sea of red
ink was an all-star production of *Julius Caesar* starring Charlton Heston,
Jason Robards, Jr., John Gielgud, Robert Vaughan, Richard Chamberlain,
Diana Rigg, and Richard Johnson. Figuring (wisely) that people would have
to be dragged kicking and screaming to such culture, Harvey reasoned that
the only way they'd make a buck was selling tickets to every high school
English class in the eastern part of Massachusetts and all of Rhode Island.

As soon as he hired me with a handshake, Harvey said, "Now that you've
got the job, could you send me some kind of resume?" I told him that I had

one with me and was surprised that he hadn't asked for it sooner. "What good's a resume?" he grunted. "Some guys have long resumes and they can't do shit. I need your resume to cover my ass with California." He looked it over and the first thing he saw was my fresh Bachelor's Degree.

"What's the *cum laude*? It looks dirty."

"It means 'with honors.'"

"I knew that. I was testing you. You're a college boy?"

"Um, yeah."

Harvey gets on the intercom. "Hey Joe, Harold, everybody. We got us a college boy."

This college boy started the next Monday and was given a desk facing a corner in the all-female accounting department. Having heard the "college boy" announcement without having met me, accounting clerks Rhoda and Ruthie decided to lay down the law the moment I arrived. Ruthie, a buxom, brassy woman, didn't just speak, she *declared*, making a standing order out of everything from "have a nice day" to "I'm going to make some coffee." Rhoda was her opposite, a chatty, demure, small-featured woman of inde-terminate age. The third woman in the department was the brittle, quick-witted, but discrete Patricia Kelly, who became a friend. But it was Ruthie and Rhoda who saw themselves as AIP's guardians.

Unfortunately, Wes Bishop, the actor-son of comedian Joey Bishop, didn't know this. He was passing through Boston on a publicity tour for a new AIP film and wanted to meet the people who were responsible for han-dling it. Wes happened to walk in the door the morning I was scheduled to arrive. Ruthie and Rhoda thought he was the new Group Sales Director for *Julius Caesar*. They showed him to my desk, read him their rules of conduct, and scared the shit out of the poor kid until Harvey rescued him and set the women straight. That's when I arrived. Having shot their wad on the wrong stranger, Rhoda and Ruthie must have gotten it out of their systems and we all got along.

It was Harvey who laid down the law to me. "Look at your shoes!" he said, pointing at my loafers. "You little *pisher*, what do you mean coming in here without your shoes shined! We may sell trash, but we don't have to look like trash."

My starting salary was a hundred dollars a week with a five dollar/day expense account. In those days a whole case of beer cost five dollars. "Here's how you fill out your expense form," Harvey said, writing down "5" on every line, Monday through Friday, and handing it to me as an example.

"What if I don't spend that much?" I asked.

"Don't be a schmuck," He grumbled. "Just write it down. Nobody checks on five dollars (he actually said "fyedollas"). Lemme show you mine." He slapped his own expense account on his desk. He had written "25" for each day. "This is 'cause I'm the boss. If you actually spend money, keep the receipt, and come to me and we'll figure out how to reimburse you. The important thing," he said, winking, "is don't make me look like a crook. I'll teach you the business, Nathan Detroit. Anybody ever call you Nathan Detroit? You know who Nathan Detroit is, doncha?"

"Sure. *Guys and Dolls.*"

"I was just testing you. Good old reliable Nathan. Just listen to me, *pisher*. I'll be your Professor Higgins. Know where that's from?"

"*Pygmalion.*"

"I figured you'd say that. College boy. Anybody else'd say *My Fair Lady*. Don't be a smart-ass. Go call people."

The next day I found a handwritten note from Harvey taped to my desk lamp: "Prof. Higgins says: shine your shoes." I still have the note.

October 17, 1970 was to be the New England Premiere of *Julius Caesar*. It was mid-August so I had precious little time to prepare a sales mailing in time for school opening after Labor Day. AIP's home office in Los Angeles was no help. The company had been built on a marketing strategy of get in quickly and out quicker before the reviews broke. They opened films on Fridays in drive-ins and prayed that it wouldn't rain over the weekend. I wasn't even sure that the press would review an AIP picture, but Bobby Epstein, who owned the Abbey Cinema in Boston where *Caesar* was scheduled to play, assured me that they would, "If not for AIP, then for the Abbey." Since the Abbey had just concluded its tremendously successful engagement of Franco Zeffirelli's film of *Romeo and Juliet*, the house was not only established as Boston's home of Shakespeare but its staff had become trained in handling rambunctious student audiences.

Even though I did a mass mailing to every public high school English teacher (no computers; I typed 500 mailing labels, copies of which held me for the next five years), I still had not seen the film I was promoting. Strangely, there was no great rush to show it to those of us who had to sell it. At last a screening was arranged and Harvey called an office recess. We filled the downstairs screening room in the Film Row building that AIP shared with MGM. Talk about contrasts.

It quickly became apparent that Caesar would die and take the film with him. Director Stuart Burge had not been given a big enough budget. Interiors worked (how much does it cost to build a fake Roman pillar?), but when it came to crowd scenes such as for "Friends, Romans, Countrymen" and the climactic Battle of Philippi, the parsimony was painfully obvious. Soon we began to recognize the same pillars that were moved around from one scene to the next. The soundtrack always carried more crowd noise than there were crowds. Whenever there was a parade, the scene always started just as the last few sandaled feet were straggling out of the frame.

Every cast member acquitted him and herself with stately aplomb except Jason Robards, Jr. who, as someone delicately reported, "was not at his best" as Brutus. In truth, he was dreadful: flat, disoriented, possibly drunk, and certainly deadly. As the heroic Antony, Charlton Heston—who looked like he fell off a Roman coin—was noble, serious, and competent. But it was uncomfortably clear that, once word got out, the only business that the film would do would be at its 10 AM school showings where attendance was forced. The nighttime dating crowd would look elsewhere.

So I made another mailing, this time to private schools.

Shakespeare's brand name did the trick. Advance sales started to come in. Harvey was amazed. Frankly, so was I. Best guess: the combination of Shakespeare, the first field trip of the school year, and teachers who remembered being dragged to see Charlton Heston in *Ben Hur* when they were kids. Harvey insisted that I send him weekly progress reports with copies to everyone up the hierarchy at AIP just short of company President, Samuel Z. Arkoff. Harvey had nothing to gain by boosting me, but he did it anyway. And he was right to do so because, when it looked like his film was going to be a hit, Heston announced that he would fly to Boston to promote it in person. Paul Levi, the advertising specialist who had the AIP account, would shepherd him around town for interviews and personal appearances. I might even get to meet my first movie star.

My long hair and short age (then 21) worked in my favor. I was anointed an expert on Boston's youth market. With some forty-seven colleges, scores of high schools, and a student population of over a million, the Hub could make or break a film. While Paul Levi set up Heston's radio, television, and newspaper interview schedule, I was asked to look into the possibility of landing the actor a speaking engagement on a college campus. As co-founder of the AFI, the attractive, articulate Heston was fond of talking to students. I called my friend Kenneth Rogoff, who still had another year to go at BU. "Kenro" booked the Boston University Distinguished Lecture Series and was able to schedule the university's largest auditorium, Hayden Hall, for the event. Posters went up.

Heston timed his appearance to the opening night of the film at the Abbey. He would work the press all day, say a few words before the showing, and work the press again the day after, leaving town before the reviews broke. The premiere tickets would sell for a premium with the theatre keeping the normal box office and everything above that going to charity. The advanced sales would create the impression of a hit.

AIP's old-time publicist Jimmy Boyle rushed from New York to Boston to supervise. He was not a Harvard man like Paul Levi, he was a colorful rough-edged flack straight out of Damon Runyon's Broadway. "We'll order six cases of champagne, see," Jimmy explained. "Make it the cheap stuff. Two bucks a bottle, max. Put 'em in two big garbage cans full of ice and cover 'em with a towel. Then buy one bottle of Mumm's and set it on top of the serving counter. The customers'll think it's the good stuff, but we'll pour 'em the cheap stuff, and let their eyes do the rest." Damned if it didn't work. The "cheap stuff" turned out to be André Extra Dry sparkling wine retailing for $1.79 a bottle. Just to play safe, we had the servers fill the plastic champagne glasses below the bar. No one caught on; in fact, we got compliments, which astonished me. So much for Boston sophisticates.

Guess who took home the Mumm's. Right: Jimmy. It was only fair. Besides, he let me scarf an unused case of André to take back to the apartment I shared with Bob Brown and Bill Wight, and we spent the weekend inviting friends to help us put it away. Ever had a champagne drunk at 9 o'clock Sunday morning? It's not pretty, it's André.

On the night of the 17th, Paul Levi arrived at the theatre with Charlton Heston. He spoke for fifteen minutes and then we all rode in George Abdon's limousine service car to BU's Hayden Hall. As we entered by the back door, Ken Rogoff told me that we had a good house and, hearing that, Heston finally acknowledged my presence. Kenro wasn't exaggerating; when we entered the auditorium it was packed to the back doors with over a thousand students, most of them young women who were thrilled to put aside homework, parties, and anti-war protests to see Moses (literally). The star spoke wistfully of "this mountebank profession of acting" and recalled how making a film for Willy ("not William; Willy's his real name") Wyler was like getting "the works" at a Roman Bath: "You go through hell but you come out smelling like a rose." Early on, he unbuttoned his suit jacket, stepped to the side of the podium, and casually flexed, revealing his build. An over-powering sigh arose from every woman in the hall. Next, fielding questions, he lamented the fate of *Major Dundee* and told how he almost ran down its ornery director, Sam Peckinpah, with his horse. He recalled how he recom- mended Orson Welles to Universal-International for *Touch of Evil* ("I said,

'You know, I hear Orson's a pretty good director, maybe you ought to see if he'll direct it'"). He dismissed praise for the chariot race in *Ben-Hur* by smiling, "It was fixed." When someone asked, "How did you part the sea in *The Ten Commandments*?" he responded, "Well, I had this stick. . ." and brought down the house. Two days later he was gone, back to Valhalla, or wherever it is that movie stars live.

I had occasion to work with Heston three more times over the years: once as press agent and twice as interviewer for films that we both agreed off the record were not particularly worthy. This was before he turned arch-Conservative and became the spokesman for the National Rifle Association. He was never less than gracious, but it has remained a curiosity for me that, just as Antony described Brutus, the elements were also mix'd in Charlton Heston. Here was a man who marched with Martin Luther King, Jr., lent his name to the Civil Rights Struggle at a time when it could have hurt his career to do so, fought for inter-racial casting, and helped create the AFI. Yet he also promoted the spread of guns, helped to publicly overthrow the Screen Actors Guild presidency of Edward Asner that led to the cancellation of an important TV series (*Lou Grant*, 1975), and gave credibility to policies that were bad for America. A terribly complicated gentleman, and gentleman he was.

After *Julius Caesar* opened, I was hired by Mr. Levi to help him in what was to be a short-lived expansion of his agency. He made the contacts, booked the tours, and released the newspaper ads. His expert media buyer, Edith Horne, bought the broadcast packages. I wrote press releases, serviced the newspapers (more about this later), and did whatever else had to be done for a variety of clients. For a three-person agency, we kept busy until the dominant agency in the city, Allied Advertising, and the big theatre chain, Sack Theatres, leaned on the film companies to pull their accounts away from small agencies like Levi's and that of another man I admired, Karl Fasick. Eventually, all the independent film press agents in Boston were put out of business.

Back when I got the AIP job, I called Carl Goldman to thank him. He almost didn't take my call; he had no idea who I was. It turned out that he had seen me so often walking around Film Row during my school years that he thought he knew me and that I belonged there, even if he couldn't remember my name. He figured if I looked familiar, I must be okay, and that's why he recommended me to Harvey. We later got to be actual friends, but I took a lesson away from the confusion: be seen. For what it was worth, I was finally on the inside. And taking notes.

Otto the Terrible

O TTO PREMINGER was his own worst enemy only when nobody else was in the room. The Austrian lawyer-turned-director-producer-actor built his legend on contradictions. He was charming and cruel, benevolent and dictatorial, cultured and crass, profligate and parsimonious, cooperative and intransigent.

"I have to be nice to Otto," fellow Austrian Billy Wilder once joked. "I still have family in the old country." And writer/director Burt Kennedy remarked on the man's artistic pretentiousness by joking, "I passed Otto Preminger's house last night, or is it a house by Otto Preminger?"

The problem wasn't being nice to Otto, it was getting Otto to be nice to you. When I was a student I managed to get a front row seat at a lecture appearance at which he was promoting his terrible new film *Skidoo*. When he disclosed that he had just dropped his option on John Hersey's novel about college life, *Too Far To Walk*, I asked if I might write him at his New York Office for a referral to Hersey. He kindly gave me his address: 711 Fifth Avenue. "Oh, that's the Columbia Pictures building," I said, eager to show how savvy I was.

"Very good," Preminger replied dryly. "Are you a taxi driver?"

When I worked with him for the first time it was for the release of his 1971 black comedy, *Such Good Friends*. He was then at the mid-point of a seven-picture contract with Paramount whom Paul Levi represented. His previous three Paramount films—the aforementioned *Skiddoo* as well as *Hurry, Sundown* (1967) and *Tell Me That You Love Me, Junie Moon*

(1970)—had earned neither money nor good reviews, and Paramount was looking to get out of the Otto Preminger business.

This was a change. Since gaining Hollywood credentials by taking over *Laura* from Rouben Mamoulian for Fox in 1944, he had built a successful career, albeit with an eye more toward *sùcces d'scandale* than by mastering the art of direction. Preminger functioned best as a producer, wrangling provocative subjects and luring exciting—and, at times, offbeat—actors to appear in them. For *Anatomy of a Murder* (1956), he focused on the best-selling book's sensational rape trial, daring to mention the "R" word, and cast, as the film's jurist, Joseph Welch, who had just eviscerated Red-baiting Senator Joseph McCarthy on national television. For the political thriller *Advise and Consent* (1962), he cast journalists Irv Kupcinet, Robert C. Wilson, Alan Emory, and White House correspondents and press photographers as themselves. He cracked the movies' censorious Production Code with *The Moon is Blue* in 1953, broke the Blacklist by hiring screenwriter Dalton Trumbo for *Exodus* in 1960, insisted upon racially diverse casts, and constantly provoked a pusillanimous press to cover his morally and politically progressive subjects.

His personal life was equally precocious. Married to Marian Mill, he had an affair with Gypsy Rose Lee that led to the birth of Erik Lee Preminger. He tripped on LSD in preparation for making of *Too Far To Walk*. He was a collector of fine art, a supporter of liberal causes, and a tireless self-promoter. On the set he would berate actors into a performance, treat his crew like slaves, and threaten studio executives with legal action when reason and charm did not get him what he wanted. He called Marilyn Monroe "a vacuum with nipples," nearly burned Jean Seberg at the stake in *Saint Joan* (1957), told Robert Mitchum to slap Jean Simmons for real in *Angel Face* (1952), and justified his fights with Dyan Cannon during *Such Good Friends* by insisting, "She's crazy, I mean, the woman divorced Cary Grant!" His last picture was 1979's *The Human Factor*, of which more than one person joked that it obviously wasn't autobiographical.

Preminger loved visiting Boston. He had held the world premiere of *The*

Cardinal there in 1963 and returned each time he had a new picture so he could chat with the press and visit old acquaintances. When *Such Good Friends* was booked into Boston area theatres in the winter of 1971, Otto booked himself into his customary suite at the Ritz-Carlton and advised Paramount that he was on the way. As their publicity representatives, Paul Levi's and my orders were to arrange interviews for Otto on the area's top radio and TV shows (easy), set up a student seminar at the Orson Welles Film School near Harvard (arranged by teacher/critic Deac Rossell who had worked with Preminger on the picture), and pack a screening with young people who, we hoped, had by now forgiven him for his earlier *Skidoo* (they had not).

The press luncheon was underwritten by Paramount but sponsored by Preminger's long-time buddy, the dapper Harold "Hap" Kern, publisher of Hearst's arch-Conservative *Boston Record-American*. As a further testament to Otto's stature, Kern allowed competing newspapers to attend. In that way, writers from all over the area could cover a single luncheon where they would hear the same quotes and yet, remarkably, come away with separate stories, most of them accurate, and all of them colorful. The guest list included the *grande dames* of the Boston movie press corps: Marjory Adams (*Boston Globe*), Peggy Doyle (*Boston Record-American*), and Alta Maloney (*Boston Herald-Traveler*). Collectively, these women were known as "the three witches of Boston." They were bright, beloved, single, and knew how to drink. I can recall monitoring morning press screenings when, for instance, Peggy would fall asleep and I would gingerly wake her during the end credits, hand her a plot synopsis, and apologize that I'd forgotten to give it to her earlier, neither of us admitting that she would need it to write her review because she had passed out. Peggy was an old-line Hearst employee of the same breed as Louella Parsons and the peerless editor Walter Howey. In fact, Peggy had started her career under Howey in Chicago when the Windy City had eight papers, each of them at the others' throats. According to her, she became a journalist by accident. She was visiting her brother, who was a copy boy at the *Chicago American*. He happened to be in the can when

Howey barked, "Doyle!," so Peggy stepped up and was rewarded for her cheekiness by being hired as the paper's first female copy boy. When Howey discovered that she could write with sensitivity, he made her a "sob sister," an old-fashioned name for a female reporter who could craft heart-rending stories about widows, orphans, and reformed sinners. It was helpful if they were true, but that wasn't a requirement.

Now comes the stuff of legend. It was neither proven nor denied, but word around Boston was that, back in Chicago in the 1920s, Peggy was not only a looker, she was the girlfriend of a capo in Al Capone's mob. Being a reporter, it was inevitable that she would, one day, write something that displeased Big Al, and she did. Capone put out a hit on her and Howey—no slouch in the influence department—supposedly intervened with the Mob and had the contract canceled as long as Peggy got out of Chicago as fast as the Twentieth Century Limited could carry her. Howey spoke to Hearst, Hearst had her transferred to Boston, and there she lived and worked until the day she died. Peggy always dodged questions about this, but late one Tuesday afternoon in her fifth floor office at the old *Record* building on Devonshire Street, we got into a discussion.

"Do you think young reporters today have any sense of the history of their own profession?" I asked. I was starting to deal with journalists as young as I was—those who had been brought into flower in the freewheeling underground press days—and I wondered what a seasoned pro thought of them.

"I'm never sure," Peggy said. "For instance, I remember a young man who started to work for us. They sent him to write a story about a new production of *The Front Page*. He said that the production was credible enough, but what were the playwrights thinking when they contrived to have the escaped prisoner hide in a roll-top desk? Who on earth would believe such a thing? Someone had to take him aside and explain that playwrights Ben Hecht and Charles MacArthur had based their play on an actual incident that happened while they were newspapermen in Chicago."

The other question was *Citizen Kane*. History records that, because it was more or less about William Randolph Hearst, the Chief's papers boycotted any positive coverage of the film or its director, Orson Welles.

"You know, of course, why Louella Parsons was so angry at Orson, don't you?" Peggy asked, deadpan.

"I'd always assumed it was because it was about her boss."

"That's not it," Peggy said, a twinkle appearing in her bulbous eyes. She leaned forward, pushing aside her work. "It was because Hedda Hopper got a screening before she did." Hedda and Louella were arch-rivals. It was hard to tell if Peggy believed it or just wanted me to.

Unlike Hedda and Louella, Peggy Doyle and her rival on the *Boston Globe*, Marjory Adams, got along. Marjory became a journalist at a time when few women took up the pen, paper, and press pass. She was the first journalism school (Columbia) graduate hired by the *Globe*, and she worked there for fifty-two years until they forced her out in a move to bring in younger staff. She was not a Boston Adams, but did nothing to disabuse people who thought she was. A round and persistent reporter, she would put celebrities through hell during their interviews, prodding and interrupting them, jamming words in their mouths. Even though she heard exactly what others heard and even if she was snockered at the time, when her piece appeared in print, it was invariably the best in town and almost always complimentary.

Alta Maloney of the *Boston Traveler* (later *Boston Herald-Traveler*), covered the beat from the 1950s until her paper folded in 1971. Where Marjory was boisterous and Peggy was meek, Alta was the mediator. Tall and classy, she was dryly funny and unfailingly tactful. She once offered to drive a tipsy Marjory Adams home from a party at my apartment by announcing, "We have to go now; it seems I've overstayed Marjory's welcome."

One more thing needs to be said of Marjory. At press luncheons she was known to eat half her meal and ask that the remainder be packed for her to take home. Sometimes she wouldn't wait for the server to return with a bag and would dump her plate, side dishes and all, into the dining room's linen napkin, then shove the wet package into her purse. Legend said that she had a plastic-lined purse for such occasions, and one theatre man swore he once saw her pour creamed spinach into it.

Everyone always assumed that Marjory ate the leftovers later, but I knew better because I once saw what she did with them. The next year, she invited her *Globe* colleague George McKinnon and me to dinner at her Beacon Hill apartment. We enjoyed several cocktails apiece and nibbled on a small container of peanuts (which Marjory, after her second Scotch, started calling "penis"), until she stood up and announced, "Well, I'm going to make dinner. I can't cook, you know." George and I looked nervously at each other as she left the room. He well knew of Marjory's press luncheon souvenirs; on the way up in the elevator we had joked that she must have a closet full of linen napkins and a freezer stocked with half-eaten, tin foil-wrapped press luncheons marked, "Charlton Heston, 1962," "Alan Ladd, 1956," "Bette Davis, 1961" and so forth. When she finally put food on the table, it was a relief to find that it was some kind of meat, canned corn, and cauliflower that she had managed to to burn in the boil-in-the-bag pouch. It was a memorable evening.

Other members of the Boston press corps were Connie Gorfinkle of the Quincy *Patriot-Ledger*; Donald Cragin of the *Boston Herald-Traveler* (alternating with Alta); Virginia Lucier of the *Framingham/South Middlesex News*, Cecile Markell of the *Jewish Advocate*, and Kay Bourne of the *Bay State Banner*. New to the beat when Otto arrived in 1971 was Janet Maslin of *Boston After Dark* (later the *Boston Phoenix*). A few years down the road she would become the chief film critic for *The New York Times*.

Three things were unvarying at a Preminger press luncheon in Boston: the menu (filet mignon, roast potatoes, green beans); the venue (the posh Algonquin Club on Commonwealth Avenue in Back Bay); and the sexism, for the Algonquin Club refused to admit women through its front door. The Women's Movement was blossoming, but the Algonquin Club cared not. The female press politely observed this restriction just as they accepted it at Locke-Ober's cafe and the Ritz bar, the latter of which refused to seat unaccompanied women, assuming that they were prostitutes.

The press may have followed rules, but Otto Preminger did not. Taken with Maslin's spunk and intelligence as well as her youthful good looks, he presented his arm to her and, while the women of the press dutifully detoured to the side door, grandly escorted Maslin through the Algonquin's main entrance. Otto smiled, publisher Kern scowled, Janet stared straight ahead, and the rest of us watched in anticipation of the institution crumbling. It did not. Unfortunately, not one word about it turned up in any of the stories, much to Otto's disappointment.[1]

It was certainly not Preminger's first miscalculation with the Boston press. Deac Rossell used to dine out on his story of the time Preminger held court in a function room at the Ritz when Marjory Adams decided she needed more quotes. Otto was sitting comfortably on a divan chatting alone with a reporter when up comes Marjory holding a scotch in one hand and her notebook in the other. Without asking if she could join them, Marjory plopped beside Otto, rested her drink on the carpet, and started writing down what he was telling her competition. The competition said nothing, but Otto turned his back to Marjory, hoping she would get the hint. She did not. Instead, she twisted on the divan to hear more clearly and, in doing so, kicked her iced drink down the side of Otto's Cashmere socks and Italian shoes.

Otto dared not lose his famous temper; the *Boston Globe* controlled the city. Instead, he smiled tightly, blotted the wetness with a linen napkin, and continued his conversation.

Marjory was undeterred. While Tito, the waiter, replenished her cocktail, Preminger moved to a dryer location.

Marjory followed him. She waddled over, sat down again, but, this time, was careful to place her drink at a safe distance. That was not enough. Very soon she picked it up to take another sip and managed to set it down, not on

---

[1] A short time later, the men-only Locke-Ober Café was crashed by a cadre of women eager to be thrown out to score publicity. The Café simply served them, immediately and quietly ended its sexist policy, and that was that.

the carpet, but on Otto's trouser leg. Preminger jumped at the cold while an embarrassed Majory took herself sheepishly away.

Five minutes later she had a fresh drink in her hand and headed back in Otto's direction. When she was halfway across the room, Preminger stood, rose to his full Teutonic height, pointed his finger at her, and bellowed, "Vould somevun pleese disarm dat voman?"

Preminger had an executive assistant named Nat Rudich. Formerly Spencer Tracy's aide, Rudich, a high-strung man, lived in constant fear of being fired. But his attention to detail was just what someone like Otto needed. It was Nat who confirmed all of Preminger's travel plans, made sure that there would be cars waiting for him, vetted prospective employees and crew members, and catered to his bombastic boss's every whim. He was a prince who was treated like a slave.

Rudich and I bonded instantly and because we shared a first name, I had to watch powerlessly as Preminger abused him time and again. Knowing that he had scrambled from New York to Boston without time to pack, Preminger lectured him on the foolishness of his actions and asked, in front of me, whether he needed clean underwear, and, if he did, to go to Filene's to buy some. Nat said he would do just that, and Otto left the room to make a phone call. I looked into Nat's eyes to offer sympathy, but his distracted stare let me know that he would have none of it. Suddenly, from the other room, Preminger screamed, "NAT!" Both of us jumped. Preminger had decided to wash his hands and needed a fresh bar of soap but was too proud to phone Housekeeping himself, so he chose to frighten his faithful assistant and the junior publicist who shared the hapless man's first name.

Nat Rudich left Otto shortly afterward and took a job in advertising for Twentieth Century-Fox in Los Angeles, a post for which he was completely unsuited. He hired another unsuited person—me—to be his New York assistant and paid for me to relocate there in early 1975. My job was doling out something called "cooperative advertising" in Fox's New York office, a number-crunching task that determined how the studio and each individual theatre shared advertising allotments. Although Nat was my boss on the Coast, my New York supervisor was a man who had become my friend while I was doing publicity in Boston, Nico Jacobellis.[2] Nico handled advertising and publicity for the New England region. Nat did not like Nico. He always phoned from California when he knew Nico was at lunch and asked me how things were going in the office. It was both discomfiting and obvious that he wanted me to spy on my friend. I confided this to a fellow New York Foxster, Hal Sherman, and he agreed with my analysis. Rather than stay in the middle of a situation that could only get worse, I sent word around town that I was looking to make a change and was hired within a week by United Artists. Nat was upset with me when I called him with my resignation. I never told Nico why I left, but I hope our mutual friend did. Thinking back on it from many years' perspective, I don't suspect that Nat had any particular reason for this chicanery. I suspect that he had writhed under Otto's heel for so long that, when he got put in charge of something, he wanted to see how much power he could wield. Nat died not long after I left Fox. If there is a Heaven, he'll be there because he already went through Hell on earth. Otto died in 1986 and, whichever place he went, he's probably giving the Boss a hard time.

---

2 Nico was the Jacobellis in *Jacobellis v. Ohio*, the landmark 1964 U.S. Supreme Court ruling that held motion pictures (in this case Louis Malle's *The Lovers*) to be protected speech under the First Amendment. It included the phrase by Justice Potter Stewart that he couldn't define obscenity, but that "I know it when I see it." Despite my interest, Nico consistently declined to discuss the case with me. He was a gentleman.

Disunited Artists

COMPARED TO Fox, which was a tightrope act, United Artists was the rest of the circus. UA's strength was the diversity of personalities and independent producers they attracted, starting with four of the most diverse in history: Mary Pickford, Charles Chaplin, Douglas Fairbanks, and D.W. Griffith, who co-founded the company in 1919. When the four principals couldn't supply enough of their own product to keep their company running, they instructed their sales people to pick up independent titles for distribution. In 1951 a consortium of attorneys, led by Arthur Krim and Robert Benjamin, purchased it from its founders and took it private. Over time UA acquired other indie distributors, went public, gained a sterling reputation, and, in 1967, was sold to the insurance conglomerate, TransAmerica. Throughout, management's ethics had remained essentially the same: they stuck to financing and distributing—"we've never owned a camera" was the company mantra—and they never took a film away from a director (although they were known to lean on them like hell).

Because of their respect for filmmakers, United Artists depended on its distribution wizards to market whatever they were handed. Usually it worked, as a phenomenal string of hits and Oscar®-winners proved from *West Side Story* and *The Apartment* to *Midnight Cowboy* and *Tom Jones*. Throw in the James Bond, Pink Panther, and Beatles movies, and UA was riding high in the integrity and box office departments.

When I fled Fox, I was hired for a newly created post of Assistant

Promotion Manager to help the avuncular Carl Ferrazza, who was in charge of UA's network of field personnel. Carl was an expert manager of people and possessed a devastatingly dry wit. Carl insisted that he didn't need an assistant, but the company forced him to hire one out of concern for his health (he was far too heavy for his own good). Above him were Vice President Gabe Sumner and Senior Vice President Freddy Goldberg. Taken as a trio, these were among the brightest and most wickedly funny people in the industry.

We inhabited the twelfth floor of UA's office building at 729 Seventh Avenue that had been built by the company's founders when Manhattan real estate was still affordable. Management offices ringed the floor on the window side and the secretaries' desks were placed in the next circle. Trench workers like me were consigned to a walled-in bullpen that was open on the far side of the building but whose main entrance was shielded from view when you got off the elevator, meaning that the first thing the famous people saw when they stepped onto the floor were the executive offices, not the people who were in charge of implementing their fame.

My desk was the first one you hit if you stumbled off the elevator and glanced instead to the right to get your bearings. I soon learned that my own status was just as shaky. When I was hired by Fox, which was a California corporation, I had to join the Los Angeles local of the Publicists Guild. UA, however, was a New York corporation, and that put my LA union status into a jurisdictional tug-of-war. I was, if you will, a demimonde: management considered me labor, labor considered me management, and the New York Publicists Guild local considered me an interloper. My desk felt like a foreign embassy on American soil. Technically, I was forbidden to do PR in New York City; I literally had to leave town in order to do my job.

A regal man named John D'Artigue was UA's publicity director. He was soft-spoken and mysterious and celebrated his Haitian roots to the extent of bragging that he took out voodoo curses on other companies' films so they wouldn't open as well as UA's. Or so he and his coterie of sycophants joked. The first thing he asked me when we were introduced was, "What's the date and time of your birth so I can do your chart?" Since I agreed with Dorothy Parker that "Astrology is Taurus," I gave John my birth date but had to invent the exact hour. Whatever I said, it made me his enemy, not because I lied, but because my chart said so. John and I barely spoke after that, but, since I was technically not in his department, we didn't have to.

In addition to being Carl's assistant, I was a fixer. Unlike at Fox, where I was asked to spy, at UA I was asked only to clean up the rare mistakes made by UA's regional publicists and, on occasion, to intervene in spats with unit publicists who ran up against producers and directors. No money was involved, only favors. I was also told not to let anyone know that I had saved their ass. (If you think cops stick together, try publicists.)

One of my first tests was placating Cornel Wilde. Wilde, an actor who had become a star as composer Frederic Chopin in *A Song to Remember* (1945) and appeared later in *The Greatest Show on Earth* (1952) and *Omar Khayyam* (1957), among others, had become a thoughtful producer/director with such films as the anti-war *Beach Red* (1967), the ecological thriller *No Blade of Grass* (1970), and the African odyssey, *The Naked Prey* (1966). But messages didn't sell, so he crafted an ocean adventure called *Shark's Treasure* which had the bad luck to be released two months before *Jaws* in 1975. The grosses for *Shark's Treasure* drowned in *Jaws'* wake, and it was decided that Wilde's increasingly demanding phone calls about grosses and publicity (of which there were neither) should be channeled to me. Day after day the poor man would call and ask for news, and I would lie that we were still awaiting it from the field. Finally I was allowed, out of compassion, to tell him that both business and reviews were "disappointing." Wilde never directed another picture.

Sig Shore was another filmmaker whose drama set in the music business, *That's the Way of the World* (1975), written by sports columnist Robert Lipsyte, was also tanking. UA had picked it up because Shore's two previous films had been the box office smashes *Superfly* (1972) and *Superfly T.N.T.* (1973) The moment *World* opened soft, Shore's calls were also diverted to me.

1975 was a tough year for Hollywood. A national recession had affected the normally invulnerable film industry. Over the previous decade, the old studios had been bought by multi-national conglomerates who tried to fit picture making into a traditional business model. In addition to UA's acquisition as a "leisure time activity" of TransAmerica, Paramount had become a "unit" of Gulf+Western Industries, Columbia was swallowed by Coca-Cola, Warner Bros. belonged to Kinney parking lots, Universal joined the hydra of MCA, and Fox became a charm in oilman Marvin Davis's bracelet. Not only didn't the Wall Street types know crap about making movies, even if one of their choices accidentally did well, the parent companies had become so diversified that the corporate bottom line would barely reflect it.

Moreover, United Artists' management chafed under TransAmerica's heavy hand. On a superficial level, this meant that we couldn't print press releases for the prestigious but X-rated *Last Tango in Paris* on letterhead that carried the sacred TransAmerica logo. On a deeper level, TA's tight grip on UA so dispirited the seasoned management team of Arthur Krim, Robert Benjamin, Mike Medavoy, Eric Pleskow and Bill Bernstein that in 1978 they up and quit, started Orion Pictures, and made a deal to release through Warner Bros.

But before it got that bad, UA tried everything it could think of to survive during a box office drought. Although they could count on a biannual James Bond movie and, if Blake Edwards felt like it, another Pink Panther, the company was not driven by today's franchise-hungry, tentpole-driven mentality. Each film was supposed to be unique. These were the days before home video, cable, merchandising, and 3000-print releases, so movies had to make money first and foremost by selling tickets. UA faced a mixed but illustrative bag during what was poised to become, by the mid-70s, the last great period of originality and creativity in American cinema. Unfortunately, that period hadn't yet arrived while I was there. The biggest hit was Blake Edwards' *The Return of the Pink Panther.* Coming eleven years after his previous Panther, *A Shot in the Dark* (1964), it was what today's baby moguls would call a "reboot." It scored well and was commended by *Variety* not only as a hit but for reviving the tradition of the press junket to promote its release.[1] UA flew over a hundred local, national, and international journalists to the La Costa resort in Carlsbad, California to meet the filmmakers. It was a triumph. When they got home, however, an embarrassing footnote hit the headlines when La Costa was linked to the Mob.

Inspired by *Panther*'s success and deluded that there was predictability to the movie business, TransAmerica urged UA to throw more junkets. Woody Allen was persuaded to give his first mass confab for *Love and Death,* his spoof of *War and Peace* that heavily referenced such classic silent Russian movies as *Ten Days that Shook the World* and *The Battleship Potemkin.* After the junket was over, Woody asked UA to arrange screenings of those very classics so he could finally see them instead of just making fun of their famous parts.

Woody was known to visit the twelfth floor. "Treat him carefully," we were warned. "He owes us his next picture and we don't want to make him unhappy." (The next picture turned out to be *Annie Hall.)* "Above all," Freddy Goldberg implored, "don't bother him with idle conversation. In fact, don't even look at him when he comes in."

Two mornings later I carried my coffee and roll into the UA building when Julie, the elevator starter, said, "Hurry, hurry" and pointed me toward the center car. Slouched against its rear railing was Woody Allen. We looked at each other and I realized he was waiting for somebody to do something. I pressed "12" and the door closed. I knew that I wasn't supposed to look at Woody, but I also didn't want to turn my back on him. So I rode up twelve floors facing sideways. When we got to our floor, I stepped aside and he floated out.

At least Miloš Forman was garrulous. We met informally while he was promoting *One Flew Over the Cuckoo's Nest* in 1975, but by the time he chose *Hair* (1979) as his next project, I had left UA. It was reported to me that my

---

1   See the chapter on press junkets with the subtitle title "Gang Bangs."

old company knew that they had a hard sell with Forman's heavy-handed treatment of James Rado's and Jerome Ragni's ebullient but dated musical. When it came time to present their marketing campaign, they invited Forman to a meeting at which, one by one, successive advertising concepts were unveiled with great flourish. Each poster was worse than the one before it. The Czechoslovakian director seethed. Finally, Forman could take no more and said, "What ees all of thees? Can't you make up your minds how to sell my feelm?"

"Here's how we worked it," Goldberg explained proudly. "We had each of our branch offices submit ideas for the poster based on their knowledge of their territory. Then we'll take a vote on the best one."

"You are going to take a *vote*?" Forman said, horrified.

"Yes," Gabe Sumner added. "It's what we call democracy."

"Do not tell me about democracy," Forman steamed. "That is how you people got Nixon!"[2]

When a picture opens poorly, the producer blames the distributor and the distributor blames the publicist. Nobody ever blames the executives who screwed around with the script until it no longer resembled the one the studio bought. (I once asked writer/director John Milius [*Red Dawn*] how this could happen—how a company could love a script enough to buy it and then ruin it—and he said, succinctly, "Because they're stupid.")

Then there are pictures that go rogue from the git-go. This was the case with *The Johnson County Wars,* a modest western that United Artists decided to green-light after the Orion executives bolted in order to prove to the industry that they were still players. In the ambitious but unsupervised hands of filmmaker Michael Cimino, however, *The Johnson County Wars* became *Heaven's Gate.* The tragic saga of *Heaven's Gate* has been meticulously chronicled in Steven Bach's book *Final Cut,* but there's a personal codicil. I

---

2   For the record, Forman denies this story, even though he comes off well and I stand by my source.

was visiting a friend at the MGM studios in California (after I'd become a critic) in April of 1981 when *Heaven's Gate* opened; by then MGM and UA were joined at the hip. We were in the Thalberg Building, a coldly historic structure where many of the creative executives had their offices. Although its corridors were carpeted against footsteps, there was an even more oppressive pall hanging in the air. The *Heaven's Gate* grosses were coming in. Rather, the lack of them. No one ventured into the hallway. Not a phone was ringing. UA had its future pinned on *Heaven's Gate*, and its future, to use a line from another movie, "was all used up." As I left the building I walked past one office after another where people were sitting but no one was working. Letters were going un-typed. Phones were going un-dialed. Profit participants were going un-cheated. Meetings were being missed. Nobody was packing yet, but you knew that the company would soon be playing bocce with people's heads.

I didn't last at UA as Assistant Promotion Manager. Just before Christmas of 1975 all the New York publicists got up and went into a meeting to which I was not invited. The next day Carl fired me, and I could tell from his voice that he was as surprised about it as I was. The reason he gave was that somebody said I was reading papers on other people's desks. I told him that, if I had, I might have had a clue what was going on in my department, because nobody ever told me anything. He agreed but said that his hands were tied. Later I learned that I was squeezed out in a jurisdictional dispute between east and west coast Publicists Guild locals, and UA management decided that the best way to settle it was by showing me the door.

Either way, I didn't care. I had read the scripts for the company's upcoming films and, aside from *Annie Hall*, they all looked pretty sad. Carl gave me the choice of two weeks' severance or ruminating at my desk to look for work. I chose the latter so I could stay in my loyal co-workers' faces. When I finally said my goodbyes it was on the night of the company Christmas party. I'd like to report that snow was gently falling on Seventh Avenue, that urchins were singing carols in the lobby of the UA building, and that a

Salvation Army Santa Claus was ringing his bell at the hookers on the corner of 49th and Seventh. Alas, the only thing that happened was that I ate a few cookies, said goodbye to Carl, his assistant Barbara McReynolds, Gabe Sumner's assistant Cathi Hollander, and grabbed the 104 bus up Broadway to go home. I opened a bottle of wine, phoned some friends, and made plans to move back to Boston where I knew people.

But, more importantly, where people knew me.

Easy Come, Easy Go

NOBODY KNOWS who Wallace Reid was any more, but he was the Brad Pitt and Tom Cruise of his day, his day being silent pictures. He was handsome, clean-cut, athletic, and had a shy smile coupled with a self-assurance that made women want to love him and men want to be his friend. He came to Hollywood from Chicago in the early 1910s hoping to be a writer, director, or cameraman, but his looks got in his way and they made him a star. He appeared in over a hundred programmers while thirsting for a substantial role. When one finally came in 1915, he took a salary cut to land it: Jeff the blacksmith in *The Birth of a Nation*. This was a breakthrough in the epochal film of its era. Soon he was signed by Famous Players studio, which capitalized on his fame by working him relentlessly, often in several pictures shooting at the same time. Already troubled by alcoholism, in 1919 Reid was injured on the location of *The Valley of the Giants* and the studio, desperate to keep filming, had a doctor fill him with morphine. By the time he returned to Hollywood, he was an addict. Rather than help him escape his illness, Famous Players fed it, milking their star for another twenty-five pictures, in the last of which, *Thirty Days* (1922), he was so zonked that he was practically a puppet. He died of influenza in 1923, but everyone in Hollywood knew it was the drugs that did him in. The rumors were confirmed when his widow, actress Dorothy Davenport, starred in *Human Cargo*, a preachy drama about the evils of narcotics, shortly after her husband's death from them. Reid was thirty-one when he died, and more than one producer said, "Thank God the sonofabitch wasn't making a picture for me!"

I thought of that story on the morning of November 3, 1975 when Hy Smith, Vice President of International Publicity for United Artists, looked up from his newspaper. It was the custom for those of us who worked publicity for UA to gather in the twelfth floor bullpen to schmooze before the phones started ringing.

Smith was a man of cutting wit, only now he looked drained of humor.

"Holy shit!" he said. "Pasolini is dead."

Pier Paolo Pasolini was the radical left-wing Italian filmmaker of *Teorama* and *The Decameron*. He was also gay and had been beaten to death by a guy he picked up, a male hustler who apparently wasn't a hustler so that, when Pasolini started to get down to business, the kid beat him up, threw him on the road, and ran over him with his own car. Twice.

Then came the Wallace Reid moment. When he finished reading us the article, Hy said to us, in all seriousness, "Thank God he finished his film for us first."

Indeed, Pasolini had only just delivered *Salo: The 120 Days of Sodom*, a film that would further widen the schism between image-conscious TransAmerica and UA. *Salo* portrayed the Italian Fascists of World War Two as degenerates who kidnap peasant teenagers to a remote villa where they inflict countless indignities upon the children before executing them in an orgy of S&M. Its graphic scenes showed beatings, slashings, coprophilia, sexual assault, and other degradations, all photographed with the camera at a distance. Critics would debate whether Pasolini did this to be discreet or, more likely, to demand that the viewer become a voyeur at the same time he chastised them for it. Either way, the effect was to create a sense of collaboration rather than superiority in his audiences. The effect was so disturbing that critic David Denby swore, "I hope to God I am not called upon to defend this film in Court."

The details of Pasolini's death remain controversial, but the consensus is that he was murdered, not by a homophobe, but by a hustler hired by Italy's right wing because of the filmmaker's left-wing beliefs. Exactly why and by whom have never been confirmed. Although teenager Giuseppe Pelosi confessed to the crime, in 2005 he retracted his statements and said they were made under threat of harm to his family. Subsequent government inquiries have been inconclusive.

Smith's comments may sound callous but, in a trade that values people by their box office potential, they were hardly unique. "This is the only industry whose assets walk out the door every night," MGM President Louis B. Mayer remarked as he watched the likes of Clark Gable, Katharine Hepburn, Spencer Tracy, Garbo, and others pass through the studio's Washington Boulevard gates in the Lion's heyday.

The ephemeral nature not only of stardom but of stars themselves was brought home to me in a personal way when I worked briefly with Scott Newman just as his career was taking off, or so he thought. Scott—son of Paul Newman and his first wife, Jackie Witte—made his acting debut in *The Towering Inferno*, the 1974 blockbuster in which his father co-starred with Steve McQueen. He had a small but important role as a young firefighter who conquered his fear of heights when he was called upon to fight a fire in a high-rise building. It was the last successful disaster picture of the 70s, although it was not the last to be made. Scott's father played the architect and McQueen played the fire chief who tries to save the all-star cast. Privately, Scott told me how producer Irwin Allen had sent writer Stirling Silliphant's script to his father with an offer to play the fire chief. While he was waiting for a reply, the cagey Allen sent the script to McQueen to be the architect. McQueen replied first but wanted to be the fire chief because, said Scott, explaining McQueen's reasoning, "he's the only character in the whole film who isn't guilty of something." Thus Newman became the architect whose specs were not followed, more or less exonerating him, too, and allowing him to become co-hero. He got his son a job as stunt actor under stunt coordinator Paul Stader's expert guidance.

Continued the younger Newman, "The dailies came back and Irwin was so pleased that he told me, 'Kid, you were great in that scene. So do you know what I'm gonna do? I'm gonna kill you off." He thereupon had Silliphant create a scene where the young fireman, having become emboldened, foolishly grabs a power cable, is electrocuted, and dies in McQueen's arms. It was a tender moment that never made it past the sneak preview (possibly because producer Allen needed the support of firefighters and didn't want to portray one of them as flawed).

When it came time to push the picture in the fall of 1974, Fox sent Scott to several cities. I was made part of a special *Towering Inferno* unit headed by David Forbes to draw attention to the Allen picture. Call it coy, but the publicity people decided not to pitch him to the press with the hook that he was Paul Newman's son, but as a young man trying to make a name for himself in a tough profession—oh, and, by the way, he also happened to be Paul Newman's son. Because no one had seen the picture yet, interest in the newbie was light, so we hung out together, saw the sights (it happened to be Philadelphia), and talked with the press, who had trouble finding a story, so they made polite eyewash.

Too often the scions of famous people say that they want to make it on their own, but they really don't. Scott did. He had a healthy pragmatism about the business he'd chosen, a robust sense of humor, and the decency to be funny without being nasty. Since we were roughly the same age, we promised to keep in touch afterward but, of course, never did.

Scott died at a friend's home on November 20, 1978 from a combination of alcohol and Valium. There was snarky after-talk about estrangement from his family and troubles with his personal life, but those who knew him believe that his overdose was accidental, and I want to agree. His famous father set up the Scott Newman Foundation to help kids trying to break the drug habit. Whether it was out of philanthropy or guilt remains the subject of debate.

Sometimes an actor suffers, not because of his own incompetence, but from somebody else's. Writer/director Paul Mazursky was casting *Next Stop, Greenwich Village* (1976) in New York and wanted to use an unknown as his autobiographical lead. One of the publicists at Mazursky's studio, Fox, thought he should check out a talented young actor who had just opened in an off-off-Broadway showcase. It was a Friday in New York and the publicist arranged for a pair of comps to be left at the box office for Paul and his wife, Betsy.

Mazursky was a prize catch for the studio. After rising to fame with the gentle but incisive satire *Bob & Carol & Ted & Alice*, he had continued to score with *Blume in Love* (for Warners) and *Harry & Tonto* back at Fox. He was known for making sophisticated yet entertaining films, balancing on the cutting edge while not, as he put it, being "too hip for the room." After several hits in a row, he earned the right, and the financing, to make this ode to his days as an aspiring actor.

Monday morning, at another publicity meeting, someone asked whether Mazursky had liked the play.

"He didn't see it," reported the man who had arranged the tickets. He was visibly irritated. "My girl called, but when Paul got to the box office, they hadn't put up the tickets, so he left. He never saw the kid."

"Well," said another publicist, "there goes that career."

The part was eventually played by Lenny Baker who, tragically, never fulfilled his promise; six years after making *Next Stop, Greenwich Village*, he died of cancer.

I never knew who the actor was that Mazursky didn't get to see. But, then, neither did Mazursky.

Everyone now knows the 1981 Broadway musical *Dreamgirls* as Michael Bennett's supreme success (emphasis on the word *supreme*), but when it tried out in Boston that November before being brought into New York, it had a huge problem that they didn't know about until press night. The role of Effie Melody White, played by Jennifer Holliday, disappeared when her character is fired at the end of the first act. She sings "And I Am Telling You I'm Not Going" and exits.

Much has been written about Holliday's in-again/out-again relationship with *Dreamgirls* over the years from when it was workshopped as *Big Dreams* to when it triumphed at the Tonys. What I remember is that night of November 23 in Boston when the entire theatre gave Holliday a raucous, cheering, stomping, standing ovation when she finished her song -- *before the intermission* – and then that same audience's mounting disappointment when she didn't show up anywhere in the second act. Apparently Bennett and writer Tom Eyen agreed, based on the reaction, because, by the time *Dreamgirls* opened at the Imperial Theatre in New York on December 20, 1981, Effie was back in.

There is a sad epilogue to this story, however. The show's dapper, beloved, mustachioed press agent, Horace Greeley McNab, did not celebrate his show's Boston opening. He was found in his Avery Hotel room the next morning, November 24, having shot himself in the head for reasons that never became known, or, if they were, were never made public.

Francis Horace Greeley McNab was born in Medford, a Boston suburb, on March 14, 1913 and raised in Everett, Massachusetts, blue collar all the way. His folks were supposedly in entertainment, and Greeley at age nine made his stage debut in vaudeville. When his father retired from performing and landed a job in newspapers, Greeley followed him and became a copy boy at the *Boston Herald*, then moved to the *Record-American*. His show-biz dreams were rekindled when he watched the stream of theatrical press agents flowing through the papers on their customary Tuesday rounds, and soon he joined their ranks.

Greeley's flair for the theatrical paid off. He wouldn't just walk into an editor's office, he would make an *entrance*, then whip out his photos and press releases with a flourish worthy of a magician. He became not just a publicist but an advance man for touring shows, locking in their dates, arranging promotional tie-ins, and educating himself on the minutiae of every play or musical he touted. His clients included *A Chorus Line, Grease, Annie, Hair, Man of La Mancha*, and *Dreamgirls*.

He could also tipple with the best of them (I met him through *Boston Herald* critic Donald Cragin, who was also a tippling expert) and would be lost to his company two or three times a year when the bottle drew him away from the footlights. In other words, Horace could drink. Perhaps that's what got to him on that cold night in Boston. Or perhaps, at age sixty-eight, with the holidays near and no one waiting for him at home, he got to wondering how much longer he could keep it up. Being unforgettable is one thing. Being forgotten is another. I remember Horace.

At five-and-a-half-hours, Abel Gance's 1927 silent motion picture *Napoleon* is both a masterpiece and a behemoth. Its proper presentation demands three interlocked projectors to present its massive triptych sequences, and a full symphony orchestra is also helpful. In 1981, director/producer/showman Francis Ford Coppola, working with historian Kevin Brownlow, reconstructed what was then a three-and-a-half hour version of *Napoleon* and roadshowed it with a score composed and conducted by his father, Carmine Coppola. It debuted that April at New York's Radio City Music Hall and thereafter traveled to selected cities, one of which was Boston. Chapin Cutler of Boston Light and Sound conquered the technical issues for its November 10 performance at the grand Metropolitan Theatre, which seated 4200 people, most of whom had likely never seen a silent movie before, let alone one of the most famous ever made.

It was a challenging but satisfying evening that was greeted with excited applause, but Maestro Coppola stopped the audience to announce, in a grave voice, that he had just received word that Abel Gance had died that evening in France. He then asked the audience to rise for the playing of La Marseillaise. We did, both exuberantly and tearfully. It was the closest I've ever come to feeling like Rick in *Casablanca* when he nods to the Café Américain band to play the French anthem in opposition to the Horst Wessel song being sung by Major Strasser's occupying soldiers. Different circumstances, to be sure, but a memorable moment nonetheless.

⚜

I was having lunch with John Milius and his then-wife Elan Oberon in New York's Jockey Club when suddenly the restaurant went silent. The reason stood at the entrance. A man had entered the room. A tall, tan, balding, trim, and fit man in a glowing white suit, Oxford shirt, and subdued tie. I leaned forward and said to John, "I think a friend of yours just arrived." John glanced in the newcomer's direction and said, "Ah! The Raisuli." Sean Connery – who had played the last of the Barbary pirates in Milius's 1975 success, *The Wind and the Lion* – saw us and walked over. I swear that the room grew bigger with each step he took. He shook hands all around and smiled in silence as John introduced me. Then he crossed the room to take his seat with the person he was meeting (publicity consultant Larry Auerbach). We learned later that the star had recently had throat surgery to remove vocal polyps and he dared not stress his voice. So I never heard Connery's Scottish burr. But there was no denying his sheer presence of which Milius had written, in his script, "He has the way about him, doesn't he?" Damn right he did. And always will.

As for John, more words are needed.

Big Bad John

A LOT of the principles by which I live were dead before I was born," John Milius sighed between puffs on the cigar he wasn't supposed to be smoking in his two-room Warner Bros. office overlooking a parking lot full of BMWs, SUVs and Porsches. The secluded building otherwise housed the offices of producer Mark Canton and actor/director Clint Eastwood. Compared to their palatial spreads, Milius's digs were positively Spartan. On his walls hung the obligatory posters for his films, which included *Conan the Barbarian, Big Wednesday, Red Dawn*, and *The Wind and the Lion*. The rest of his office, which he shared with his assistant, Leonard Brady, was stocked with military artifacts, photos, plaques, and mementos, most of which might have been more at home in the Pentagon. There were also shelves of books ranging from literature to politics that you just know had actually been read.

In short, Milius' headquarters was a cross between a boy's tree fort and Elba, reflecting his demimonde status as a Hollywood insider who was treated like an outsider. The 2014 documentary, *Milius*, by Zak Knutson and Joey Figueroa, beautifully presented this paradox.[1]

Nevertheless, when this was going on in the early 2000s, Milius was in demand, albeit not as a director of his own scripts, but as a doctor for the flawed scripts of others. When asked why the studio bosses resisted

---

[1] Disclosure: the author not only appeared in the documentary but provided some of the video and much of the audio interview footage from which it was constructed.

green-lighting his own projects, he surmised, "I think they go around and say, 'He's too much trouble' or 'I don't want to deal with him because he won't do what I want him to do.'" He also claimed that it was because he was a political Conservative in a Liberal town. That never washed with me; true, John was a Conservative—the old-fashioned, pre-Neo-Con kind that believed in freedom for everybody, not just for themselves and bankers. But his talent was so undeniable and he was so professional that even the most doctrinaire Liberal was thrilled to engage him. A staunch traditionalist, John detested all things "hip" and "cool." He belonged to the NRA,[2] and had a broad range of military contacts. "I have always been on the other side of the cultural war," he said with relish. "I have always been an example from the beginning of that which was culturally incorrect."

Milius was widely regarded as the best writer of the so-called "USC Mafia," a tight-knit group of filmmakers who resuscitated—though some say homogenized—American cinema in the 1970s. Perhaps it was his politics that kept him from being as prolific as his friends and collaborators Steven (Spielberg), George (Lucas), Francis (Coppola), and Robert (Zemeckis), but the simple fact was that his tastes were different. As a consequence, so was his box office clout. In the mid-2000s, after we'd finished the bulk of our interviews for my *Backstory 4* monograph, he and his wife, Elan, moved to Connecticut. He continued to doctor scripts of people half his age who could land the budgets that eluded him.

Like the man, each Milius film was conceived in struggle, born of grit, and tempered by the fires of studio development hell. It's a grueling ordeal, but he survived over three decades an astonishing number of gauntlets. "I'm probably going to be the last writer to have twenty-three credits," he

---

2   While I visited his office on Friday afternoon he was on the phone with DreamWorks executive Jeffrey Katzenberg about where they and "Steven" were going to go out shooting over the weekend. I had to admit that idea of E.T.'s daddy and a former Disney VP toting loaded shotguns gave me an image it took me a decade to shake.

lamented. "People don't get a lot of sole credits any more, they get rewritten so much. There were so many movies I shoulda done that were done by inferior people, and they can never be done again." Indeed, a comparison of his original scripts to the films made from them by others proves that they were wrong and he was right. How does this happen? Said Milius, "It's Hollywood. That's how it happens."

His taste in film—his own and other people's—is decidedly classical. Raised on Ford, Hawks, Lean, and Kurosawa, shaped by filmmakers as disparate as Fellini and Delmer Daves, Milius favored history books over comic books, character over special effects, and heroes with roots in reality, not stardust. His reputation as historian informed his scripts with a keen sense of time, place, and custom, and when they described complex military procedures and maneuvers (such as *Rough Riders* or the still-unproduced *Son Tay: The Greatest Raid of All*), they are both vivid and forthright. If there is a burr under his saddle, it was that so much of what he wrote for others wound up being directed badly. Nevertheless, he persisted with his own projects with the confidence of a battle-hardened general who knows how to win the war if only those damned politicians would just let him.

The burly, bearded Milius was a captivating raconteur. A conversation with him was like sitting around a campfire, and—unusual for Hollywood—his tales were rarely about himself, but limned the drama of history. When he intoned, "You know, it's interesting . . ." it invariably was. He insisted that he honed this ability as a surfer, yet the precision of his language exceeded the argot of those who hang ten. Milius's stories reflected his own deeply held ethic embracing the values of tradition, adventure, spiritualism, honor, and an intense loyalty to friends.

At the time we worked on the *Backstory* monograph, John and I had known each other for something like twenty-five years. Though I had first heard of him from actor/producer George Hamilton, who touted him as the "truly talented young writer" who had just written *Evel Knievel* (1971) for him, we only met after he'd made his directorial debut with the stunning *Dillinger* in 1973. I was then a publicist for the Sack Theatres chain in Boston that was showing the film (made for AIP, incidentally), and I discovered him to be refreshingly honest and happily indifferent that his political conservatism placed him at odds with most of his peers, and most certainly with the local press.

This, plus his fondness for macho themes, not surprisingly made him a frequent critics' target. Pauline Kael, the late *New Yorker* reviewer, once wrote that if there were to be any animals shot during the making of a Milius film, Milius himself got to do it. Other legends held that one of his contract terms was that the producer must give him a new gun; that he almost killed John Huston; and that he once actually refused to accept money for a writing assignment. (In order of debunking: he wanted to shoot only those animals needed for food, not for sport; the gun rule only lasted for his first few scripts; it was the emphysemic Huston who insisted on a too-long desert hike; and John did, indeed, turn down Paramount's rewrite money for a Tom Clancy film, though he happily accepted tribute of a Chevy Suburban filled with Cuban cigars.)

John once told me that I was the only liberal film critic he liked. Whether this says more about him or me, we never decided. The subject arose over *Red Dawn* in 1984. He had just come from Washington, DC and a tour of the Pentagon conducted by General Alexander Haig, Ronald Reagan's former Chief of Staff. John excitedly described the experience: "they have separate floors for each branch of the services, they have these neat uniforms and armor and grand oil paintings hanging everywhere, and you have to get around in a golf cart . . ." Listening to his enthusiasm, I soon realized that he was describing the building more than the institution. Finally, pausing to light a cigar, he asked, "You ever been to the Pentagon, Nat?"

"Well," I offered nostalgically, "I demonstrated outside of it a couple of times."

John raised his eyebrow, puffed his cigar thoughtfully, and said, "We have more in common than you like to think, and it bugs the shit out of you."

Like Ford, Hawks, and other filmmakers he admires, Milius' work addresses heroes, leadership, loyalty, duty, friendship, professionalism, and the difficulty maintaining those ideals in an amoral and confusing world. In his lexicon, the worst thing to be is stupid, and the worst sin is to be dishonorable. Although he privately chafed at his public image as a gun-toting, Liberal-baiting provocateur, he allowed himself to be painted as such, at times even holding the brush. He played the Hollywood game like a pro, yet stuck to his own rules; he was a romantic filmmaker who avoided love scenes; his movies contained violence, yet no death in them was without meaning. Most frustrating, his best-known writing was in films that other people wound up directing, sometimes without giving him credit, and often botching it (notable exceptions being *Jaws* and *Apocalypse Now*).

No one was more aware of these paradoxes than Milius himself. For example, the day after *Farewell to the King* opened disappointingly in 1989, I dropped by his Mandeville Canyon home overlooking one of Los Angeles's most picturesque vistas. As we walked through the living room we were trailed by an attentive terrier tap-dancing behind us on the tile floor. John waited for the tiny thing to catch up, and then gazed disdainfully down at it.

"That's Posie," he grunted. "He's Elan's. A guy like me, you'd figure I'd have a dog named Fang."

John Milius, the youngest of three children (Bill and Betty are older siblings), was born on April 11, 1944 to Elizabeth Roe and William Styx Milius of St. Louis, Missouri. The elder Milius was fifty-six at the time, and the vast age difference kept him, by his younger son's admission, "distant, sort of a Churchillian, statesman-like figure." When John was seven, his father retired, sold the family shoe manufacturing business, and moved everybody to Southern California, joining the Golden State's long postwar boom. By the age of fourteen, John had become both an avid surfer and a juvenile delinquent, two pursuits that went hand-in-hand "in the old days," as he would later call them in his autobiographical *Big Wednesday* (1978). He acquired the nickname "Viking Man" for his flamboyance, and began honing his narrative skills in the story-swapping sessions the beach community shared when the tide was out.

"Surfers in those days were more literate than the image of surfers to-day," he explained wistfully. "You must remember that surfers then had a great beatnik tradition. The first time that the great waves of Waimeia Bay were ridden, Mickey Muñoz quoted the St. Crispen's Day speech to the other surfers before they rode." But such traditions were invisible to parents, and John's shipped him to the Lowell Whiteman School in the mountains of Steamboat Springs, Colorado for eleventh and twelfth grade.

"It was a new school at the time," he recalls fondly. "We built it our-selves, and I mean that literally: if we wanted a place to live or have a class in, we had to get the wood and build it." The rustic experience—and the mentoring he received getting it—ignited John's creative spirit. By the time he returned to California he was developing into a first-rate raconteur and a recidivist surfer. Undecided whether to become an artist or a historian, he spent a summer in Hawaii where, on a day too rainy to surf, he wandered into a Kurosawa film festival. That did it. Returning home, he enrolled in the then-undergraduate Cinema School of the University of Southern California at a time when the term *student filmmaker* wasn't even a gleam in Eastman Kodak's yellow eyes. By the time he got out in 1968, that had changed; soon after, so would Hollywood.

USC offered no automatic entree to pictures. The film industry was practically a closed shop when Milius and his generation (George Lucas, Steven Spielberg, Martin Scorsese, Brian DePalma, Randal Kleiser, etc.) sought access. What blew the doors open was a combination of fresh talent and the fact that the old-line studios didn't have a clue what the burgeoning youth market wanted to see, and a plummeting box office proved it. Thus, when Milius *et al* arrived, the time was as right as it was for Patton at the close of World War II when he urged America to invade Russia. Unlike the Third Army, however, the USC Mafia struck hard against the major studios, finding allies and exploitation in the likes of independent producers such as Roger Corman, Samuel Z. Arkoff, Joe Solomon, and Larry Gordon. With the collusion of Francis Coppola, who had made inroads as the first film school graduate to land a studio deal, the movie brats changed the shape of film, both artistically and commercially. By the time *Jaws* consigned all previous movie grosses to Davy Jones's Locker in 1975, it could be said that the New Hollywood had its finger firmly up the pulse of the public. And John Milius was its most celebrated writer.

During our sessions, John mused about taking a teaching post in a New England college, but rejected the idea the instant he brought it up. "It would be nice to retire to someplace like that and teach," he said, "but those are all politically correct schools, and I don't think that I would last a day at one of those places. I'm a victim of my times; I don't fit in at all any more. Years ago I would've had it made. Now I'll probably be an outlaw till the day I die."

If John felt out of place, his work did not, at least not the old work. In 2009, *Red Dawn* was needlessly remade, changing its original premise of a Soviet invasion of America's heartland to a Chinese invasion, changed again in post-production to a North Korean invasion when a financially strapped MGM realized they would lose the Chinese market.[3] Producers culled a newer roster of young actors and actresses to replace those whom Milius had cast in the original. In a 2010 interview, Milius deemed the remake idea "stupid" and its anemic 2012 release only confirmed Hollywood's paucity of new ideas. In 2011, Milius's 1982 *Conan the Barbarian* was remade with Jason Momoa as Robert E. Howard's Cimmerian hero. The filmmakers ignored Milius's and Oliver Stone's earlier script (which, itself, had admittedly ignored the Howard source material) and the picture was released to little interest.

In 2001, Milius scripted his own sequel titled *King Conan* fully intending for Arnold Schwarzenegger to reprise the role that had made him a star, adding years and wisdom to the character. Ignoring the 1984 sequel *Conan the Destroyer* from producer Dino DeLaurentiis, *King Conan* begins as Conan, in order to secure peace for his people, supplicates himself to a

---

3   It didn't help. MGM's bankruptcy delayed the film's release until 2012.

feudal overlord with soul-withering results. "Freedom brings with it a lot of baggage that isn't necessarily what you expected," was how John explained it. It was a mature and geopolitically astute screenplay that acknowledged that Schwarzenegger had become twenty years older, but the project was put on hold in 2003 when the actor became Governor of California. Unwilling to find another Conan and unable to land a deal to direct it without him, Milius optioned his script to Larry and Andy Wachowski, the brothers whose über-hip 1999 *The Matrix* had made them Hollywood powerhouses. The Wachowskis did a rewrite that so displeased Milius that he disowned the project, and by 2004—when Larry Wachowski transitioned into Lana Wachowski—it looked as though *King Conan* would join that group of legendary scripts that everybody wanted to see but nobody wanted to make. Meanwhile he was working on a project that he asked me to keep hush-hush, but which it is now quite safe to reveal. He called it *The Sopranos* set in ancient Italy. HBO and millions of viewers called it *Rome*.

In 2010 Milius suffered a stroke that rendered him unable to write and barely able to find the words to speak. It was not just a sad but a cruel fate for the preeminent storyteller of his film generation. But by then there was a new film generation that wasn't interested in telling his kind of stories. Undeterred, by 2013 he had recovered enough to resume working on the project he was writing when he was felled, *Genghis Khan*, and once again found his talent and writing back in play. It would appear that the man who once lamented "I am upholding traditions that were dead before I was born" was creating new traditions in a creative rebirth.

Mythconceptions

S UPERSTITIONS ABOUND in Hollywood, and for good reason: since nobody knows what makes a hit, people spend a lot of time trying whatever they can think of and covering their asses. Superstitions persist even after they are debunked, in which case they are gamely cited as "the exception that proves the rule." Boat rocking is not a Hollywood sport, nor is artistic daring; as Dorothy Parker once observed, the only "ism" that Hollywood believes in is plagiarism. This is why, over the years, the following truisms have guided and/or thwarted many a filmmaker:

1. "Don't put guns in the poster. Some newspapers (including *the Christian Science Monitor*) refuse to accept ads showing artillery. Besides, you'll get letters from people accusing you of promoting violence."

    Somehow this edict never applied to westerns or, starting in the 1960s, James Bond, which practically fetishized pistols.

2. "People won't go to a movie with snakes in it." There may be some truth to this (*Anaconda* and *Snakes on a Plane*), but Arnold Schwarzenegger wrestling with a big one in *Conan the Barbarian* may have broken the curse. And, of course, there's Python (Monty). But the pseudo-prohibition remains.

3. "Never put Nazis in the ads." This might stem from Hollywood's Jewish roots. In fact, studio movies didn't even mention Nazis until Hitler in-

vaded Poland because the film companies were afraid of losing their Euro-pean markets (which, by then, were occupied by the Third Reich). Even-tually that rule tumbled: "*Where Eagles Dare*" was rank with swastikas, and so was *Ilsa: She-Wolf of the SS* as was, more recently, *Inglorious Basterds* (2009). Interestingly, when Paramount/Seven Arts made *Is Paris Burn-ing?* in France in 1965, the prop Nazi flags were sewn in black and white (the film was made in black and white) so as not to offend the sensibilities (and memories) of Parisians.

Of course, the ultimate proof that the three previous movie maxims are bogus is *Raiders of the Lost Ark* whose artwork included snakes, guns, *and* Nazis.

4. "Movies about movies don't make money." Sadly, this may be true, but only because bad movies about movies occasionally get made and re-prove it. For every *Sunset Boulevard, The Bad and the Beautiful, Two Weeks in Another Town, Barton Fink, Singin' in the Rain, The Big Picture, The Player,* or *Trumbo,* there are—hey, wait a minute, all of those did pretty well. So where does the truism come from? Is it because the Powers That Be don't want outsiders finding out about insiders? Or is it what Pauline Kael once said: that anybody who writes about Hollywood is automatically writing satire. And satire, according to George S. Kaufman, "is what closes on Sat-urday night."

5. One of the most persistent movie taboos is that playing Jesus kills an ac-tor's career. Like so much about Jesus, this is also myth. One of the first to play him (or Him, if you prefer), H. B. Warner, made more than a hundred pictures subsequent to Cecil B. DeMille's 1927 *King of Kings,* in which he essayed the title role. Since it would be untoward for the actor playing Christ to be involved in a scandal, DeMille put a stringent morals clause in Warner's contract, at least for while the film was in production. When MGM remade the film in 1961, teen heartthrob Jeffrey Hunter had no

such clause, but his career didn't notably take off after he wrapped it. He veered into television (including the pilot for *Star Trek*) and European movies when his Hollywood career dried up. He died in 1969 following a stroke.

The doom-and-gloom legend may apply to Enrique Irazoqui, who played Christ in Pier Paolo Pasolini's lean 1964 production of *The Gospel According to St. Matthew* and had but a handful of acting jobs after that. But the curse was clearly lifted on Max von Sydow, who played Jesus in George Stevens' lugubrious *The Greatest Story Ever Told* (1965). In this case the film died, not its star's career, and von Sydow was still making films forty years later.

James Caviezel, who appeared in Mel Gibson's graphically violent 2004 *The Passion of the Christ*, resumed mortal roles afterward with neither a boost nor an obstacle to his career. Willem Defoe, who appeared as a human Jesus in Martin Scorsese's controversial 1988 *The Last Temptation of Christ*, was moved beyond words by the weight of the role, but his distinguished career kept going despite the film itself being crucified by the Fundies. Robert Powell notably played the lead in Franco Zefirrelli's reverent 1977 TV mini-series *Jesus of Nazareth*. He successfully balanced theatre, screen, and TV appearances thereafter, as did Victor Garber, who was a sweet-faced singing and dancing savior in the 1973 screen adaptation of the stage musical *Godspell*.

But it was Ted Neeley whose passion as Christ I witnessed in person. A soft-spoken young man from the town of Ranger, Texas, Neeley was a drummer and singer whose emotionally charged voice and broad vocal range were topped by sad eyes and a gentle but commanding presence. He and his group, the Ted Neeley Five, had played clubs and other traditional rock band engagements in the early 70s, and when he got to New York he tried out for Tom O'Horgan's stage production of the hit Andrew Lloyd Webber-Tim Rice record album, *Jesus Christ, Superstar*. Jeff Fenholt won the title role, but Neeley was hired as understudy and to watch from the chorus. One of his fellow choristers was Carl Anderson, who understudied Ben Vereen as Judas.

When filmmaker Norman Jewison was engaged by the Robert Stigwood Organisation to direct the inevitable screen adaptation, both Neeley and Anderson were hired instead of Fenholt and Vereen, marking a rare instance of understudies winning roles away from the stars.

As it had on records, the film of *Jesus Christ, Superstar* drew its share of protests from the usual religious nuts while more evolved audiences appreciated the creators' attempt to make the Christ legend accessible to a generation that had outgrown religion. To capitalize on the release of the film by Universal Pictures, the Stigwood Organisation mounted a nationwide concert tour of The Who's *Tommy*, which they also controlled, and cast Neeley as the deaf, dumb, and blind pinball-playing protagonist. Hoping that *Tommy* would benefit from *Superstar*'s publicity, RSO contrived for *Tommy* to shadow *Superstar* as it opened city by city across the country. What they did not do, however, was promote it. They left that to the local impresarios. And the local impresarios left it to Stigwood. Thus, when Teddy arrived in Boston, he discovered that the people who had put *Tommy* into the spacious Orpheum Theatre on lower Washington Street—a rifle shot away from the Hub's fabled adult entertainment district known as the Combat Zone—had done little to tell anybody that it was there. Neeley stewed as he gamely performed to three-quarters-empty houses. After opening night curtain, we were connected by a mutual friend, Russ Manker, who had known him in New York theatre. Meeting Neeley backstage, I found him despondent. Unlike other cities he'd played, Boston seemed to be on automatic pilot. He graciously agreed, however, to do interviews on behalf of *Jesus Christ Superstar*, which had just opened in town, and, in fact, wanted to use the opportunity not only to plug *Tommy* but to praise the film's director, Norman Jewison.

We took Peggy Doyle of the Boston *Record-American* to lunch, then walked around the Boston Common watching the swan boats and talking about everything except *Tommy*. Eventually, we made our way to the theatre where the movie was playing and arrived in time for Teddy's "What Do You

Want Me To Do?" monologue with God. We stood quietly in the back of the auditorium and he whispered how uncomfortable he had been shooting the sequence in Israel, trying to look focused while cutting his bare feet on the sharp rocks and fighting against being blown off the mountaintop by the intense cross-winds.

As he described making the shot, a woman customer walked up the aisle and looked at Teddy. Teddy smiled back. Then a look of utter astonishment crossed her face. She turned around, saw Teddy on screen, then turned back to see him in the flesh. She had, quite literally, seen Jesus. I nodded a slight "You're right"—what else do you do?—and she floated into the lobby with a glow that approached beatification.

Teddy and I lumbered back to his hotel. Along the way we stopped for coffee, to buy a newspaper (no reviews yet), to check out some T-shirts, and so forth, like the Stations of the Cross, only through the Combat Zone. He was billeted at the Hotel Avery. As we entered the lobby he heard me gasp.

"What do you know about this place that I don't?" he invoked.

"Who booked you in here?"

"The company."

"They have a great cocktail lounge," I said, trying to sound positive.

"I haven't had the time to check it out. But that isn't why you gasped, was it?"

No it wasn't. The Avery was where reporters met sources who didn't want to be seen. It was so dark, the cockroaches needed flashlights, and so scuzzy that, when the piano player made her music, the keys stuck together. At least the drinks were strong; they needed the extra alcohol to disinfect the glasses.

The hotel was located at the outer reaches of the Combat Zone, so it was no surprise that they rented rooms by the hour. As the old joke goes, they changed the sheets every day—from one room to another. But the real attraction of the Avery was that, if a press agent or road manager booked his company there, he got his own room for free. This was never advertised, but everybody knew it except the hapless performers and crews who found "Hotel Avery" on their itineraries. The Avery has long since been demolished as part of Boston's urban renewal, but I'm not entirely sure that it didn't just crumble to dust one day on its own.

"We were ripped off," Neeley admitted. "Management clearly wanted to bank on the movie, and that says it all. I'm trapped in *Tommy* with a contract that says I have to stay with the tour. We all do. They say they have an advance man promoting the show, but I've yet to see the good he does."

After the engagement of *Tommy*, Teddy and his cast moved on to the next city. Meanwhile, *Jesus Christ Superstar* was still playing in Boston without fulfilling its commercial goals, either. One day I received a letter in my publicity office. It was a request for a signed photo of Ted Neeley. Ordinarily I would refer such letters to the studio's publicity department, which was equipped to deal with such things. That is, if I didn't disregard it entirely, as we were told to do, because the way that modern studio publicity departments deal with such things is not to deal with them at all. This letter, however, was from the mother of a child who, she said, was hospitalized and needed an emotional boost to speed his recovery. True or not, it was a well-written letter, so I did something I swore I'd never do: I forged Neeley's signature to a photograph, dedicated it to the sick child, and sent it off. What the hell. Who'd know?

A month later, the mother sent me a note thanking me for getting the photograph to her son, and that it gave him the positive attitude he needed to endure his surgery and start on the road to recovery.

Over the years, many people have done terrible things in the name of Jesus and were not punished. As small as my forgery was, I like to think it was one of the good things done, if not in the name of Jesus, then in the name of Teddy Neeley, A.D. 1973.

Robert Altman
Got Me Banned

IDISCOVERED Robert Altman before Pauline Kael did. In early 1968, Floyd Fitzsimmons, the New England field publicity representative for Warner Bros., handed me a letter of invitation to a sneak preview of a new film called *Countdown* while I was in his office trying to bum TV commercials for Warner Bros. movies. At Boston University's Cinema at West Campus, we used 16mm television spots as previews of coming attractions since we couldn't handle the 35mm trailers distributed by National Screen Service. We would acquire as many TV spots as possible when the films and their advertising campaigns were new, and store them until the movies themselves were released in 16mm for us to book. But back to Altman.

Countdown (1967) was an innocuous title but I recognized it as the long-awaited screen adaptation of Hank Searls' 1964 science fiction novel *The Pilgrim Project* that I had noticed on the production charts a year earlier. The book's concept was more politics than science or fiction: when NASA learns that Russia is about to send a cosmonaut to the moon, they adapt a Gemini space capsule to send a single brave American astronaut, Lee Stegler (James Caan), ahead alone with enough provisions to last until a way can be found to bring him back. Of course, Stegler realizes that he will never return, and he duly accepts his mission to plant the American flag on the lunar surface ahead of the Commies.

I had never heard of the film's director, Robert Altman. In those days, there was no easy way to research credits. But I went to the preview anyway because no student in his right mind turns down a free weekend movie pass or, in my case, the chance to suck up to Warner Bros.

Perhaps this is why I liked *Countdown* more than I later learned I should have. The first person who tried to talk me out of liking it was Altman himself, who dismissed his early effort saying, "I just did it to get out of television." What I appreciated about *Countdown* was what later became an Altman trademark: overlapping dialogue and a naturalness of performance that made me think I was watching real people, not actors. In fact, that achievement was what got Altman barred from the studio by Jack Warner himself.

"They were talking about this big career that I was gonna have," he recalled for the American Film Institute. "The last day of shooting, Jack Warner came on the set. I had gone to the toilet so I was not in the room, and when I came back, he was not on the set. I had missed him. The next morning I got a call from one of the producers who said, 'Don't come in today because they're not gonna let you in the gate.' I said, 'What are you talking about?' He said, 'Jack Warner . . . looked at your dailies last night and he just went crazy. He said, "That fool has actors talking at the same time"' and they barred me from the lot. I said, 'I have the right to edit my film' and they said, 'yes, you do. You can do that but, if you persist in doing that, as soon as you turn in your cut, nobody's gonna look at it and they're just gonna toss it out. Warner, he doesn't like you.'"

Warner—who, as a reference point, later hated *Bonnie and Clyde*—was not impressed with the tyro cast that Altman had assembled in addition to Caan: Robert Duvall, Michael Murphy, Ted Knight, Joanna Moore, and Barbara Baxley. Moreover, the narrative style was antithetical to the genre—intense rather than manipulative—yet I was struck by its originality. Apparently this is exactly why Warner Bros. wound up dumping the picture. By the time of *M*A*S*H* in 1970, the critics had finally caught up with my infatuation with this quirky but emotionally honest filmmaker.

In January of 1973, I took over the publicity department of Sack Theatres, Boston's major exhibition chain, when their Publicity Director, Jane Badgers, bolted to do press for the Chateau de Ville Dinner Theatre circuit. No sooner had I learned where the free passes were kept than I was asked to set up a studio sneak of a new United Artists film called *The Long Goodbye*. It was Robert Altman's latest.

Studio sneaks are different from publicity screenings. The latter—like the one I had been invited to for *Countdown*—are designed to begin word-of-mouth. For the former, the Directors Guild contract provides that a filmmaker is entitled to two public showings of his version of his film before the studio can tamper with it. This allows for the director, editor, and sound mixer to fine-tune the picture in front of a virgin audience. Wise producers schedule their film far enough away from Los Angeles that rival studio spies can't sneak in.

They have good reason to fear the Hollywood rumor mill. The studio sneak of Universal Pictures' *The Great Waldo Pepper* (1975) was a disaster whose story is told by its screenwriter, William Goldman, in his book *Adventures in the Screen Trade*. *Waldo Pepper* was about a barnstorming young pilot, played by Robert Redford, and his pretty wing-walking partner, played by Susan Sarandon. The film flies along on its high-spirited way until Sarandon is killed in a stunt gone wrong. Goldman describes the moment at the studio sneak when they lost the audience: "They felt tricked, they felt betrayed, and they hated us."

I confess that I was the publicity representative from the theatre chain who set up that screening in late 1974. I remember seeing ashen-faced Goldman and director George Roy Hill in the lobby of the Sack Cheri theatre as the audience poured out, not waiting for the end credits to finish. Neither the audience nor the film ever recovered. That's how important studio sneaks are.[1]

---

1   Goldman later reported that they should have gone back for half a day and taken a shot of Sarandon in a lake waving her fist at Redford, signaling to the audience that she was all right. But retakes weren't the ritual then that they have since become.

So *The Long Goodbye* was important. I was advised that, not only was Robert Altman going to fly from Los Angeles to Boston for the sneak, so were editor Lou Lombardo, producer Jerry Bick, and actor John Schuck (not in that film, but a friend from M*A*S*H days who was about to co-star in Altman's *Thieves Like Us* [and later for me in *The Waldorf Conference*]). Knowing I was an Altman fan, the theatre chain's Vice President, A. Alan Friedberg, allowed me to play hooky to accompany the filmmakers and arrange for their comfort.

Not wanting to be embarrassed by a low turnout, however, the theatre chain and United Artists bought full-page newspaper ads advertising the sneak. This upset the filmmakers. Standing in front of the Cheri with the *Boston Globe* spread in front of them, producer Bick marveled at how beautiful the ad looked. "Of course it does," grumbled Altman. "We paid for it."

"What's wrong with that?" asked the perpetually nervous Bick.

"You don't get it, do you?" chided Altman. "If you advertise a Robert Altman film, we'll get all the Robert Altman fans, and there aren't enough of those. We need people who don't know who I am if we want an honest reaction." The director shook his head in disgust at the studio's logic.

"I'm kind of a cult," he later admitted. "A cult is not enough people to make a minority. But you're encouraged because you have that group of people. It's 'C'mon, Bob, you can do it.' You're responding to that cheering section no matter how small they are. Then there's a point where too much acceptance of success will disturb the artist. The artist at that point becomes a stimulator of money. You get into that game where an artist will look down at what he's doing and change his perceptions. I like to surprise people with something they've never seen. People will travel a long way to see something they've never seen before. What the artist likes is that look in their eyes, and he says, 'I made this!'" He then pronounced the upcoming sneak preview worthless.

Worthless it may have been, but the audience laughed in all the right places and stayed in their seats throughout. Riding to Anthony's Pier

4 seafood restaurant after the show for a late supper, I sat beside Lou Lombardo, who described the unusual challenge of editing the film.

"It was Bob's idea to make every shot a moving camera shot," he said. "In every shot the camera is either zooming, panning, tilting or dollying, even if the characters are just standing there. It's his visual counterpart to Philip Marlowe's constantly shifting point of view as he solves the mystery."

Based on Raymond Chandler's novel, *The Long Goodbye* follows private investigator Philip Marlowe, played by a goofy Elliot Gould, as he tries to solve the murder of his friend, Terry Lennox (Jim Bouton), who was involved in the disappearance of a bag of money belonging to gangster Marty Augustine (Mark Rydell). He also tries to locate his lost cat (Morris from the TV cat food commercials) and find missing writer Roger Wade (Sterling Hayden) who has abandoned his wife (Nina van Pallandt). Scripted by Leigh Brackett, who handled similar chores for *The Big Sleep* director Howard Hawks twenty-five years earlier, *The Long Goodbye* was updated from the novel's 1953 setting to modern-day Los Angeles.

"That's because Philip Marlowe will always be out of place no matter what era he lives in," Altman said, turning around from the front seat. "He is always the most moral man in an immoral environment. That's why it's set in Los Angeles. Plus," he said, summing up his film as if practicing sound bites for its eventual publicity tour, "if you'll notice, he doesn't solve any of the mysteries he's hired for. He gets double-crossed, beaten, lied to, and, in the end, he kills his best friend. We changed the ending from the book to show that, eventually, he's just had enough. By the way, did you like the two dogs humping in the road?" (Sure enough, there had been two dogs going at it in a road in Mexico.) "That happened while the camera was rolling," Lombardo chuckled. "We'll take it out if the MPAA complains."

"Editing on the moving camera was both confining and liberating," Lombardo continued. "It sets up a rhythm where you're always kept off guard. It was like working for Sam"—he meant Peckinpah, for whom he'd edited *The Wild Bunch*—"Sam tried to mess with you, too, not so much by cutting as by intercutting, I mean slow motion, regular motion, multiple views of the same thing, like that."

"Whose idea was the slow motion?" I asked, remembering John Ford's famous complaint, "I can kill three guys and have them buried in the time it takes Peckinpah to have one guy hit the ground."

"We played with it," Lombardo said diplomatically, "but it was all in the script.[2] Like in Kurosawa."

The car arrived at the restaurant, a Boston tourist magnet whose glamour exceeded its cuisine. Nevertheless, every visiting Hollywood type demanded to eat there because Anthony Athanas, the owner, served an impressive lobster, a creature that seldom made it onto California menus in those days. Anthony also prided himself in running a class establishment and, in ye olde Yankee parlance, that meant that all male customers had to wear a tie.

Robert Altman did not wear ties.

Anthony insisted.

Some restaurants keep house ties on hand for unadorned guests. All of Anthony's were in use. I offered Bob mine. He refused.

But Anthony was a diplomat as well as publicity-savvy. To be fair, he had allowed me to make reservations, a privilege he only extended to VIPs. As a further compromise, he seated the Altman party at a table as far from the entrance as possible. Not for privacy, for secrecy.

"Nat," the restaurateur said, taking me aside, "I will make this one exception because you are here, but, in the future, I don't care who it is, no necktie, no table."

"Sure thing, Anthony," I lied.

Altman *et al* got their lobsters. I stuck with the scrod. The studio paid the bill.

The next year, still working for Sack Theatres, I was pleased to arrange a

---

2   Screenplay by Walon Green and Roy N. Sickner, rewritten by Green and Peckinpah.

studio sneak of *Thieves Like Us*, Altman's next film, the one with John Schuck. Along with Altman this time came writer Thomas McGuane, who was adapting his novel *92 in the Shade* for Altman to direct (McGuane wound up directing it himself); producer Jerry Bick; executive producer Elliott Kastner; and a female Boston critic who was McGuane's special guest.

"Will he be wearing a necktie?" asked Anthony Athanas when I called to reserve a table.

"I can't guarantee it," I said.

"Then I can't guarantee a table," Anthony countered, and reminded me that he didn't reserve tables anyway, except for celebrities who wore ties.

"What if he doesn't?" I asked.

"Then don't bother bringing him. In fact, don't bother bringing yourself again. I remember last time."

"Then we'll go to Jimmy's," I said. Jimmy's Harborside was Anthony's closest competitor, literally across the street from him, as well as a more congenial place to eat, I thought. When a limo driver brought people to Jimmy's, Jimmy allowed the driver to eat for free. That was sharp.

"In that case," barked Anthony, "Don't bother coming here even with a tie," and he hung up. I guess he wasn't all that diplomatic after all.

By the time my dinner diplomacy failed, it was too late to go to Jimmy's either, so the Altman party enjoyed a noisy after-hours meal at the Charles Playhouse Restaurant. Most of the conversation was aimed at Elliott Kastner and little of it was complimentary. "How much did you make on our backs, Elliott?" asked Altman. "How come, of all the films you've produced, the only one who makes a profit is you?" Astonishingly, Kastner smiled and absorbed insult after insult, even when it was obvious that they were not offered good-naturedly but were, in fact, all-out attacks on his character. It was a good show and I was prepared to offer sympathy until the waiter brought the bill.

Ordinarily, the highest-ranking person at the table would make a show of picking up the tab, stick it on his credit card, and quietly put in for studio reimbursement. Protocol indicated that this should have been Kastner, the executive producer. Instead, he just stared at the bill like it was a tray of cold sores. No one spoke. Altman and the others watched him.

"I didn't bring my wallet," Kastner said quietly. Attention shifted to Altman. Altman rolled his eyes, then turned to me. "I authorize you to pay it and put it on Elliott's advertising campaign," he said.

As totem poles go, I was so far on the bottom, I was underground. Unknown to them, I was under strict orders from my theatre chain not to spend a dime on these people; if we didn't play the picture, we'd have nothing to leverage the expenses against. I wished we'd all worn neckties. With Kastner and Altman at a standoff and none of the actors about to reach for the bill (surprise, surprise), I swallowed and stood for the charge. Later, A. Alan Friedberg himself generously reimbursed me out of his own pocket. I'm sure he found a way to make the studio—but probably not Elliott Kastner—pay him back. It was a year before I returned to Anthony's Pier 4 with Peter Bogdanovich, who wore a tie (he has since switched to ascots) and interviewer Pat Mitchell. I never liked lobster anyway.

Despite getting boned over dinner, I stayed in contact with Altman, who soon let me call him Bob. When I gave up publicity and became a critic, I would interview him whenever he came to Boston to flog a film, and sometimes in between I'd call him if I needed a good quote. In Los Angeles, I hung out at his warehouse-like Santa Monica facility, Lionsgate,[3] where the indoor air was often redolent with something other than smog. That was where we gathered shortly after he returned from shooting *Popeye* in Malta to discover that thieves had stolen his state-of-the-art editing equipment. Despite the loss, he exuberantly collected a dozen friends in the stripped-down offices to watch a rehearsal of Frank South's one-act play *Rattlesnake in a Water Cooler* with actor Leo Burmeister as a westwardly mobile Easterner forced to face the limitations of his, and the country's, shaken dreams. Bob had hurriedly mounted the piece to distract himself not only from the theft

---

3   The connection with today's Lion's Gate Films is too convoluted to explain here.

but also after learning that his next film, *Lone Star*, had been canceled by its studio. The plug had been pulled in the worst possible way: rather than get a call from the studio, Altman read it in the papers. The affront was such that he told a writer for *Penthouse* that there weren't any studio heads that he would like to sit down to dinner with. He later regretted saying those words, but not for having the thought behind them.

"I just don't come off well in print," he lamented. "You've got to understand. I just want to keep a low profile for now, at least until I have something I want to talk about. I'm trying to get some control back. I want the press to look up all of a sudden and ask what happened to me. Then I'll give them the answer."

Bob was a spirited ringleader. Like the local delinquent who lures the neighborhood kids to join him in mischief, he was at once charismatic, prickly, stimulating, and nurturing. But just because he was sensitive to people's personalities, that didn't mean that he was sensitive to their feelings. So observant was he that, if he wanted to, he could devastate with a single, well-placed comment. In my case, we were casually discussing how each person has his own reality and I offered, attempting to agree with him, "It's like something Sartre said. . . ."

Bob cut me off sharply. "Sartre didn't just say it. *I* did."

He could also be illuminating. "I've never seen a bad performance in any of your films," I once asked. "How do you explain that?"

"I hire good actors." A beat, and then he elaborated, "I don't know how I know. I think I don't restrict the actors. I allow them to do what they can do, or what they will do. In fact, I insist on it. By the time a film is cast, about eighty-five percent of my creative work is finished."

"What do you tell the actors to make them do what you want?" I pursued.

"There's a word that's in the directors' manual. It's '*action*.'" He smiled conspiratorially. "I don't talk to the actors much. By the time we get to working and shooting, they know the kind of film we're going to make and what their contribution is to be. There's not much discussion that goes on."

"Let me ask you about another film," I said. "In *The Wedding. . . .*"

He interrupted me. "It's not *THE Wedding*, it's *A Wedding*. *THE* wedding is *MY* wedding. *A Wedding* is my *film*."

"Okay, okay," I laughed. "In *A Wedding* there's a scene where Lillian Gish, who plays the matriarch of the family, dies while the ceremony is going on. The shot of her that you use is clearly a freeze-frame. You can tell by the grain. Why did you do that instead of having Lillian Gish just hold her breath?"

"Because she was eighty-five," Bob said, "and I was afraid that if she stopped breathing she'd never start again."

His refusal to answer a direct question was also typical of the obtuse way he attacked filmmaking. He turned genre after genre on its ass: a western that wasn't a western (*McCabe and Mrs. Miller*), a mystery that wasn't a mystery (*The Long Goodbye*), a political thriller that wasn't a political thriller (*Nashville*), a fantasy that was set in the real world (*Brewster McCloud*), a glossy Hollywood movie that satirized glossy Hollywood movies (*The Player*) and a film noir set in broad daylight (*Quintet*).

Quintet was a sore topic. "*Quintet* is a film that even the Altman groupies don't like," he admitted. Set in a frozen world of the future (it was originally written to be filmed in the shell of the 1963 World's Fair in Flushing, New York), it starred Paul Newman in a mystery which, even after repeated viewings, remains impenetrable. I ventured that it might be his least accessible film.

"Then why are we talking about it?" he asked me pointedly.

"Because it's a Robert Altman film," I said. Score. "Now, one last question." He sighed. "You made *Vincent and Theo* about the relationship between Vincent van Gogh and his brother. If anyone would know this, it would have to be you. How do you pronounce *van Gogh*?"

"Ah," he began. "In America it's 'Van Go'. In England it's 'Van Gok'. In France it's 'Van Gog'. And in Holland they say, 'Vincent.'"

For all his plaudits and accolades, Robert Altman was the least pretentious director I have met despite many people feeling that his films were the opposite. I think that's because he challenged viewers to watch his films, not as works of art fixed forever in time, but as living things, experiences that give insight rather than lessons. He was the last person to attach timelessness to his work, even though it is inevitable that some of them will earn that stature.

"The film, when it's born, is about the only shot it should get," he said. We'd been discussing the trend in "Director's Cuts" or "Restored Uncut Versions" appearing on home video. "I think it's interesting," he allowed, "and I think in many cases you see that it's a better film when cut in a different way. But these are all afterthoughts. I don't save footage thinking, 'Oh, well, some day we'll put it back in.' You have your fight at the time. Once they're born, that is what's out there and that is what they are."

It was years before I could ask him about *Countdown* and why he repudiated the film that, after all, coined what would become the "Altman style."

"I'll tell you why," he finally explained. "The studio shot a happy ending,"[4] At the end of the film, James Caan makes it to the moon but lands shy of the previously sent life support station. Just as his oxygen is about to run out he sees, far in the distance, a flashing red beacon that will direct him to safety as the end credits roll. "That's gratuitous," Bob said, "I was never gonna show him rot and die on the moon, but I wanted the audience to know he was going in the wrong direction and consequently his future was . . . limited." Then he added, again with that smile and twinkle in his eyes, "as were all the futures of all the people on the earth!"

Another joke. But one which—in keeping with the path of his whole career—held more truth than if he had played by the rules. There's a difference between never lying and always telling the truth. Robert Altman found a way to do both at the same time.

---

4   Producer William Conrad shot the ending.

Shitheels

MARTIN RITT grabbed my wrist. We had just recorded an interview about his new film, *Norma Rae* (1979), in the studios of WEEI-FM, the CBS radio station in Boston where I was Entertainment Director from 1977 to 1981. We had been discussing the Hollywood Blacklist and how Ritt had been brushed by it when his career was just starting. Unable to act or direct because of pressure brought upon broadcasters by hate groups and misguided patriots, he'd found a home in New York's Yiddish Theatre and made ends meet for himself and his wife, Adele, by teaching drama and hanging out at the race track.

During the interview, I had remarked that CBS had a proud legacy of fighting the Blacklist by enabling Edward R. Murrow and Fred W. Friendly to go after Senator Joseph R. McCarthy on their TV show *See It Now*, hastening the Red-baiting senator's fall from grace. As soon as it was over, Ritt said to me in a voice cold enough to freeze the microphones we'd been using, "Perhaps they did, but you should also remember, if you forget everything else, is that, when the Blacklist took hold, CBS was the first network to turn over names and use *Red Channels* to keep people from working."

It was impossible to ignore Martin Ritt. Marty—that's what people called him, including writer Paddy Chayefsky, who, it is said, named the hero of his most famous script after him—was a bulldog of a man. He had a bulbous nose, tired eyes, and hair that looked thin even before it started falling out. He wore jumpsuits for comfort, not as an affectation, and they became his trademark, except when he donned a suit to go into hotels or receive the awards that came to him late in his grumpy life and exemplary career.

Although born in New York, he gravitated to the American south for school and then for most of his film work. Among the productions he placed in that environment over the course of twenty-five years were *The Long, Hot Summer* (1958), *The Sound and the Fury* (1959), *Sounder* (1972), *Conrack* (1974), *Norma Rae* (1979), *Back Roads* (1981), and *Cross Creek* (1983). He was always a good interview and we enjoyed many of them during our twenty-year critic-director relationship. Perhaps because I met him first as his publicist (for *Conrack*) and only later as a critic, he knew that I had a knowledge and competency, not to mention respect and affection, on which he could depend.

"I like to set my stories in the south," he said during one of our interviews, "because the essence of drama is change, and that section of the country has undergone more change than any other. There were so many violations of the human spirit that existed there. They exist all over the country, of course, but there they seem exacerbated. You've got your Carson McCullerses and Faulkners and Tennessee Williamses, and you've got your fat sheriffs. It's a very complicated and dense psychological forum. I went to school down there and it stuck with me: this massive contradiction, day by day. I still feel it's a place where extraordinary American films can be made. Also, the country itself is pretty. It has a lot going for it."

Never one to dodge a fight, Marty still chose his wisely. Many's the time I asked if I could write his biography and, even though he considered me worthy, he consistently declined. "The shitheels come out of the woodwork every time I make a movie," he said, citing *New York Times* art critic Hilton Kramer (who suddenly became a movie critic whenever Ritt had a new film) and a cadre of other right-wingers who attacked his person instead of his work. "Why should I have to take their shit between pictures?" He also refused to let well-meaning liberals off the hook. When asked by members of the African-American press why he, a white man, made *Sounder*, a film about black sharecroppers during the Depression, he shot back, "I said, 'Fellas, make your own God damn pictures; get off my back. I've spent a lifetime believing in integration. You want to make another film, make it. Why do I have to deliver a film that you approve of?'"

When he directed Jane Fonda and Robert DeNiro in *Stanley & Iris*, which became his last film, he said, "We've had trouble from some right-wing people about Jane.[1] I guess nobody had heard from [the groups] in a while and they've had no moment in the sun. And all through this discussion with Jane nobody has even mentioned that she was right about the war." I used that quote in an article I wrote about him for my reactionary tabloid, *The Boston Herald*. When the piece appeared in print, it was the only line my editor had deleted. "I'm not surprised," Marty said when he saw the paper. "What surprises me is that you're surprised."

The occasion for that particular interview was a life achievement award from Boston University's film school, an institution with which he had no connection save his friendship with me when I taught there, several seminar visits, and the admiration of tenured B.U. Professor George Bluestone, who had miraculously navigated the school administration's right-wing waters to secure the honor. The date was April 19, 1988 and I was asked to deliver the appreciation at the ceremony. Adele Ritt and their daughter, Martina, would also be attending, along with the press and such distinguished B.U. alumni as the AFI's Jean Firstenberg, producer Victor Pisano (a classmate of mine who had worked with Ritt), director Fred Barzyk, and broadcasters Stephen Schlow and Francine Achbar.

Marty and I arranged to meet privately for dinner the night before. "I eat at 5:30 sharp, whether you're there or not," he warned. I was, and I briefed him on the political minefield that Boston University's School of Communications had become. He took it in stride. "I'll be happy to receive

---

1   Fonda famously visited North Vietnam and posed with weapons, earning the enmity of some veterans groups who called her "Hanoi Jane."

the award," he said, "but I won't show up in a black tie. I don't wear those clothes. I'll wear a suit, though." As usual, we both groused about how hard it was to make worthwhile films within a system that increasingly craved frivolity. "It's always tough doing serious pictures," he grumbled, "but what the hell are you gonna do? If I don't do that, I'll go to the race track every day and I don't think I can quite stand that." His love-hate relationship with Hollywood was never far from conversation. "Very few people survive here. Certainly, when you get older, fewer. But money is the bottom line in Hollywood and, if you use any other criteria, you're kidding yourself. If you make money—unless you're breaking the law in some way—they're going to hire you."

Although he was best known for his films, Ritt's legacy reached back to the Group Theatre of the 1930s and 40s. He acted in the original production of Clifford Odets' *Golden Boy* as well as serving as its stage manager, and began a long career helming such plays as Arthur Miller's *A View from the Bridge* and a revival of Sidney Howard's *Yellow Jack*. Steeped in the Group Theatre's immersion in the Stanislavski "Method," he was tarred with the right-wing's red brush during the 1950s when people like Elia Kazan named names and destroyed many of the people they themselves had mentored into the Party. Ritt survived and, by 1957, had returned to Hollywood to direct *Edge of the City*. It led to other jobs, not only because of its modest commercial and critical success but because Ritt knew how to work with the emerging generation of actors such as Paul Newman, Joanne Woodward, and John Cassavettes.

Throughout his career, he made it look easy, and that's hard. I once asked him ponderously why the visual style of his films was so perfectly integrated with their themes, and he complimented his cinematographers. I asked him why his dialogue always sounded true, and he complimented his writers. I asked him why the acting was uniformly focused and authentic, and he complimented his actors. Then I went and asked his cinematographers, his writers, and his actors, and they all complimented Marty.

One of his credos was that a man has to take responsibility for his own actions. He always swore that he never set out to make message pictures, and yet everything in his canon carried a message. He admitted to making only two overtly political films: *The Front*, about the Blacklist, and *The Molly Maguires*, about the mining labor movement betrayed by infiltration, both of them scripted by Walter Bernstein, a fellow blacklistee. He made five films with blue-eyed Paul Newman and had the gall to shoot three of them in black and white. And he remains the only person to ever make two films for Producer Robert Radnitz.

One incident, in particular, encapsulates the rough-hewn charm that Martin Ritt not only possessed but that he demonstrated to others. In September of 1972 a studio sneak was scheduled in Boston of Ritt's comedy-drama *Pete 'n' Tillie* starring Walter Matthau and Carol Burnett. It was a rich comedy-drama about a charming but mismatched couple that get married, have a child, lose the child, and nearly lose each other, but survive. It needed an audience reaction to adjust its difficult tonal transitions. Ritt, who didn't like previews, reluctantly agreed to allow the studio sneak for which Matthau and Burnett accompanied him to Boston.

It turned out to be a busy press weekend in the Hub and for me, as I was filling in between PR jobs by freelancing for *Boston After Dark*. Arriving on the plane from California with Ritt, Matthau, and Burnett were Jacqueline Onassis and her daughter, Caroline. Publicist Jane Badgers met the flight and gasped when she saw, first, Mrs. Onassis, then Matthau, then Burnett alight. Typical of Burnett, she turned to Badgers and joked, "Just my luck! If that damn plane had gone down, I'd have gotten *third* billing."

The movie people took dinner that night before the preview in the main dining room of the old Ritz-Carlton hotel, the summit of Brahmin elegance. Ritt deigned to wear a tie for the occasion. The Hollywood group made their noteworthy entrance and was shown to their table against the Arlington Street windows of the hotel. This was the side with the grandest view of the Boston Public Garden.

Then the Onassis party entered. Astonishingly, Nino Todescu, the Ritz maitre d', sat them in the center of the vast dining room.

"Why?" he was asked.

"Because, with famous people, it's better to seat them in the open so everyone can easily see them, rather than cause a commotion as people contrive to walk past their table."

A few posh heads in the dining room casually looked toward Jackie O, but the ones who were gawking most was the Hollywood contingent.

Pete 'n' Tillie was a delicate balancing act. Its skillfully comic first half lulled audiences into thinking they were watching a pure comedy, and they began shifting uncomfortably when the second half became not only serious but funereal. It was a brave gamble that worked on paper but not fully on the screen, even though the talents involved in the project were all at the top of their game. The most difficult moment occurred when Pete and Tillie lose their child and a devastated Tillie rails against God, "I spit on you." At the preview, she repeated it for a fair amount of time and it was clear from the noises the audience was making that it had to be shortened. When the film was released months later, it was, and it played well. Previews can be helpful that way.

Ritt was a master storyteller even away from the camera. "There was once an actor in the Yiddish theatre named Menachem Goldberg," he recalled, lifting his muscular, squat frame into standing position to perform the story. "He was a great star. And one day, during the intermission, he had a heart attack backstage and died. The company was devastated. Not only was Menachem Goldberg dead, but they might have to give back all the ticket money. The Stage Manager was designated to make the announcement. He stepped out in front of the curtain and quieted the audience.

"'Ladies and gentlemen, I have terrible news,'" Ritt began, assuming a Yiddish accent and acting the role of the beleaguered Stage Manager. "'Menachem Goldberg is dead.' A hush falls over the audience. All of a sudden, a little old lady yells from the back of the top balcony, 'Give him an enema!'

"The audience is stunned. The Stage Manager doesn't know what to say. 'Please, madam, this is serious. We can't go on with the show. Menachem Goldberg is dead.

"Comes down the voice again, 'Give him an enema!"

"'For heaven's sake, madam,' the Stage Manager says, 'Menachem Goldberg, he's dead. An enema, it wouldn't help!'

"Says the old woman, 'It wouldn't hurt!'"

Marty would direct nine more films before dying in 1990 of complications from diabetes. His legacy is a remarkable example of what a filmmaker can do if he has both a conscience and the skill to weave meaningful ideas into entertainment that lifts the human spirit. But he never did bring jumpsuits into fashion.

Only the Press Agent Eats

PUBLICITY IS the world's oldest profession. Some people mistakenly think that prostitution is the world's oldest profession, but before the first hooker went into business, some poor damn publicist had to get out a press release on her. I was that publicist from the time of my first job in Boston from the summer of 1970 to the end of 1975 when I walked out of that Christmas party at United Artists vowing never to do publicity again. And yet I proudly keep up my union membership in the Publicists Guild (even though I had to bury my card to avoid conflict of interest when I became a critic) and I remain generally sympathetic to publicists themselves.

Publicity is ephemeral, though I prefer to think of it as being stealth. I used to teach my students that advertising is what you pay for but publicity is what you get for free. That's a workable distinction except for remembering that, while publicity is free, somebody still has to arrange it. Show business has several words for publicity, each of them shaded to specific needs. *Publicity*, of course, is exactly what it is: gaining public attention for a product by any means that does not involve the purchase of advertising. For this reason—because it comes at you from places you don't expect—publicity can be more effective, much as rumor can defeat truth. Its drawback is that, unlike advertising, it can't be quantified and, therefore, the publicist's job is constantly at risk.

Tub-thump is a term popularized by *Variety,* formerly the bible of show business. Its derivation is said to be the ancient art of drawing attention to a traveling show or an arriving general by parading through the center of town banging on drums. *Hoopla* is a term for boasting about something, possibly derived from its sound when shouted by the human voice, like "Hubba-hubba," "Extra! Extra!" or "Laaaaaaadies and Gentlemen!"

Ballyhoo, like *hoopla*, is an onomatopoetic term whose origins are similarly murky, but whose meaning is clear: a noisy, even vulgar, display contrived to gain attention. *Hype* is short for *hyperbole*, the overuse of superlatives in service of a product undeserving of them. Today this is more commonly found on Internet videos: "The greatest song ever," "the best dance of all time," etc. Needless to say, none ever is.

The only term that has no moral place in publicity is *public relations*. Both the phrase and the concept were invented around the time of World War I by Edward Bernays, the self-proclaimed "father of public relations." It means propaganda, and it has been wielded with enormous expertise to cleanse products, people, and ideas of the stench of opprobrium. A press agent admits he's a press agent, but a public relations person thinks he's doing a service. It's like the old joke about the guy who propositions a woman in a bar by asking, "Would you sleep with me for a million dollars?" When she says, "Yes," he asks, "Okay, what about for ten dollars?" Becoming outraged, she huffs, "What kind of a woman do you think I am?" To this, the lothario replies, "We've already established that. Now we're just haggling over the price."

Finally there's *exploitation*. In a show business context, exploitation is pointing out the most attractive aspects a product in order to raise interest. Although the word has negative connotations elsewhere—to "exploit" someone is to abuse him without adequate compensation, like textile workers at the J.P. Stevens plant—its meaning within the entertainment industry is historically more benign.[1] It just means to make use of any tools at hand. Yee haw.

---

1   On this note, I once asked Robert Altman if his movie, *O.C. and Stiggs*, was a youth exploitation film. "No," he said, "it's an *adult* exploitation film."

I'm no moralist, but I never saw it this way. To my literal mind, exploitation was exploitation. If I wanted an entertainment reporter to interview a client, I asked him nicely, but he was always aware that my studio's advertising department was spending significant money in his publication, so it was hard to turn me down. The content of the resulting story was not affected; in those days, editorial and advertising departments were kept rigidly separate. Or perhaps it was affected because, while editorial respects advertising, advertising likes to lean on editorial unless a principled publisher or station manager intervenes. But as far as deciding what to cover, mainstream newspapers and broadcasters always favor advertisers over independent sources. Always. Editors and broadcast executives insist that this is because their customers are mainstream, but no one who has to play the tug-of-war really believes this.

I hated asking people for favors even though we told ourselves that what we were doing was in the public interest. True, it was only a movie, but I took it seriously. After 1975, when I switched sides and became a journalist, I held onto this inside knowledge of the game and playfully irritated publicists by reminding them that I knew the tricks, so don't try using them on me.

One of the more flamboyant conventions of movie publicity is the press junket. In a press junket (q.v., *The Return of the Pink Panther*), a film company will fly a hundred or more reporters from key markets to a central city, usually New York or Los Angeles, where they will be wined, dined, shown an upcoming movie, and allowed to interview the filmmakers. Interviews for the print press generally take place in a hotel function room set with round tables, like a wedding reception, at which one seat is kept empty for the person being interviewed. They usually answer softball questions for twenty minutes before hopping to another table and another set of equally softball questions. Television interviewers get private time with the VIP, usually seven or eight minutes, but it's on an assembly line basis as they trek room-to-room and the VIP remains seated. It's maddening for everyone involved—try answering the same banal questions seventy-five times—but it does the job.

Before the age of the manufactured blockbuster, films opened in only a handful of theatres in key cities, then widened their bookings if initial success warranted expansion. This is no longer the case. Distribution has become an all-or-nothing gamble in which films open on as many as five thousand screens at once, and the first weekend's grosses dictate instant success or failure. P&A (prints and advertising) costs have skyrocketed. There was a time when, if a film was advertised on TV, you knew it was a stiff. Now if a film *isn't* advertised on TV, you think it is. Against this template, independent features and documentaries don't stand a chance. Back when publicity held more sway than advertising and press junkets were rare, celebrities were flown from key city to key city where they were interviewed at press luncheons by competing journalists who agreed to share access. These were held in the most prestigious hotels and restaurants in town on the theory that, if the film wasn't strong enough to draw coverage, the meal would.

With the youth market becoming increasingly important, and Boston being one of its top five centers, my beat became a regular stop-off for these VIP tours. Boston press luncheons were usually held in the Ritz-Carlton, Four Seasons, or the "57" Restaurant (which was rumored to be involved in a complex kickback scheme between the restaurateur and a local theatre owner).

The protocol at these confabs was unwavering. The press would assemble at noon, start drinking, and at about 12:15 the press agent would enter with the movie star, director, or producer (seldom the writer) in tow. Celebrities who knew various press members from past encounters might hug and fuss, while newcomers would make businesslike introductions. Questions would flow; the only taboo subject was, "What did you think of the picture?" Reporters who attended such affairs learned early in their careers to cut the food on their plates ahead of time so they could take notes with one hand while eating with the other (this was before small tape recorders). When a reporter got her or his answer, another would ask the next question with deference. Although reporters got to finish their meals, the interviewee seldom got to even start his, and was advised to wolf something down beforehand. At these affairs, the only person who was able to finish his meal was the one who had set it all up; thus, only the press agent eats.

Remarkably, there were few spats between reporters. Each publication at the luncheon had its well-defined market, and each press member was extraordinarily skilled. Unlike some cities that were still fighting the newspaper wars, Boston was cordial. *The Boston Globe* was slightly upscale, the *Boston Record-American* was blue collar, and the *Boston Herald-Traveler* was whatever was left (unable to find it, it folded in 1972), and *Boston After Dark* (later the *Boston Phoenix,* now gone) was considered "underground." *The Patriot-Ledger,* covered by Constance Gorfinkle, served the area of Quincy, the *Framingham News,* whose reporter was Virginia Lucier, addressed the South Shore, the *Bay State Banner,* whose Kay Bourne also wrote general assignment pieces, represented the city's African-American community, and Cecile Markell sought comments for her *Jewish Advocate* readers. I particularly admired Bourne and Markell, who had the ability to extract angles for their parochial audiences from the gush of general quotes that flew around the room, but everyone there was a seasoned pro.

Other papers entered the market after I stopped doing publicity (I even wrote for some of them), and other colleagues emerged, but these were the mainstays when I broke into the luncheon PR circuit.

Some visiting celebrities actually enjoyed these mass feeds. John Wayne would stride into the Ritz and bellow, "Where's that old broad, Marjory?" meaning Marjory Adams, the cantankerous but supportive writer for the *Boston Globe,* who beamed with pride at being singled out by her old friend, the Duke. Frank Langella held court when he winged into town to promote *Dracula,* announcing regally, "Of course we realize that vampires don't really exist, except for the next hour, when we all agree that they do." Jane Fonda, freshly back from Vietnam to promote her anti-war movie *F.T.A.*[2], entered

---

2   The letters stood for "free the Army" although they were widely understood to mean "fuck the Army." The documentary does not appear on Ms. Fonda's IMDb credit page.

the room cautiously, sat facing the press as if expecting a firing squad, and slowly defrosted once she realized that, as arts reporters, they were on her side. I was embraced in front of my colleagues by director William Friedkin, renewing our friendship and making my competitors jealous. I'm sure Billy meant to do both.

George Hamilton made one of the more notable entrances. I met him twice, first as a press agent (when he'd mentioned John Milius) and then as a reporter. For the first, he dispatched me ahead of time to where the press was gathered with instructions to report back to him everyone's name and what he or she was wearing. He then memorized the list, strolled into the dining room on his own, and greeted everybody as though he knew them. When I interviewed him years later I asked him about it. "It's a trick," he acknowledged. "It doesn't really fool anyone, but it's a nice gesture."

Press luncheons can last up to two hours, which is sometimes ninety minutes longer than the conversation. This is primarily true of people who are either at the start of their careers or who have only the briefest of stories to tell. Adrianna Caselotti was an 18-year-old girl who gave Snow White her voice in *Snow White and the Seven Dwarfs* in 1937. For the film's 1983 reissue, she was sent around by the Walt Disney Company to reminisce about the experience. Caselotti, by then sixty-four, was bubby and engaging and winningly recalled the few memories she had of her historic role. There weren't many of them after 46 years, but she utterly charmed the room, which was the publicity-savvy Disney folks' whole point. After the coffee and dessert dishes had been cleared, Karl Fasick, the popular local Disney press representative, signaled the waiter, who brought in a basket full of gorgeous bright red apples. "Anybody want to make a wish?" he asked playfully. Presenting magic wishing apples to the now-grown-up Snow White was a marvelous touch, but the punch line was Adrianna's. As she picked out the biggest and juiciest of them, she held it in her delicate hand, closed her eyes, and said, "I wish, I wish, I wish for residuals."

Such stories make entertainment writing sound like fun, but there is tarnished side of the tinsel. Critics who voice strong opinions can receive strong counter opinions from their readers, listeners, viewers, and, on occasion, bruised filmmakers. This is to be expected; art provokes passion. With film critics, however, the element of commerce is never far away. Other than war correspondents, movie critics have the most dangerous job in journalism. Let me explain. When a sports writer knocks an athlete, or a political columnist attacks an elected official, a society reporter angers a blueblood, or a restaurant critic pans a local eatery, none of them is going after a large advertiser. But a movie critic is the only journalist whose very job is to criticize one of a newspaper's or TV station's biggest spenders. You never see anyone routinely dumping on real estate companies, department stores, supermarkets, or (especially) car dealerships. They're sacrosanct. They'll pull their accounts faster than you can say "Freedom of the Press." But the movie critic paints a bull's-eye on his back every time he enters a screening room.

Back in the 1970s, Boston TV critic Pat Collins benefited from this. Hired by the local NBC-TV affiliate, Collins made an early reputation for herself by slamming a number of films. This enraged the leading local exhibitor, Ben Sack, who, against the advice of his staff, issued orders banning her from advance screenings. He even tried to prevent her from buying tickets once the film opened. The effect was predictable: Collins' TV bosses backed her to the hilt and Sack's actions earned her national publicity and a network job offer. By the time her successor, Pat Mitchell, likewise drew Sack's enmity, he had the good sense to keep silent, forcing Ms. Mitchell to use other means to advance her career.

Celebrities can be quirky. Paul Newman posed an unusual problem for press agents. For a time, he refused to make personal appearances unless the studio stacked several cases of Coors beer, his well known favorite, on the doorstep of his Connecticut home as an inducement to leave the house. When facts emerged about Coors' anti-Union, anti-gay, and anti-civil liberties policies, Newman publicly switched to Budweiser. (No reports on whether he still wanted five cases of it.)

Walter Matthau was the bane of publicists who failed to understand his droll humor. Time and again he would be quoted as saying, "This film is dreck, don't see it, it's too good for anyone to waste ticket money on." It was his tactic to attract customers to his work by trashing it. When Jack Lemmon directed him in a drama titled *Kotch* about a senior citizen, Matthau started his interviews by saying, "What's all this about a movie called 'Crotch'?" Matthau—trained as a classical actor but driven to comedy by his basset hound face and loping walk ("I'm the Ukrainian Cary Grant," he often said)—could raise a laugh without even opening his mouth, just by looking nonplused. He was also the rare comedian who could be a straight man. At a dual press conference with George Burns on behalf of *The Sunshine Boys* in 1975, the elderly but spry Burns fielded the predictable inquiries about his sex life.

"Has your age affected your dating?" a woman reporter asked.

"Not at all," Burns said. "At my age, just putting a cigar into my cigar holder is exciting."

"By the way, George," Matthau cut in. "You're going to be 80 next month. When did sex stop for you?"

Burns took a puff on his cigar and said, "About eight o'clock this morning."

Entering a much newer generation, Tom Cruise recalled the difficulty he encountered on his first LA venture.

"I remember when I came out to California," he said, "and was reading for television situation comedies. I was in a meeting and did a reading for a guy and I was terrible. The guy said, 'so how long are you gonna be in town?' I said, 'I dunno, a couple of days.' He said, 'oh, a couple of days?' I thought he was going to ask me to come for a callback and read again. I was about to get excited, when, instead, he said, 'A couple of days, huh? Well, you might as well get a tan while you're here.'"

Some actors find press luncheons a cross between a tennis match and target practice. They want to be polite, but they're also never far from wondering how they may be misquoted if they don't finish a thought or speak clearly enough to be heard. Accuracy is up for grabs. Cliff Robertson solved the problem by rehearsing his anecdotes and performing them in response to expected questions. Charlton Heston talked like he read it off tablets. Paul Newman developed the technique of telling stories one way when he was being interviewed for broadcast and another way, slower and more linear, when his words were intended for print. Groucho Marx may have famously said, "If you want a reporter to get a joke right, you have to tell it to him wrong," but Newman wasn't taking any chances.

Writers Stirling Silliphant, William Peter Blatty, Oliver Stone, and Larry Gelbart not only went over transcripts, they expanded their comments. At least they did for me when I wrote about them. I didn't consider that a breach of ethics; where history is concerned, I prefer accuracy to ambush. Besides, do you have any idea how much a free Silliphant, Stone, Blatty, or Gelbart rewrite is worth on the Hollywood market? I even had two quite disparate people—actor Charles Haid and television producer Don Hewitt—contact me after our interviews to ask if I needed additional material or clarification of what we had discussed. In both cases, their integrity spoke for itself.

For a Disney film called *The World's Greatest Athlete*, the decidedly un-Disney Jan-Michael Vincent triggered controversy even before he faced the Boston press. Quoted in a published article complaining about "all the fags" in Los Angeles, the magnetically handsome young actor was warned, in print, by Stuart Byron, Boston's first openly gay critic, that his remarks were offensive. Moreover, Byron suggested, if Vincent opposed being turned into a gay icon like Tab Hunter, he shouldn't gallivant around the screen in a loincloth, as he did in his new movie. The Disney people expected sparks to fly when Byron attended the Vincent luncheon, but Byron—himself a former press agent (for Embassy Pictures)—declined, saying that he didn't want that to be the story that got covered. At the luncheon, Vincent ordered a shot of tequila and proceeded to sip it slowly to make the local Disney people uncomfortable (it did). He played with the glass, repeatedly lifting it to his lips and barely tasting it, as though he was less interested in getting a buzz than in warning the studio reps to keep their distance. Naturally, Marjory

Adams ignored his game and cut to the chase. Referring to an earlier film, *Going Home,* in which he played a violently troubled youth, she asked, "How could someone with such a sweet face play a rapist and killer?"

Responded Vincent, "Sometimes it's more effective for someone with a sweet face to do bad things."

"I knew that all along!" Marjory chortled. "I just needed to hear *you* say it."

Questions lobbed at celebrities can throw them. Gene Wilder once stopped answering my technical question about *The World's Greatest Lover* to ask, "Are your readers gonna know what we're talking about?" I responded, "Yes, I'll use italics."

"What Gene is saying," chimed in Dom DeLuise, who was part of the press tour, "is that he's been interviewed a lot of times and these are the *new* questions."

The subject happened to be something that actors love talking about: pain. Showing the pain beneath a comic façade is the greatest thrill a comic actor can have. Wilder, whose ability to combine discomfort and surprise distinguished his performances in *Bonnie and Clyde, Young Frankenstein,* and *The Producers,* waxed eloquent.

"The question you ask, if it gets beyond a role they just offer you for money, is, 'What pain do I want the audience to know I feel?'" he said. "What have I lived through in my life that I'd like to share with the audience, to make them suffer, but that I will understand and be able to act better because of it? Instead of just playing superficial things. You've got to start examining what you went through in your own life."

Added DeLuise, whose best roles also were built on pain (*Fatso, The End*), added, "I think you've got to start with something real. As grotesque as some of the things are that I do, they're always based on something. People say, 'Gee, you just get up and do it,' but that's not true. I think a great deal about what I'm doing. Often I think about my own personal tragedies to make people laugh and let them enjoy me comically so that I don't have to necessarily be having a flip time. I could be having a very serious time, thinking about serious things, but coming out with funny ideas."

The pain lurking beneath the pleasure was also raised by Dustin Hoffman. He was speaking of *Ishtar*, which itself became an emblem of pain lurking beneath pleasure, at least for the company that financed it. Unfairly criticized for cost overruns, the film's two stars—Hoffman and Warren Beatty—spent most of their interview time deflecting press questions about the budget. This came across as evasive rather than charming. Example: Hoffman to Beatty: "Did you have bowel problems on location?" Beatty: "No, did you." Hoffman: "Did I! Mine came out like a Jackson Pollack painting." Hoffman brightened when critics noted the pain his character suffered despite the cheerfulness of his veneer. A past master at creating finely textured performances, Hoffman was particularly flattered to be told that he had achieved this. More pain came in the process of finishing the film itself. Written and directed by the brilliant but eccentric and reclusive Elaine May, it seemed that she, Hoffman and Beatty each had final cut. At one point, according to lore, each of them had her and his own separate version.

"We were in the cutting room; it seemed like forever," Beatty recalled, "and we'd make a contribution to the editing or mention this or that, and we'd have a dialogue going on, and, at a certain point, Dustin goes out of the room."

"I couldn't stand him any more," Hoffman joked.

Beatty continued, "And I wanted to take particular pains not to go out of the room at the same time because I didn't want anybody to think we were having a kind of a confab, but I had to go to the bathroom. So I waited and I waited and finally I just can't stand it any longer, so I say, 'Well never mind diplomacy, I gotta go to the bathroom.' So I go into the bathroom and I see Dusty's shoes under a stall, and I hear him ripping the sheets of toilet paper and putting them down on the seat, and I say, 'That's right, put paper down, you paranoid sonofabitch.' And he wouldn't say anything."

"He's cleaning this story up," Hoffman gloated playfully. "He said, 'you scared, cowardly &%$#, you....'"

"So I go into the next stall," Beatty continued, "and I'm thinking he's gonna really hit me with something—throw water over on me—something horrible.

So I got up on the toilet seat and I looked over between the two stalls, and it wasn't him. There was some other guy, and he's cowering down there. And I said, 'Oh, I'm terribly, terribly sorry. I thought you were Dustin Hoffman.'

"And he said, 'No! No! No! I'm not even *on* that picture.'"

Shit Happens

SOMETIMES IT'S better to know what to forget than what to remember. For this chapter, we are going to forget names because many of them belong to people who are still around.

Once upon a time there was a female critic who hit on the male filmmakers she interviewed. Not all of them, but enough that people talked about it behind her back. She held a powerful position, was a gifted writer, and was attractive. She was also married to another writer who, as luck (hers) would have it, traveled a lot. This placed the hitee in a vulnerable position: If he refused her advances, she might trash him in print. If he accepted them, he risked her guilty reaction. If they both had a good time, of course, it could result in a positive article. So the odds were two out of three it would go badly. The problem then became how to say No in a manner that wouldn't create a rift in The Force.

Into this no-win situation fell the publicist.

On this occasion, a private lunch interview was set up in the Star's suite between She Who Shall Not Be Named (hereinafter referred to as SWSNBN) and a major Movie Star. "Private," in publicity parlance, didn't mean "alone," it meant "one-on-one" (which still sounds lewd) in that the press agent, who happened to be a woman, was present while the reporter spoke to the Star. SWSNBN was disappointed that the press agent would sit in, but she bowed to what the publicist insisted was studio policy. Throughout lunch, SWSNBN sidled closer to the Star, laughed at his jokes, and flirted. She was not subtle; her batting eyes threw off enough breeze to flap the curtains. The Star—who, after all, seduced interviewers as part of his job—quickly caught on and sidled away from SWSNBN, regaling her with stories of how he had met the woman he married.

SWSNBN persisted. By the time coffee was served, she and the Star had practically played musical chairs around the room service table. Once the interview was over, the critic slapped her notebook shut, grabbed her wrap, and left in a more businesslike manner than the one she had used during the interview.

"Do you believe that?" remarked the Star after SWSNBN left.

The press agent explained SWSNBN's penchant for proposition and added, "and she has such nice skin."

"Yes," agreed the Star. "But look what it's stretched over."

The interview ran as predicted, as did the review: Both were businesslike.

Knowing that everybody was wise to her did not thwart SWSNBN. Soon it was my turn to accompany her on a drive-along assignment in which she would write about a day in the life of a Movie Star for whose life I was, for that day, responsible. This one was a wee bit more complicated because, when the day's press activities were over, the Star and I were scheduled to visit his brother in a nearby town. Since SWSNBN had kept her distance all day long, I decided that my charge was safe and I lowered my guard.

The moment the last interview was over, however, SWSNBN, rather than go back to her paper and write up the aforementioned day in the life, switched into siren mode. The Star, also unguarded, was smitten by her charms and, before I could stop him, he invited her along on our road trip. This was Plan B—both of them obviously had the same idea—so I jumped into the front seat of the limo, left them together in the back, and figured that the odds were in his favor. By the time we got to where the Star's brother was staying, the Star wanted out. He pulled me aside to tell me what she had been trying to do in the back. I asked him, man to man, if that wasn't what he'd been looking for, and he said that he was just trying to endear himself so she'd give his film a better review. I told him to stick to acting from now on and let me do the publicity, but not in those exact words. His only response was, "Help!"

I spent the rest of the evening playing Puritan, asking everybody if he or she needed another soda, and reminding the Star of our 8 AM live radio interview the next morning. He pretended to protest my intrusions (signified by a wink). She grew irritated (signified by a scowl). The brother didn't have a clue about the backstory and, at one point, it looked as if she was going to switch her sights to him. After four hours of playing keep-away, the star, SWSNBN, and I all got in the back seat of the limo and returned uneventfully to the Star's hotel.

When I offered to drop SWSNBN off at her apartment, she said that she'd grab a cab. The Star had already taken the elevator upstairs to his suite and I couldn't think of a polite way to linger without betraying my skepticism. I decided that the Star was a big boy, and that I was off both the hook and the clock. I don't know whether SWSNBN followed him upstairs. All I know what that she hated his film and wrote a snarky interview.

Famous people are unusually vulnerable to the whims of the press, who may be out to get a story at any cost. Often there is a "we made 'em, we can break 'em" mindset that befalls the Fourth Estate just as there is an "I made it on my own, who needs you?" attitude that can infect a celebrity.[1] Tension also comes from the simple fact that celebrities give dozens of interviews and can never be sure if they are being accurately quoted. In most cases, of course, they simply can't remember what they said. Then there's the problem that verbatim speech may be what the subject *said*, but not what he or she *meant*. Lauren Bacall once took me to task for making her look illiterate in an interview. "I wrote a *book*, for heaven's sake," she lectured. "I'm an *author!*" So I showed her the transcript, and she spent the next hour correcting what the tape recorder flawlessly heard.

---

1   Fred Allen said that a celebrity is someone who works hard all his life to become known and then wears dark glasses to avoid being recognized.

Perhaps Hollywood people are entitled to be prickly. They live in an age in which they are cyber-stalked, hacked, and photographed in the most unflattering circumstances and there's no studio publicity machine to protect them. At the same time, some of them court scandal so they can monetize their fame. Maybe that's to be expected; after all, if you take the most talented and attractive people in the world and put them in one town, critical mass is bound to happen. Desperate people will often do anything to get ahead, and sometimes they do it wrong. There's the old joke about the starlet who was so stupid that she slept with the writer. Said Dick Powell (the writer, not the actor), "If you change *writer* to *producer*, the joke doesn't work, but the starlet does."

In the golden age of Hollywood, a studio staff publicist's job sometimes called for him to procure girls for visiting male exhibitors, investors, politicians, and celebrities. This doesn't happen as much as it used to thanks to the breakdown of the studio monopolies, the enforcement of anti-pandering laws, and the rabid interest of the tabloid press that no longer butters its bread in the studio commissary. But the practice of procurement was common in the 20s, 30s, 40s and 50s when Hollywood controlled the papers and fan magazines, and shop girls had stars in their eyes. The casting couch was real; Darryl F. Zanuck, when he ran Twentieth Century-Fox, had a standing order with the studio switchboard not to put calls through between four and five PM. That was when he "interviewed" talent. The women who were interviewed this way became known as "the four o'clock girls."[2] Such shenanigans were rife among extras in the silent days but dropped off with the inauguration of the Central Casting agency in 1925 that institutionalized the hiring of extras and set standards of decency. Speaking parts were another story.

"The most beautiful people in the world gravitate to Hollywood to be stars," explained producer Larry Jackson. "And after a while they give up but stay around anyway and mess up the gene pool."

---

2   Marilyn Monroe was a Fox contract player at this time, but insiders insist that Zanuck never laid a hand (or anything else) on her. That's because she belonged to Joseph Schenck, Zanuck's boss. Or so they say.

When I was doing publicity in Boston in the 1970s, it was soon enough after America's Summer of Love that it wasn't that hard for visiting filmmakers to get laid on their own. Sometimes they had need of recreational drugs in those carefree pre-cocaine and heroin days. It was too risky to try to score them on the street, but I had kept my college contacts, so the holy trinity of pot, hash, and mushrooms was never a problem. The risk was they might render the celebrity incoherent for the next day's interviews. Fortunately, people like director Bob Rafelson thoughtfully brought their own stash. The brilliant but erratic helmer of *Five Easy Pieces, Head, King of Marvin Gardens* and *Black Widow* generously offered to pass around the joint of which he was partaking in his ninth floor Ritz hotel suite, but I declined for pragmatic reasons. I flashed on Jane Fonda's rant against Rex Reed for reporting that, during their magazine interview, she had been sitting cross-legged on the floor smoking pot.

"Of course I was!" she said between interviews as I was showing her around Boston for *F.T.A.*. "That's because he was sitting there cross-legged smoking with me. Only he didn't print that part."

So I played it safe with Rafelson, a puckishly funny man who, like his films, looked at life from obtuse angles.

"When I was in the service," he recalled once he was relaxed, "I was an announcer on the base radio station, the Far East Radio Network. The kind of music I hate most in the world is Hawaiian music and, of course, they assigned me to host 'The Hawaiian Hour.' To make it worse, it was an overnight show. I got into the habit of putting on a long record and taking a nap, waking up when it was over to announce the station ID. One time I fell asleep and woke up at the last minute and was still groggy, so instead of turning on the mike and saying, 'This is the Far East Radio Network,' I said, 'This is the Near-East Radio Fart-works.' I was off the air the next day."

Rafelson was no stranger to spontaneity, and one instance of it nearly cost him his career. In 1979 he had just started directing Robert Redford in the film *Brubaker* about a prison warden who cleans up a corrupt Southern correctional farm. Within a matter of days he had fallen behind Twentieth Century-Fox's optimistic shooting schedule and the studio dispatched a company representative to the rural location to find out why. What happened next is unclear, but tempers flared and Rafelson allegedly slugged the studio guy. That served as his letter of resignation. Soon after, his empty director's chair was filled by Stuart Rosenberg, who had scored a 1967 hit with the Paul Newman chain gang picture, *Cool Hand Luke.*

As a testament to Hollywood friendships—the real kind, not the red carpet kind—Rafelson's friend Jack Nicholson, with whom he had made three earlier films, immediately hired him to direct his remake of *The Postman Always Rings Twice,* released in 1981. The film didn't work, but Rafelson did.

The intoxicant-of-choice before and after the industry's flirtation with drugs was, of course, alcohol. Reporters were old hands at this. The classic image of the hard-drinking reporter, press agent, or macho movie star became a stereotype because it was true. Many a newspaper writer filed a story and hit the local bar for a drink, only not necessarily in that order.

Stars also imbibed on the road. John Wayne, despite his fame, came to Boston armed, not with a six-shooter, but with a bottle of vodka and insisted on riding in the front of the limo with the driver. Joan Crawford forsook her trademark Pepsi-Cola on several television appearances and quaffed vodka during the commercials. Shelley Winters was more delicate: her handlers were instructed to have a glass of white wine ready for her as soon as she walked onto the set to shoot. Dean Martin didn't really drink on the air, but Jackie Gleason did. Humphrey Bogart was known to have his assistant standing by with a napkin-covered scotch and soda that was held at the ready until the stroke of 5 o'clock, quitting time. The last take of the day on a movie set is called the "Martini shot" for obvious reasons, and the tradition of "wrap beers" for the crew is an old, respected, and expected one.

It wasn't necessarily that these screen legends were alcoholics, only that they sought fortification before coming face to face with the press. There was also an unspoken rule that you never wrote that an actor was tight (perhaps because, half the time, you were, too). Today, access to celebrities is so heavily controlled, and the press is so predatory, that both sides seem to have forgotten that they need each other. The energy that the paparazzi expend chasing fleeing stars, the twenty-four-hour guards that celebrities must hire to protect their families and their privacy, and the endless TV shows and Internet websites who dig for dirt on people no one would otherwise care about, are not only mind-boggling, they have turned what used to be a craft into a racket that no longer has room for the one thing that made it popular in the first place: humanity.

I miss it. And I know I'm not alone.

Liar's Poker

TAKE A dollar bill. Look at the serial number. Now imagine that the bill is a poker hand where the twos are deuces, the threes are threes, and so forth, up to the zeros being tens, the ones being aces, and there aren't any face cards. This is the tool of Liar's Poker, a game of bluffing that can be played when you're with a group of folks who have lots of paper money in their pockets and too much time on their hands. Although it's a barroom game, Liar's Poker can also be found on film sets where boredom runs rampant between, as they say, moments of stark terror.

No one knows where it started, but here's how it's played. The object is to bet according to how many of each digit you think there are, not just on the bill in your hand, but on the bills in the entire game. Your thumb may be caressing four threes, but if you think the total of threes sitting around the table is seven, that's your bet. If the next person raises it to eight and you think he's bluffing, you call him on it. Everybody shows his bill to settle it. Whoever comes closest without going bust wins the bills that were in use. Then people whip out fresh singles and the cycle of loss continues.

We were sitting in a bus in Texas Canyon, a six-pack's drive out of Tucson, Arizona, on a cold spring day in 1976 waiting for the rain to stop so we could resume filming. Joe Camp, whose Mulberry Square Productions had made a fortune with *Benji* in 1974, had decided to go from canines to camels with a comedy called *Hawmps!* Based on a true incident in which the U.S. Cavalry experimented with using camels instead of horses to patrol the newly acquired western territories in the late 1850s, it starred a herd of familiar faces such as James Hampton, Christopher Connelly, Herb Vigran, Denver Pyle, Slim Pickens, Lee de Broux, Gino Conforti, and Jack Elam.

Being a star has its glamour, but it's the character actors who have the most fun because the weight of the film does not rest on their shoulders. If they're popular as people, they work constantly, moving from one film to another while the star is still waiting for just the right script.

James Hampton, then known to millions as the bugler on the TV series *F Troop,* may have been the co-lead (with Christopher Connelly, formerly of TV's *Peyton Place*) in *Hawmps!,* but he didn't have a flicker of star temperament. He told of the time when they were shooting *F Troop* on an unusually crisp morning at the Warner Bros. Ranch. The director had just called for a take when one of the horses decided to poop on the ground.

"In the morning cold," Hampton recalled, "it sat there, festering and steaming, and had to be removed, so the director called out, 'Craft Services!'"

On a film set, the Craft Services guy handles incidental chores from stocking the snack table to hauling away trash. In this case, he was expected to take care of the road apples.

"So there's the Craft Services man leaning on his shovel," Hampton says. "He's tired, he's got his pension, and he had to get up early. He looks down at the pile of horseshit and says, 'While it's still steaming, it's Special Effects.'"

Slim Pickens was next. A former rodeo cowboy with a Texas drawl you could stretch from Houston to Fort Worth, Pickens built a solid career in westerns until Stanley Kubrick cast him for just that reason in *Dr. Strangelove, or: How I Learned to Stop Worrying and Love the Bomb.* As Major "King" Kong, Pickens rode an H-Bomb rodeo-style to its Russian target, ending both the movie and humanity with one big bang. After that, his career exploded through pictures such as *Will Penny, The Ballad of Cable Hogue,* and *Blazing Saddles.* Now he was recalling how Kubrick put him through his paces.

"They had me strapped upside down to the bomb," he said, drawing it in the air with his hands. "The bomb was hung from the roof o' the sound stage and I hung below that, and they aimed the camera up and dollied it back while they projected the background behind me to make it look like the bomb was falling." Cleverly, the bomb itself hid the ceiling wires because the camera was aiming directly up underneath it. Kubrick would use the same trick to make the astronauts float in space four years later in *2001*.

"Well," Pickens continued, "they'd do take after take and I'd be there with the blood rushin' to my head. They'd do a couple of takes, then I'd get off and throw up, then I'd get back up agin. One time I got bored so I climbed up on top of the bomb and started doin' a jig. Stanley caught me and wasn't happy. I said, 'I did bad, huh, Stanley?' and he said, 'Yep, Slim, you did,' so I got back under the bomb agin and we'd shoot some more and I'd throw up some more, but finally we got it.

"I'll tell you somethin' else ya might not know," he said, leaning in. "Y'know when we're goin' through the survival kit and I'm readin' off the list of the chocolate bars, the nylon stockin's, the prophylactics, and then say, 'shoot, a guy could have a pretty good weekend in Vegas with this'? Well, if you look at my mouth, I'm not sayin' *Vegas*, I'm sayin' *Dallas*. But while they were editing the film, Kennedy was shot, and they changed *Dallas* to *Vegas*, so I had to come in and loop the line."

Another seasoned cowboy actor was Denver Pyle whose silver-haired, walrus-mustached presence marked him early-on for westerns, even though his roots were in farming. Best known as Sheriff Hamer, who is taken hostage by Bonnie and Clyde in the 1968 film, Pyle in his long career also appeared in *The Alamo, Shenandoah, Home From the Hill* (where he met young Joe Camp), and several Disney films. Pyle's sternly handsome appearance and authoritarian manner were in contradiction to his dry humor. Not so Gino Conforti, a mischievous comic actor who played an Arab camel wrangler named "Hi Jolly" in the film, but whose long stage and TV career included everything from bothersome hotel managers to a denizen of a nudist colony.

"This camel is sick," he said once during a take. "Notice the swelling on top!"

While these seasoned veterans traded stories, the most seasoned veteran of all, Jack Elam, was sizing everybody up. Elam—whose wall-eyed stare made him suitable as either a creepy villain or a comic sidekick—was a former accountant whose doctor told him that he'd go blind if he didn't give up adding figures. Since he was a film production accountant, he traded columns for dialogue and never looked back. At the right moment, he said, more innocently than it turned out he deserved, "Anybody here interested in a little game of liar's poker?"

"Sure," "of course," "yeah," "why not?" came the consensus as everyone started reaching for loose singles. Again, Elam didn't move, only watched.

"Okay, then," he drawled, a smile growing on his face. "I'm game if you are." And with that he took a wad of bills from his pocket that would have choked a camel, carefully removed the rubber band holding it, and started riffling through it in search of the perfect dollar to open with.

It was a massacre. Having a head for figures and probability put Elam at immediate advantage. Plus his eyes, which were straight out of Edgar Allen Poe's "The Tell-Tale Heart." Being slaughtered at liar's poker by Jack Elam is nothing to be ashamed of. After all, you can't lose a game unless you're invited to play in the first place.

Hawmps! led me to someone who became not only a friend but a con-spirator, though the only thing we ever stole was time. Deborah Walley was an actress who often played the bad girl opposite Hayley Mills' good girls in various Disney movies of the early 1960s and was, therefore, more inter-esting. She also played Gidget in *Gidget Goes Hawaiian*, appeared in beach blanket movies, and co-starred in the aforementioned *Benji* for Joe Camp. During *Hawmps!* she was married to Jonathan Reynolds, one of the film's technicians, and it was through him that I met her when I visited California on some now forgotten press junket.

Deborah was born, not in a trunk, but in a refrigerator; her parents were with the Ice Capades and, by age fourteen, she was acting in summer stock. One of her first films was *The Bubble* (1966; a.k.a. *Fantastic Invasion*

of Planet Earth), an early 3-D movie, but it was the other film she made
that year, *Spinout*, from which she drew the most renown. Her co-star was
Elvis Presley.

But one cannot live on Elvis alone, and so, when the acting work
stopped, Deborah relocated to the artist-friendly town of Sedona, Arizona,
where she began a children's theatre. As time went on she developed projects for Sea World, wrote an ambitious animation project based on Aesop's
Fables, published a folksy book called *Grandfather's Good Medicine*, and
looked for projects that fed her spirit as well as her income. Once a year she
would be lured back to Los Angeles for the annual celebrity show that was
held at the Beverly Garland/Howard Johnson's Conference Center in North
Hollywood. It sounds grotesque, but it really wasn't: the massive ballroom
was outfitted with tables and celebrities were flown in to meet and greet fans
and sell autographed photos, books, and memorabilia. One could just as
easily see a former Mousketeer as bump into the legendary Mickey Rooney
(I did both). Stars of westerns, serials, long-canceled TV series, and pop
stars sat with pen in hand ready to exchange a fan's $10 or $25 ticket (no
cash changed hands) for a signed photo or to pose for a snapshot.

Some people call such gatherings sad and speak of them in terms of
faded glory, but to those who attend them they are a joyous occasion to celebrate memories, thank ones idols for their past work, and reminisce about
better (or at least younger) times. True, there are a few whorish brokers who
gather multiple autographs hoping to sell them at a posthumous profit, but
they are minimal and marginal. Mostly, the pervading emotion is love. Plus,
as Deborah said the first time she invited me to one, "Where else can you get
an all-expense paid trip to Los Angeles where you can have a reunion with
the people you used to make movies with?"

Deborah was one of the "Elvis Girls"—the King's co-stars from various films—who would hang out, reminisce, and, oh yes, earn pocket money.
After I moved out to California in 1993 I used to spirit Deborah away at

lunchtime (that's the conspiracy part of it) and we would drive to a reserved table at the nearby Eclectic Cafe and Wine Bar on Lankershim and Magnolia where we would talk about everything *but* Disney and Elvis.

The last time I saw her was in 1999. We'd kept in touch at Christmas, of course, but I didn't get the usual card in 2000. On May 10, 2001 I read that she had died of esophageal cancer. Her sons Tony and Justin survive her, and also some memories I still have of the bad girl who stole my heart when Hayley Mills did not.

Taking Flack

FAME IS not normal. It is not natural to be approached by a total stranger who knows who you are and what you've done without your knowing the same about him. Famous people are expected to be nice to others simply because they are recognized and, if they aren't nice, they risk offending their public. If you are truly famous they may even begin to think of you as a "thing" instead of a person—that's how Marilyn Monroe described it—as if being famous means you have no feelings. Tabloid journalism (there's an oxymoron for you) has drawn a line in the sand as surely as the paparazzi hounded Princess Diana's limousine into a brick wall. The celebrity who voluntarily exposes himself to public scrutiny knows, or should know, that he is sacrificing privacy. Unfortunately, once privacy has been forfeited it is impossible to reclaim.

That said, when a celebrity agrees to make a personal appearance to publicize a product, there used to be ground rules. A press agent brokers access, which can be at a press conference, red carpet walk, book signing, shopping center opening, premiere, or similar event where the public's presence is accepted but also controlled. On these occasions, paparazzi are expected and tolerated, even exploited. This is different from those occasions when a VIP tries to have a personal life and the remora swarm. Lawmakers try to balance the public's right to know with the famous person's right for the public not to know. Even legitimate acquaintances and co-workers know the unwritten rule: if you've worked with a VIP in the last six months, it's okay to approach him or her in public and say hello. After that, assume forgetfulness. And never, ever be the first to recognize a famous person in a public setting lest it confirm their identity to nearby strangers.

That's the game in Hollywood, New York, and places where recognizable figures routinely appear. In the provinces, a new game is afoot. Here's what happens if you're a celebrity visiting a strange city, say, to do publicity. You step off the plane (first class, of course) and stare straight ahead so you don't make eye contact with anyone who was on your flight and who spent the last four hours thinking, "Hey, isn't that so-and-so?" You watch for a uniformed limo driver holding up your name on a piece of paper. That can be dangerous, too, because as soon as people see the sign, they'll know it's really you (so sometimes you use an alias; I knew a famous actor who always checked into hotels as Harry Potter). But you keep walking. Then a total stranger approaches you and says, "Mr. So-and-so? I'm so-and-so representing your studio and I'm going to be your contact while you're in town. Here's your interview itinerary. May I have your claim checks so the driver can get your luggage while we wait in the car and go over your schedule?" With that, the complete stranger you just met is going to be responsible for your life and safety for the next few days. If the studio has done its job they will have given you this person's name. If not, your spider-sense had better be working.

First come the autograph hounds. Every city has a gaggle of people who somehow know who is coming and what hotel they're using. They are generally harmless; all they want is a smile, an autograph, and a snapshot. Some press agents call them "the little people" and accept their fan-like behavior because they usually show as much interest in people who aren't famous as people who are, and it's an ego boost for up-and-comers. Many of them have developmental or emotional problems, but few pose an actual threat. Plus they buy tickets, albums, videos, and books.

But tell that to Michael Caine. We had arranged a bookstore signing of the paperback edition of *Sleuth* when he came through town publicizing the movie in January of 1973. The fan lines were, as they say, out the door in anticipation of his arrival. Caine, one of the most charming people around, had been keeping the press in thrall all day and he was looking forward to being with civilians as our car arrived at the Paperback Booksmith on Boylston Street in Back Bay, Boston. He leaped out enthusiastically to greet his fans and took a seat behind a stack of books, ready to inscribe them. He had hardly signed four of them when he made a dash for the car, his pale face looking even paler. "Get out of here, pull away now," he urged the driver. "Go!"

"What's the matter, Michael?"

"Just leave. Please, we 'ave to leave."

We tore off into traffic, the limo driver expertly dodging the aggressive Boston drivers. Several blocks later Caine calmed down enough to explain, "I looked up, and there was a man dressed in a dark raincoat —."

"I know him," I interrupted. "He's one of the little people. He's harmless."

"'ow do you know dat?" the actor asked sharply. "As soon as he stepped up to me at the table, he said, 'Don't worry, Mr. Caine, if anything 'appens, we'll take care of you.'"

I waited for more information, but Caine was shaking. "What do you think he meant?" I asked.

"I'll tell you wha' he meant," Caine continued. "It was a threat. You know that I just married a Muslim woman. Shakira is Muslim. It's considered a crime worthy of death to marry outside the faith, and it's the mission of any Muslim to kill bof' of us."

Caine had married the beautiful actress Shakira Bakish on January 8, 1973 just before leaving for the *Sleuth* press tour. The fan's words, whether innocent or malicious, created a palpable fear for the actor who felt vulnerable in a strange city. He was calm by the time we got back to the hotel.

Robert Radnitz didn't need protection, he needed a doctor. An accomplished producer who enjoyed success and accolades with *Sounder*, he was also an unbridled eccentric. He always wore— and, what's more, traveled in—white tennis clothes, except he never had a tennis racket. He bragged that, when he was on the road promoting a film, he flew home every Friday night so he could be with his family, and then he returned to his publicity chores each Monday. To him, this meant loyalty. To his publicists, it meant losing half of Friday and Monday making airport runs. Maybe he had a thing for airline food. He also believed in the value of B-12 vitamins as a source of energy, and this required his press agent to drop everything once a week to arrange for a local Doctor Feelgood to administer a shot of B-12 to Bob's rear end. Since the vitamin and the injection required a prescription, this took a little doing and a lot of discretion. But when you spend $2 million on a picture and it returns rentals of over $8 million even before TV and video sales, the studio allows you to indulge in a little harmless B-12 now and then.

There can also be such a thing as being too protective. When *Saturday Night Fever* opened just before Christmas in 1977, Paramount Pictures sent its newly minted star, John Travolta, through the major youth market cities to publicize it. Paramount had been touring stars for half a century by then, but the film's producer, the Robert Stigwood Organisation—who, as noted earlier, had done such a bang-up job deserting *Tommy*—insisted that they knew better. Instead of a single seasoned press agent with deep contacts, RSO flanked the 23-year-old Travolta with a staff of young flacks ready to block anything they didn't like or know about. It turned out that there were a lot of both.

"Don't ask him about Diana Hyland," they said (sadly, the actress, with whom he had been in a relationship, had died earlier in the year). "Don't ask him about *Welcome Back, Kotter*" (his hit TV series). "Don't ask him about his co-star" (he and his *Fever* love interest/co-star Karen Lynn Gorney reportedly didn't get along). "And don't take pictures of him with his mouth open or while he's talking or eating." And this was *before* Travolta's involvement in Scientology became an issue.

"We're shooting video," I said. "It's for *Evening Magazine*. What's he supposed to do, answer questions in writing?"

"I'll get back to you on that."

"No," I insisted, with my very tall cameraman, Jim Arnold, and the petite host, Robin Young, beside me. "You make up your mind right now whether you're here to do publicity or be a problem, or we're out of here. Why not ask John? He seems nice enough."

"That's impossible," said the assistant. He glanced toward Travolta, who was sitting on a sofa across the room having a cordial discussion with the print press.

While the Stigwood wonks confabbed, I called the producer, Tom Houghton, back at the TV station and filled him in. He had a one-word solution: "Bail."

We started to pack up our equipment and this drew the attention of the assistant, who approached us. "Are you leaving?" he said.

"Looks that way."

"What about the interview with Mr. Travolta?"

"Mr. Travolta is doing just fine. If you don't want us to do our job, we don't want to get in your way."

Years later I reported this encounter to James Bridges, the writer-director who had made *Urban Cowboy* and *Perfect* with Travolta. He shook his head.

"They almost killed his career," he said. "John is one of the most pleasant, decent, professional actors I've ever worked with. He was down for a while, and his comeback is entirely his own achievement."

I thought about that when I read the scathing reviews for *Moment by Moment, Staying Alive,* and the other films he made before *Pulp Fiction* restarted his career. It was clear to me that the bungling by his Stigwood "handlers" had angered the entertainment press in his name, and they were unwilling to cut him any slack during the lean years. His own people had sealed him in a prison from which only his talent could liberate him. I have been overjoyed at his return and his longevity.

Stars meet thousands of people over the span of their careers. They remember very few of them, but they learn to project a sort of friendly familiarity unless something tells them to either shut down or open up. Woe be unto the co-worker, fan, journalist, or press agent who confuses conviviality with intimacy. Actor Robert Montgomery was once asked what Greta Garbo was like and he said he didn't know, even though they both worked at MGM. "But didn't you make *Inspiration* (1931) with her?" the questioner persisted. Montgomery replied coolly, "Making a film with Garbo does not constitute an introduction."

Spiked

A SPIKE is what a newspaper editor sticks stories on that he kills. "Killing" is deciding not to run a story by spiking it. It refers to the days when reporters typed on paper and, when an editor thought the results weren't worthy of ink (or for any other reason), he would impale the pages on a large metal nail with a green base that stood at threatening attention on his desk. Every editor had a spike. So did publishers. Editors tended to use theirs for pieces that simply didn't work, or for which there wasn't room in the paper. Publishers used (and still use) theirs for stories that might upset advertisers or threaten political cronies. Spiking is not restricted to newspapers; television and radio use it, too, only they don't have a physical spike, they just never air stories that threaten the status quo. At the moment there are six communications conglomerates that control ninety percent of broadcasting, cable, and print.

You'd think that, with a twenty-four-hour news cycle, broadcasters would run every legitimate story that they could find. God knows they run enough useless ones. But you'll probably never see any major exposés of oil companies, automobile manufacturers, Big Pharma, or other advertisers. Only local garages that charge too much.

When I was a freelancer at the Rupert Murdoch-owned *Boston Herald*, I seldom had stories spiked. This is not because I was a hotshot writer, it was because I was a freelancer and they would have to pay me a kill fee of 50 percent if they decided not to run one of my assigned pieces. Usually they were honorable about it, and sometimes even ran an otherwise doomed story in a single edition just to give me something to mail out to my relatives. That's right, Rupert Murdoch. Despite everything else, good or bad, he's a newspaperman first.

On the whole, my editors were sharp. At the *Boston Herald*, for whom I wrote freelance pieces from 1976 to 1991, Bill Weber was my immediate boss, and the assistant editor was Terry Byrne, whom we lovingly called "Ilsa" (coined from the exploitation film *Ilsa: She-Wolf of the SS*) because of her demanding criteria. They knew when and how to shape a story, and they trusted their writers. Only once did an editor (not Terry or Bill) whack away at my copy out of sheer malice. It was for my review of Haskell Wexler's 1985 film, *Latino*. Wexler is best known as the peerless cinematographer of *Who's Afraid of Virginia Woolf?*, *In the Heat of the Night*, *Bound for Glory*, and *Coming Home*, but he also directed *Medium Cool*, about the 1968 Chicago riots, and a number of progressive documentaries. In the best tradition of agitprop cinema, he directed a picture criticizing United States intervention in Nicaragua during the Contra-Sandinista conflict. I gave the film a positive review and interviewed Wexler, whom I found sympathetic and stimulating. The morning my review came out, he called me and angrily accused me of ambushing him. I hadn't seen the paper yet, so I went out and bought one, only to discover that one of the paper's senior editors had rewritten my review to remove positive statements about the film while keeping my byline intact.

Correcting facts is legitimate and appreciated. Altering a critic's opinions is not. In fact, it's grounds for execution (I may be overreacting). When I cornered the editor about it, he insisted that he had merely cut it for space, but both of us knew he was lying. Fortunately, there is a delicious epilogue to this incident. Twenty-two years later, that editor, by then promoted to Murdoch/NewsAmerica's highest echelons, was implicated in the 2011 News of the World phone hacking scandal in which some of Murdoch's reporters and editors illegally invaded the private social media accounts of celebrities. When I told this to Wexler at a political event in 2012, we agreed that karma can be a bitch.

Spiking, like getting fired, is something that needs to happen at least once to anyone who considers himself a professional writer. It builds character. Once I even spiked myself. In early 1980 I found myself on a transcon flight with a Hollywood director whom I happened to know socially. In the course of our conversation, he mentioned that he knew Steve McQueen, who, it was rumored, was having health issues, specifically cancer. McQueen wouldn't talk to the tabloids, of course, but my friend told me that he had spoken with McQueen, who was a health nut and said he was just taking vitamins.

"I know those so-called vitamins," my director friend said, "and the only reason to take that particular combination is if he was trying an herbal treatment for cancer."

What to do. Here was a good source on a hot story, but not only was it obtained outside of an agreed-upon interview, it could be traced back to my friend if I tried to confirm it with McQueen's people. So I sat on it. Months later the story broke in, of course, the tabloids. Which I suppose made me a bad reporter, depending how you feel about ethics.

I also sat on a story about Jack Larson even while I was writing it, but in a different way. In journalism, the thing about the story that snares the reader is called the "hook," but what keeps him reading is called the "angle." With Larson, the hook I used was that he had written the libretto to the Virgil Thomson opera *Lord Byron* and was coming to Boston to hold a Harvard seminar with the famed composer. This was in 1986 after Larson had succeeded Gertrude Stein (*Four Saints in Three Acts*) as Thomson's collaborator. I managed to interest my paper in an interview, pitching that it was a major musical and academic event. Jack and I already knew each other through writer-director James Bridges (Larson was producer on many of Bridges' films, but all of us knew them as longtime partners), so our talk was relaxed and wide-ranging. We covered the rigors of precision writing, of working with Thomson, and the importance of finally getting a recording of their elaborate work. What I didn't put in the story was that Larson, in his younger days, was an actor and had played cub reporter Jimmy Olsen opposite George Reeves and Noel Neill in the wildly popular original *The Adventures of Superman* TV series. I wrote the article strictly from the opera angle and, when it was published, Jack, who had given other interviews later while in town, called me and laughingly reported, "Yours was the only article that didn't mention Jimmy!" That's pretty much what my *Herald* editor Bill Weber said when I showed up at the office, only he wasn't laughing.

"Why didn't you put that in the story?" he asked.

"Because the headline would've been 'Jimmy Olsen Writes Opera,' right?"

"You bet," he said.

"That's why I didn't."

Bill eventually understood that it was a matter of pride, not subterfuge, and he became one of my defenders. He was also a collaborator in the *Herald*'s ongoing competition against the city's leading newspaper, *The Boston Globe*. For all the camaraderie those of us generally shared on the movie beat, we were still loyal to our individual rags. There's not much controversy in covering movies, although I had a soft mandate from my paper to be on the lookout for it. I became the *Herald*'s self-appointed specialist in the business of film. Our problem was that, if there was anything newsworthy happening in the New England movie business, the executives who were involved always called the *Globe* first because the *Globe* just ran the story as if it were a press release; they had nobody on staff who knew anything about the film business. I did. Thus the *Herald* had the sources but the *Globe* had the connections.

The frustration was constant. No matter how many exclusive stories or interviews I broke in the *Herald*, people assumed that they read them in the *Globe*. And I wasn't alone in this; the *Herald* had a scrappy, skillful staff that struggled to put out five editions every day, and we chafed when we would run a story on a Tuesday but nobody would remark on it until the *Globe* ran their version on Wednesday as if they'd discovered it.

The one time I actually had fun along with the frustration was when I had been given a tip that the city's major movie house chain, Sack Theatres, was about to be sold to the national Loew's Theatres. This would be more than a real estate transaction; Greater Boston was already headquarters for three national chains: Showcase Cinemas (a.k.a. Sumner Redstone's National Amusements); General Cinema Corporation (king of shopping center theatres); and Hoyt's (Australia-based but growing in America). The entrance of Loew's would make it four, elevating Massachusetts to supreme importance in U.S. exhibition. It doesn't seem like a big deal now when sales and mergers happen all the time and are covered everywhere, but in the 1980s there were very few of us writing about the business—as opposed to the gossip—of the communications industry.

Bill and I huddled at his desk. It was 6 PM and the sun was going down. The game was afoot. I needed either a formal confirmation of the sale or two independent sources, as well as the details. Having been publicity director for Sack Theatres a few years earlier, I knew all the players. But they also knew me and, after a few furtive calls, I realized that they had all been warned not to speak to me until the story had run in the *Globe*. The *Herald*'s first edition (the "bulldog") had a close deadline but because of arcane union rules involving freelancers, my own deadline was even closer. Sack's corporate offices were closed and nobody was answering the company phone, even the private numbers.

Then I remembered the ol' jumpline trick. When a company's main number ends in zero, there's a good chance that if you keep adding ones you'll eventually hit an inside line that somebody will answer out of curiosity. I kept dialing until somebody picked up: the Vice President of Publicity (my old job). God knows why she answered, but once she did, I signaled Bill and he rolled his chair over to share the earpiece. I took a chance and said I needed to confirm some details for the story that we were about to run. But I kept interrupting her to ask about various employees we both knew and liked. This confused her about which paper I was writing for and, who knows, made her forget that we were on the record. Not only did she wind up confirming the sale (with a quote I slipped to Bill who took it straight to typeset), but I kept her talking until the *Globe*'s deadline had passed.

Then I did something for which I probably ought to be ashamed, but I'm sure the spirits of Ben Hecht and Charles MacArthur would approve: I phoned the *Globe* to tell them that the *Herald* already had the story and not to bother.

Speaking of Ben Hecht, he once quoted *New York Journal* City Editor Sherman Reilly Duffy as saying, "Socially a journalist fits in somewhere between a whore and a bartender, but spiritually he stands beside Galileo. He knows the world is round." I'm not sure that applies any more. These days, the notion of "journalistic ethics" is nostalgia. The competition for eyes, ears, and smart phones devolved into a desperation that takes the form of telephoto lenses, phone hacking, bribing sources, and blackmail ("I won't run this embarrassing story if you give me an interview"). There was a time when you didn't run a story that was obtained drunk, high, or during a liaison. You didn't bring a celebrity's family into the story unless they agreed. And you didn't use comments meant for one story within another unrelated story. When I do recorded interviews I offer to provide a transcript if there's time. This is not merely a courtesy; it's a safeguard against someone saying that he's been misquoted. If you have the corrections written in their own hand, there's not a whole lot they can complain about. I also ask people to re-state something if it doesn't make sense the first time or might be a tale told out of school. Do I sound co-opted? This is show business, folks, not world politics.

And yet scruples still survive. Film critics, like politicians, are sometimes offered gifts with all they imply. Should entertainment writers accept free movie tickets? Meals? Junkets? Presents? Alcohol? Drugs? Hookers? Some media outlets insist on paying their reporters' fares to press events, thinking that this insulates them. For fun, we used to debate whether it was okay to accept a free meal from a studio if we puked before leaving the restaurant. What about Christmas gifts? Free videos? One measure was that if a gift was worth over $25 we had to refuse it, and if it was worth under $25 we'd be insulted to accept it. Times have changed, of course. Now the reporters who cover celebrities are often as famous as the celebrities themselves. Media conglomerates own both sides of the street: studios, networks, and the outlets that cover them. Synergy is another word for conflict of interest. Sure, it's only a movie, and show business isn't the same as curing cancer or ending world hunger. But the thing about a daisy chain is that, once it starts, it doesn't end on the entertainment pages, it infects every story, from those that show up on the news pages to those that, for reasons of undue influence, do not. Spike that!

Stir Crazy

IT WAS called "dinner theatre" but purists insisted that it was neither. Nevertheless, the combination of food followed by a live play—popular in suburban America in the 1970s—was a marvelous way to bring the thespic experience to wider audiences, even if the most intellectually challenging part of the evening was deciding whether to have the surf or the turf.

The phenomenon existed in other major markets, but the dinner theatres I knew ringed Boston at a time when suburban dwellers resisted traveling into the city for culture but could be persuaded to sample it when it was brought to them. Strictly speaking, the hideously decorated Chateau de Ville Dinner Theatres were glorified banquet halls that just as easily accommodated weddings and bar mitzvahs as the bus-and-truck productions of *Hello Dolly!*, *The Odd Couple*, and *Forty Carats* and other scaled-down Broadway hits. They were famous for the immense chandeliers that hung in their foyers, but the real marvel was their meticulously trained serving staff that could swoop down and serve five hundred dinners in a matter of minutes, then clear the whole mess away an hour later in time for curtain. Truth be told, they turned out a remarkably good product as long as you weren't looking for *haute* in either cuisine or culture.

These dinner theatres, like others around the country, were the stage equivalent of shopping mall movie houses. That is, when the population fled from the cities to the suburbs in the 1950s and took their entertainment dollars with them, the men who sold tickets realized that they could never lure their customers back into town for a show, so they brought the show out to them. Some dinner theatre chains mounted their own productions while other scheduled prepackaged touring shows with slightly faded TV and movie stars whose names still had drawing power with a slightly older demographic. Like high school drama departments, they mounted safe and well-known shows like the three named earlier. Nothing too ambitious, controversial, or complicated.

Which was good all around, sort of. American legit theatre underwent a huge jolt of commercialization in the early 1970s—1972 to be precise—when the musical *Pippin* became the first Broadway show to be advertised on television. The gamble paid off and a relatively mediocre musical (Bob Fosse's and Stephen Schwartz's adaptation of the legend of Charlemagne had more dazzle than razzle) became a hit. Their success encouraged other productions to take to the tube, and regional theatres took note. Soon national revival tours were mounted and booked of *Camelot* starring Richard Harris, *The King and I* with Yul Brynner, and *Man of La Mancha* with Richard Kiley in their original roles, and a succession of Tevyes in *Fiddler on the Roof*. Often these productions would be booked into arenas rather than legit theatres, but in all cases they were heavily advertised in an effort to attract people who didn't usually go to theatre. The result was both charming and frustrating; box office workers told of having patrons ask to swap their front row tickets for some that were "farther away from the screen" or people who wanted to attend the 6 PM performance instead of the 8 PM, not grasping that live theatre is a once-an-evening event. And this doesn't even begin to address the problem with audiences who brought babies, hot meals, and candy wrappers as they would to a movie. Good thing this was before cell phones.

Suburban dinner theatre was a different breed. Like a family restaurant, informality itself was the attraction. Although the venues were Equity signatories, which guaranteed a level of professionalism, the professionalism didn't go past the footlights. At the Chateau de Ville, whose publicity was run by Jane Badgers (who had moved on from Sack Theatres where I inherited her job), a show would be booked into all four venues. The star would take up residence in town and would commute from one Chateau to another for the duration of the run. Like all theatre folk, they would get out and see the sights during the day and be ready for curtain by nightfall. Thanks to Jane's desire to have them feel at home while on the road, she took them to lunch, dinner, and gatherings at people's homes. Because Jane and I were both in the PR business, as well as friends, she often asked me to come along, sometimes as a ringer doing eyewash (unpublished) interviews, other times as part of the retinue.

We brought writer/comedian Milt Kamen, who was a frequent guest on TV variety and talk shows, to Fun Wong, my favorite restaurant in Boston's Chinatown. Kamen felt comfortable enough to talk about his appearances on the Ed Sullivan, Merv Griffin, and Mike Douglas TV chat shows, and recalled how, as a Catskill Mountain comic, he had seen and recommended a young Woody Allen. He then recited a litany of truisms about Chinese restaurants that included, "Always eat what you see the staff is eating" and something I have yet to have confirmed, which is that Chinese restaurants make the best coffee, but they save it for their own employees.

The elegant Joan Fontaine appeared in *Cactus Flower* and insisted to all who would listen that she and her sister, Olivia de Havilland, were not, in fact, the rival siblings that gossip columns had claimed they were since the 1930s. She denied it so often and so forcefully that it only reinforced the rumors. After she died in 2013 everybody admitted it was true.

Stubby Kaye, famous for *Guys 'n' Dolls* and *Li'l Abner* on Broadway, was a slightly testier luncheon companion. He was appearing with Arnold Stang (another name from fifties TV) in Neil Simon's *The Odd Couple* and the two of them carried their onstage antagonism offstage. One night their enmity became part of the show. At a particular moment, Stang, playing Felix (the neat one) lectured Stubby, playing Oscar (the sloppy one), about the difference between spaghetti and linguini. In the play, Oscar picks up the plate of food and flings it against the wall, saying, "Now it's garbage." The night the pasta hit the fan, Stubby seized the plate from Stang and lobbed it straight at his head. There was that moment when the audience realized that the actors had broken character and didn't know whether to laugh or be quiet, so they chose the latter and stayed that way until the end of the play.

Jane arranged for her stars to hang out with local movers and shakers once the publicity needs had been addressed. After all, stars are people too. Mostly. TV Producer Raysa Bonow hosted a luncheon for Tab Hunter, who was touring with some now-forgotten show. Hunter was an enthusiastic guest who preferred horses to Hollywood. (Eventually he retired to his horse farm and wrote a vastly entertaining memoir, *Tab Hunter Confidential: The Making of a Movie Star.*) Boston talk show host Sonya Hamlin did similar honors for Van Johnson, a noted recluse when living in New York, but who blossomed under Sonya's nurturing presence. Trademark red socks and all, Johnson enthused about his career, but never to the point of bragging about being America's favorite boy-next-door for so many years. Betty Hutton was the tomboy-next-door who brought her energy and comic skill to two of Preston Sturges' best films, *The Miracle of Morgan's Creek* and *Hail the Conquering Hero,* and was tapped to replace Judy Garland in *Annie Get Your Gun.* Hutton was barely in her fifties when she strutted her stuff on the Chateau's stages. When we had lunch, I couldn't take my eyes off her; she was tanned and youthful-looking and effervescent to a point that exceeded the conversation. It later came out that she was having emotional issues, to say the least (probably bipolarity), and shortly after she wrapped her theatre tour she took a job cooking and doing housekeeping for a Rhode Island monastery. Mostly, I remember her skin moisturizer. It made her glisten. No, not glisten, glare. She wore so much of it on her face that, when we went to air-kiss goodbye, my cheek skidded across hers and came to a stop somewhere around the back of her head. (On the other hand, I kissed Betty Hutton!)

The Chateau de Ville enterprise faced legal action in the late 70s over allegations of unpaid theatrical royalties. After that, the curtain came down on their productions and they fell back to hosting catered affairs. Only the chandeliers remained.

There are still a few dinner theatres around the country because there are still people who are hungry for the magic of seeing other people perform in person--even if they have to saw through rubber chicken beforehand.

Graffiti Contest

BOSTON MOVIE magnate Ben Sack built a screening room atop the Music Hall Theatre on Tremont Street in Boston. If memory serves, it seated thirty, but memory fails when it comes to the House of Pain. In an era when movies were discovering Dolby stereo and rediscovering 70mm, the Sack Music Hall screening room was content to show everything in 35mm mono, usually to the detriment of the picture. The stalwart projectionist who was crammed into the tiny booth with two full-sized projectors was never allowed to upgrade. This is the way multi-million dollar movies were screened. Most of Sack's theatres were no better.

Each theatre chain had its own screening room for its executives, but Sack's did double duty not only for private trade screenings but to run advance showings for the critics, for which a fee was charged to the distributor. When neither Sack nor the critics were using it, it might run pictures for the company's Vice President A. Alan Friedberg, General Manager David Traister, and such others as they might invite. It was here that Ben Sack would decide, not whether to play new movies—he owned so many theatres that he had to play most anything with sprocket holes—but how much to bid for the right to exhibit them. He almost always won his bids because he had so little competition, among other reasons.

Ben Sack lucked into the movie business. A butcher during World War Two, which becomes interesting when you consider food rationing, he later opened a smelting and precious metals reclamation plant in Somerville,

Massachusetts that gave people cause to call him a junk man, particularly when they unfairly held him accountable for the films he ran in his theatres. Legendary was the manner in which he acquired his first theatres: He had left a gin rummy game without his favorite gold pen and, when he returned to claim it, another player asked him to co-sign an IOU. The man defaulted on the marker and Sack acquired the man's collateral, a movie theatre. Instantly, Ben Sack thought he was a showman, and through the sheer power of his aggressive personality and the good luck to hire talented executives like Friedberg, who forged alliances with film companies, he quickly became a force to be reckoned with.

"I have a God-given gift for finding hits," Sack told the press on many occasions, as well as anyone else who would listen. The fact is, when you play everything, you're bound to have a hit now and then. Soon he was announcing that all he had to look at was the first reel of a film before his holy gift kicked in.

Sack was finicky about who else used his screening room. Employees were never granted access for parties or recreation, even if they offered to pay the projectionist out of their own pockets. The press cringed when told that they would be seeing pictures there. Having been both Sack's publicist and, later, a critic, I understood why it was uncomfortable to be there: we never knew if anybody was listening in on our conversations. Plus the place was simply uncomfortable. I remember watching *Deliverance* there and empathizing with Ned Beatty.

Access to the screening room was at the very top of the Music Hall, *nee* Metropolitan Theatre, built by Paramount Theatres in 1926 as a grand movie palace modeled, in part, after the Paris Opera House. Time had not been good to it. Its 4,100 seats were constantly being rearranged so that those whose upholstery was intact would be in the orchestra, with the tattier cushions relegated to the second or third balcony. Although the hall was rented on a four-wall basis for rock concerts, bus-and-truck musicals, and the Boston Ballet's annual *Nutcracker*, movies were its prime source of income.

Its elegance could be deceiving. A ladies committee for a charity group searched the building high and low for a room to hold a pre-show cocktail reception and was thrilled when they walked into a lower-level hall decorated with mirrors and gold leaf, only to be told that it was the ladies lounge whose toilets occasionally backed up.

To get to the screening room, you took a huge elevator (used in the old days to carry fifty patrons at a time) to the top floor, or you walked up the carpeted side stairs. You knew how far you had climbed by how sticky it got. At the top floor another staircase, nearly hidden, led to a windowed attic storeroom from which the light-tight screening room was a few steps away. Stacked at the entrance to the screening room were dozens of yellow plastic sacks of pre-popped popcorn that could be dispatched to whatever Sack Theatres concession stand needed them. If they were to be used at the Music Hall, an ingenuous system was used: instead of popping corn at each concession stand, ushers simply tore the bags open and dumped their contents down a chute that fed the candy counters from three stories up. Heat lamps freshened it for sale below and fans blew the seductive aroma into the lobby. It sounds mechanical, but decades of crowds proved it to be the only way to handle 4,100 hungry customers.

The Sack screening room saw its share of adventure. When *Last Tango in Paris* was a *cause celebre* in 1972 it was this intimate setting that became the hottest ticket in town. Eager to manage the pre-release word-of-mouth, United Artists asked us to schedule invitational showings prior to its February, 1973 Boston premiere. The room became as hot as the tickets and guests were known to fall asleep as it unspooled. (Not until the film opened officially was it discovered that it was the pretentious movie itself that put people to sleep.) The picture was so controversial that UA assigned a special press agent to supervise our screenings. Frank Warren (not his real name) was dynamic and excitable. No, make that unstable. He not only insisted on vetting our guest lists (even though he didn't know one opinion maker from another), he disinvited people just to show that he could. One night between arguments he casually mentioned that he had bought Pauline Kael. Flabbergasted, I pressed him. I disagreed with Kael's taste but I knew she was beyond even the whisper of corruption.

"Not exactly bought," Frank qualified, but here's the way it worked. Afraid they would have censorship problems with *Last Tango's* X rating, the company felt that they had to legitimize it with a major review in a major publication. Frank said that he told Kael that, if she liked the film, UA would run her review in a double-truck (two-page) newspaper ad. She did, and they did. Her review gave the film prestige, and the two-page newspaper ad gave her national notoriety. Kael's rave review ran in the October 28, 1972 issue of *The New Yorker*, and thereafter was reprinted in key cities nationwide where *Last Tango in Paris* was scheduled to open. The dates don't match—by 1972 Kael had been well established at *The New Yorker* since 1968— but that's the story I was told. Many critics over the years have contrived their reviews so that quotes could be lifted out of them. Few have been assured of it in advance.

One picture we were not allowed to screen was Woody Allen's 1973 comedy, *Sleeper.* We were told by the film company that Woody preferred the critics to see his films with audiences in public showings or, for major New York and LA critics, alone, one by one, in private screenings so they would accord him the benefit of the doubt and presume that all the jokes worked. Nevertheless, in November of 1973 I was ordered to set up a screening of *Sleeper* at the Music Hall for *Boston Phoenix* critic Janet Maslin whose husband, Jon Landau, was a rock critic and co-founder of *Rolling Stone* (and, within a year, the discoverer of Bruce Springsteen). Rank has its privileges, so I asked Janet if I could sit in. She said yes, and advised me that she wanted to bring along some friends. "Don't worry," she assured, "they're okay." Indeed they were. They were the Beach Boys, who had played a concert in Boston the night before.

As far as I'm concerned, the most important screening held at the Sack facility was for A. Alan Friedberg in July of 1973. Alan, an urbane man and a brilliant business strategist, was supposedly being romanced by Universal

Pictures to join their executive ranks. Part of their seduction included seeking his opinion on upcoming projects and troubled new releases. One of the latter was what compelled him to ask me to join him on a hot summer afternoon, taking off from work early. As we walked from the Sack Offices in the Savoy Theatre up Tremont Street to the Music Hall, he explained that Universal had a small youth-market movie that had not been well-received in studio screenings. They were going to dump it in the drive-ins rather than waste advertising dollars on a high-profile first-run release but, because Boston was an important youth market, they wanted Alan to watch it to see if he would give it at least one prestige booking on the way to oblivion. He asked me along to give him my opinion, he said, because I was closer in age to the youth market than he was.

I wondered whether the prospect of playing hooky from work on a weekday might cloud my perception, but once the picture began, both of us became completely immersed in its guileless blend of character, music, comedy, and nostalgia. Immediately after the end credits finished, Alan phoned Universal, committed to playing the film at the chain's flagship Cheri Cinema complex, and urged them to treat it like the remarkable motion picture that it indeed turned out to be. The film was *American Graffiti,* and it opened in key cities on August 11, 1973, going on to not only earn scores of millions of dollars but establish its young director, George Lucas, as a visionary force in cinema.

I'm not saying that *American Graffiti* wouldn't have been discovered without me. I'm just saying that we saw it first in the Sack Music Hall Screening Room, a.k.a. Ben Sack's House of Pain.

Brief Encounters

THE FIRST time I met Paul Newman, one of us was one or two sheets to the wind. I was standing in the back of a too-small theatre supervising a preview screening of *The Effect of Gamma Rays on Man-in-the-Moon Marigolds*, which Newman had directed, and which he had come to town to promote. I was thoroughly engrossed in the picture when somebody tapped me on the shoulder and asked, "How's it playing?" I turned around, annoyed at the interruption, and answered, "Pretty well, and the director's going to be here any—" and then stopped talking because the director had arrived.

I'd seen bluer eyes, but these had Paul Newman behind them. Aware that I was a couple inches taller than he, I spread my feet apart so I could be shorter without noticeably stooping. It seemed like the polite thing to do. Then I saw that Newman's eyes were not only blue, they were also red and white. Newman hoisted a can of Coors beer, took a few sips, and looked past me, saying, "I hope we have focus." I assumed he meant the picture; he had just wrapped a long day of interviews for it, which starred his wife, Joanne Woodward, and their daughter, Nell Potts (who has since given up acting to run Newman's Own Organics). It's some kind of poetic justice that Newman, who played a womanizer so often in his movies, should become one of the more sensitive directors of women, but *Marigolds, Rachel, Rachel,* and *The Glass Menagerie*, all starring his wife, are remarkable works. So was the man himself. An adherent of the Method school of acting taught at the Actors Studio—an institution he quietly supported at a time when its finances were tight—he became adept at insulating himself from the characters he played, and yet integrated his own personality into theirs. A neat trick, and hard-won.

"I have to separate what I find difficult and what the character finds difficult," he explained between beers. "A lot of times the actor makes the mistake and confuses the two issues. I find that I have a temptation, as a person, to understate things, so graphic language makes me uncomfortable. An actor's discomfort sometimes works very well for him. It is not beyond the realm of possibility to mistake discomfort for rage, at which time the actor's way ahead of the game."

That realization worked to his advantage at the Actor's Studio. "When I first auditioned for Actor's Studio in 1950," he continued, "you had to do two auditions in order to get in." He performed his audition scene with a female applicant. "This girl had already passed her first audition and I was straight out of Yale University. I think I'd been in New York for about three weeks. Her partner had gone off to summer stock someplace, so it was okay for me to do her second audition with her. Well, when I heard that Elia Kazan and Cheryl Crawford and Frank Corsaro and Karl Malden and Kim Stanley and Geraldine Page—I mean, all those people were sitting out there—I was so terrified that I was visibly shaking. And that's where the scene was supposed to be. They mistook this terrible case of nerves that I had for unlimited rage, and I got in on one audition, one of the few guys that ever did that."

An irony of celebrity—particularly commercial celebrity—is that, the better you are, the less they let you do. In Hollywood, casting against type is a career liability. At this point in his career (before he aged into *The Color of Money*, *Nobody's Fool* or *Road to Perdition*), Newman felt confined. "I suppose one of my great regrets is that I don't see variety," he said, finishing his beer and effortlessly winging the empty can into the trash (this was before recycling) as the end credits and the house lights came up. "I'm very envious of guys like Olivier and Guinness who seem to have an absolutely inexhaustible supply of characters, all different."

He jogged down the aisle and took his place at the front of the house as a wave of recognition rocked the audience to their feet. He bashfully tried not to acknowledge the applause which, of course, only made it louder. The intensely private Newman was at once a child of the crowd and above it, a uniquely approachable God whom people respected enough to give him space.

Back in 1980, Newman and writer-friend A. E. Hochner gave bottles of their popular recipe for salad dressing to friends at Christmas. They got so many requests for more that, in 1982, they started producing it commercially. A few years later their product line had increased to one hundred varieties and, in 2005, the Newman's Own Foundation announced that they had given $450 million after-tax profits to charity. If the Nobel Peace Prize is even given to a salad dressing company, it should be Newman's.

❦

Richard Chamberlain, who shared Newman's attractiveness but none of his brooding, struggled his whole career to ditch his pretty boy image. First as TV's Doctor Kildare in the 1960s, for which his popularity was attributed more to his teen idol looks than his acting chops, he had to go to England to gain respect, which he did with acclaimed performances of *Hamlet* (1969) and *Richard II* (1971) in London. But the movies gave him money, and he did well with *The Thorn Birds, The Towering Inferno, The Three Musketeers* and *The Four Musketeers*. It was the latter that brought him through New England for publicity and, as he wrapped a grueling day of interviews, he sprawled on the sofa of his hotel room and rubbed his temples.

"Are you sure we're finished?" he said.

"Yes."

"Are you absolutely sure? Not one last person waiting in the hallway?"

"Nope, you can relax now."

"Good. I will. And thank *God* I can call my *analyst*."

Of course, there was no analyst, there was only a serious actor who overcame the handicap of being a movie star to show that he also had talent.

Chamberlain was only joking, but there are times when a celebrity, even an actor, can get tired talking about himself. Back in 1974, they warned that Jeff Bridges was difficult. Despite his nice-guy image, he brooded and snapped at you, they reported. So when they sent him to town to talk about his quirky *Hearts of the West*, the studio's instructions were, "Don't work him too much! Make it a light schedule!" Mindful of that, he was booked for only three or four brief sit-downs per day. Then the first thing he said when he saw the printed schedule was, "How come you don't have me doing more?"

"I was told you wanted a light schedule," I explained.

"Who said that?"

I named the head of publicity.

"Oh, no wonder," Bridges said, shaking his head. "They had me booked on such a tight schedule in New York that I barely had time to go to the bathroom. They were killing me. So I had to get on their case. Sometimes you have to be like that or they take advantage of you. Now," he said, smiling and hunkering down, "let's add a few things and really sell this picture."

Hearts of the West was a lovely, funny, romantic film that not only showcased Bridges to advantage but also allowed Alan Arkin, Blythe Danner, and Andy Griffith to shine. Despite an earnest publicity push and good reviews, however, nobody wanted to see a western set in the early days of silent movies. It remains a cult favorite. Bridges, of course, kept right on working and finally won his Oscar® in 2009 for *Crazy Heart*, although he deserved it a dozen times earlier for *Starman, True Grit, Tucker, The Fisher King*, and, God knows, *The Big Lebowski*.

"Say goodnight to the sofa, honey. Now say goodnight to the chair. That's right. I love you, too." The person whispering gently into the phone was Ernest Borgnine. Borgnine, the bad-ass bully of *Bad Day at Black Rock*, the rowdy brigand of *The Wild Bunch*, and Sgt. Fatso Judson who beat Frank Sinatra to death in *From Here to Eternity* was saying goodnight to Tova, his fifth wife ("It took me this many to get it right"), three thousand miles across the country. He had come to Boston to promote Robert Aldrich's brutal and brilliant *Emperor of the North Pole*, which Fox had just changed to *Emperor of the North* fearing that people would think it was about Santa Claus. Hardly. Borgnine played a ruthless train conductor during the Great Depression bent on keeping hobos like Lee Marvin and Keith Carradine from riding his rails at any cost.

I knew Borgnine from the movies, including *The Dirty Dozen, Flight of the Phoenix, Willard, The Catered Affair* and, of course, *Marty*, which won him an Oscar®. When autograph hunters swarmed around him outside of the hotel, however, they knew him as Commander McHale from the *McHale's Navy* TV series. Such is fame.

Borgnine was joined in Boston by Nico Jacobellis, the Twentieth Century-Fox advertising-publicity representative and a *paisan*, and the two of them spoke in Italian to each other when not talking to the press or me as their assistant. At one point in the two-day appearance schedule, Nico left us alone, and I asked Ernie (that's what he said to call him), "Do you know Marjory Adams?"

"Marjory?" he said, "I've been wondering where she is." I told him that she had twisted her ankle and was writing newspaper columns—having been forcibly retired from the *Boston Globe*—out of her Beacon Hill apartment. "C'mon," Borgnine said, "let's pay her a visit."

We took the limousine to Marjory's home on Revere Street, climbed to her floor, and waited while she hobbled to the door. She and Borgnine hugged like the old friends they were. She laid out drinks and peanuts, sat with her foot propped up on an ottoman, and Borgnine sat on the other. The ottomans were two feet square, a deep olive green, and the stocky Borgnine sat perched on his like a St. Bernard waiting for a treat. They had a wonderful visit and you just know that Marjory once again had the best lead of all the interviews Borgnine had done while he was in Boston, for it began, "When Ernest Borgnine rang my doorbell. . ."

Borgnine died in 2012 at the age of 95. He had just finished a picture. He was also still married to Tova. Indeed, he did get it right.

When Marjory died she left me the ottomans. Plus the memory of knowing her.

⚬⟞⟨⟩⟞⚬

"One more, please. We have one last person," the Orion Pictures press agent told Gregory Hines apologetically. Hines had endured some 75 ten-minute taped TV interviews for 1984's *The Cotton Club*, a story of mobsters, love, and show business, and had taken off his microphone in anticipation of being able to go home and relax. But now there was one more person to see, one more time to answer the same inane questions, one more need to keep from getting slap-happy at the film company's efficient publicity machine.

The last person happened to be me.

Scheduling mistakes are inevitable when there are so many people to coordinate, and nobody on the press list understood this better than I did, having worked for film companies. But now I was a critic and interviewer, and that made the Orion people jittery. It shouldn't have, but it did. Hines knew nothing of this, of course, as he gamely re-attached his microphone and took his still-warm seat yet again.

I wish I could remember what we talked about. Maybe it was the revelation that, despite his being one of the world's top tap-dancers, he liked to improvise his steps and had difficulty repeating them for audio in post-production, so director Francis Coppola had the sound man wire Hines' trousers with wireless mikes that recorded his dancing live. Or we probably talked about his non-dancing role in Mel Brooks' *History of the World: Part*

I, or his upcoming *pas de deux* with Mikhail Baryshnikov in *White Nights*. And I'm glad that the videotape caught it all, because I wasn't really paying attention, not while I was marveling at the graciousness that this talented man showed to the last reporter who'd been waiting in the hall when all he wanted to do was go home.

<hr />

Jack Larson was a great gadfly and a good friend. He, his partner James Bridges, and I shared many dinners, and Jack and I shared others after Jim died. When he died in 2015 (Jim left us in 1993) I thought back on all the stories he had told me over the thirty years we had known each other, how he staunchly refused to write his book, and how many of the stories that he told me could never be printed even if he did write it. One that could be told involved a guest appearance he made on a 1996 episode of the TV series, *Lois and Clark*. In "Brutal Youth," cub reporter Jimmy Olsen (Justin Whalin) is subjected to a device that ages him prematurely, and, in his old man stage, the producers had the wit to have him played by Jack, who had portrayed Jimmy Olsen in the original *Superman* TV series in the 50s. It was clever stunt casting and, shooting the climax where Superman rescues Jimmy and flies him to where he can reverse the aging process, Dean Cain (playing Superman) had to carry Jack aloft on a flying rig. "Don't worry," Cain assured Jack as they set up the shot, "I've done this before."

"All right," Jack responded, "but I must tell you that you're not the first Superman who has held me in his arms."

<hr />

"You Americans!" Christopher Lee intoned stentoriously. "You insist on drinking your beer chilled! That's probably because you don't know what good beer tastes like!" I had just offered the tall, imposing Lee a lager from the hotel room mini-bar and he would have none of it. Fortunately, I had not spoken to him of *Horror of Dracula* or the other gothic Hammer films for which he was best known (and highly regarded) in the States. Instead, I tried to win him over by praising his performance as Mycroft Holmes in Billy Wilder's little-seen *The Private Life of Sherlock Holmes*. He acknowledged that Wilder was the best director he had ever worked with and he appreciated the chance to expand his range.

But Lee was already on edge, and I was partly to blame. Fox had sent him to Boston to meet the press over *The Three Musketeers*, in which he played the villainous Rochefort. My job was to arrive unannounced, pull him discretely away from the press, and slip him cash for his expenses as mandated by the Screen Actors Guild. Then I was to return to New York. Yes, that made me Saruman's bagman. When I arrived in Boston, however, Hope Miller, the skilled and stylish woman who had taken over my old job as Sack Theatres Publicity Director, had been told by a meddling third party that I had swooped into town to steal credit for her exemplary scheduling of Lee's press tour. Unable to reveal why I was there (the SAG expenses were none of the exhibitor's business), I sat in silence. It was years before Hope and I could untangle the chicanery and resume our friendship, which exists to this day.

⚫━━━⚫

John Williams had just been made conductor of the Boston Pops Orchestra and, through my film connections, I wangled one-on-one time with him for CBS radio when he arrived in town. I had visions of asking him about his movie scores and side work such as scoring Robert Altman's home movies. Instead, we got talking about his plans for the Pops, whose musicians had become flabby under their previous maestro, Arthur Feidler, and how he intended to keep doing movies, using the acoustics of Boston's famed Symphony Hall to record tracks. That prompted me to compare his two most recent works, *Star Wars*, for which he won the 1977 Academy Award®, and *Close Encounters of the Third Kind*, for which he was nominated but did not win.

"*Star Wars* is in the best Hollywood tradition," I began, showing off my knowledge of music, "but I think *Close Encounters* is more experimental. Its use of tone progressions, dissonance, and interpolation is much more adventurous than *Star Wars*, don't you think?"

Williams thought for a moment and made me a fan forever when he gently brushed aside my pretensions by saying, in that soft but authoritative voice, "Well, one is always happy to win an Oscar. . . ."

Mentioned In Passing

HIS REAL first name was Federico, after the director whose movies his father produced, but he called himself Freddie and asked others to call him that, as well. He was seventeen when we met in 1972, had already been kicked out of several of the best schools in Europe, and was coming through Boston to learn the American end of the film business from his father, Dino. Dino, as in De Laurentiis.

John "Jack" Markle, the Columbia Pictures New England field publicity representative, had set up an interview schedule for the prolific De Laurentiis, who had a multi-picture deal with the studio. I was engaged as Jack's assistant with the specific duty of looking after Freddie. It made kind of sense: Jack and Dino were in their sixties, I was within five years of Freddie's age. That's if you count chronologically. In worldly years, compared to him, I was an infant.

"Come, let us go shopping for trucks," the dark-haired youth said in perfect, Italian-accented English learned at one of his ex-schools. The scion of the stocky and dynamic Dino and the graceful and hauntingly beautiful Silvana Mangano, Freddie inherited the best of both parents: he was charmingly aggressive and stunningly handsome.

"My father, he is training me to be a producer. I will work as his assistant, then I will make my own pictures," the youth said with the assurance of a dauphin. "This is why we must find a truck. A Chevy Scout."

"Don't they have trucks in Italy?" I asked.

"Yes, but we are making the next picture in America."

"You want to buy a truck today?"

"A Scout."

"You want to buy a Scout today?"

"No, no, no! I want to *price* a Scout today."

"I don't think I understand."

"You will."

Boston had no shortage of automotive dealerships, but it was obvious from the first one we visited that Freddie was only window shopping. Scouts had been around since the 1930s, but recently—in anticipation of what would become the SUV boom—they had matured into sleek, powerful 4x4 all-terrain vehicles.

By the third dealership, the two of us had become more relaxed with each other and he began to confide in me.

"My father's next film has Charles Bronson," he explained. "My father is the only man who can work with Charlie Bronson. Charlie's wife, Jill Ireland, she is the only woman who can stand to act with him. So we are a team."

"I see that," I said, "but what has that got to do with buying a truck?"

"The interviews he is doing today with the reporters, they are not important. He is just doing that to draw attention away from the real reason he is here."

"Which is —?"

"He is visiting your First National Bank of Boston. They have a lot of money in Columbia Pictures and he wants to have some of it for himself."

"And that's why you want a Scout? To carry the money in?"

Freddie saw the humor but didn't laugh.

"We will not buy one Scout. We will buy five."

He could see me trying to count them in my head.

"Five Chevy Scouts. We will charge all of them to the budget of the film: One for me, one for my father, two to destroy in the movie, and one for Charlie Bronson to drive home."

One more dealership and we headed back to the hotel to join his father, whom I had not yet met. Freddie made the introductions. Dino was indifferent.

"I have found the Scout," the boy announced. Dino nodded slightly and turned back to the Columbia personnel, signaling for his son to join him.

"By the way," Freddie said, whispering in my ear. "The picture, it will be called *The Stone Killer*."

The Stone Killer was released the next year, 1973, and did as well as Charles Bronson films usually did at the box office: better abroad than at home (something that always irritated the ultra-American Bronson). Appearing in the cast with him were Martin Balsam, Norman Fell, and Lisabeth Hush. But the outstanding performance was by his Chevy Scout.

Not long after that, Freddie did, indeed, become a producer, turning out *King of the Gypsies* in 1978 and *She Dances Alone* released in 1981. On July 15 of that year, while scouting locations for *Dune*, he was killed when his plane crashed in the Alaskan wilderness. He was 26.

<hr />

Eleanor Perry also died that year. She was sixty-six and was responsible, with her husband, Frank, in 1962, when she was 28, for redefining American independent film when they made *David and Lisa*. It's hard now to fathom the impact that this small black-and-white movie had on the film industry. As with *Marty* in 1955, *David and Lisa*—about two mentally troubled young people who find salvation by trusting each other—reminded audiences and critics that a personal story, well told, was more powerful than any widescreen, Technicolor epic. It was Eleanor Perry who adapted Theodore Isaac Rubin's clinical novel, *Lisa and David*, for her husband, Frank, a former documentarian, to direct. The Perrys scraped together the film's modest budget (reputed to be $100,000), hired little-known actors Keir Dullea and Janet Margolin for the title roles, got maverick distributor Continental Films to market it, and pulled off a miracle. This won them a studio deal from United

Artists for the nuclear war parable *Ladybug, Ladybug,* which did not do well. Then they hit their stride with *The Swimmer, Last Summer,* Truman Capote's *Trilogy,* and *Diary of a Mad Housewife,* which was a smash. After that, their marriage dissolved and, with it, the magic.

Eleanor continued to write, notably adapting 1973's *The Man Who Loved Cat Dancing,* starring Sarah Miles and Burt Reynolds, while Frank made another nine films, including the cult hit *Mommie Dearest,* before dying in 1995.

Eleanor and I met in 1979 when she published the *roman-à-clef, Blue Pages,* about a woman screenwriter and her philandering husband during the making of a film not unlike *The Man Who Loved Cat Dancing.* The title *Blue Pages* refers to the color of the paper on which a script's final draft is printed, and the book began with the maxim, "The writer is the woman of the film industry." This led us into a frank (sic) discussion of Hollywood politics.

"The business people wish they could do without writers," Eleanor said. "Writers are just damn nuisances. Anybody who cares about something besides money is trouble."

Eleanor wrote with her heart and her mind, and she played out their conflicts on the page. "At the beginning of a project, I fall in love with the producer," she said. "I fall in love with how nice they are and how wonderful the project is going to be. And then, of course, after the first draft, the whole thing goes to hell. I hate to sound like I'm complaining—God knows writers like myself in Hollywood get paid very well—but I may never write another screenplay."

She never did. Or, if she did, it was never produced (unfilmed scripts, like producers' promises, have no value, only lamentations). Several months later I visited her in her New York apartment where we had drinks ("I must have some bourbon around here somewhere," she said, indulging me and chiding me at the same time) and buoyed each other's spirits. In other words, we reconnected. I was a devotee of her script for *Last Summer* (1969) about bored upscale teens who tease each other with sex and eventually cross the line to rape. What it said about the origins of sexism, status, and empowerment struck me as profound as well as shocking, and she was pleased when someone saw beyond its provocative content. Our conversation then turned to courage, something a writer has to have every time she faces a blank sheet of paper, but also needs once those pages are full and she has to defend her talent to people who have none.

It was not only her commitment to her craft but her ability to inspire that led me to writing my own script about troubled teens. Called *Townies*, it was about two blue collar youths whose friendship is tested when one of them commits a terrible crime and confesses to the other, placing him in jeopardy.

"Oh, you've just *got* to write it!" Eleanor coached enthusiastically. "All that teenage sex will sell!" I thought she was joking. She wasn't. "But," she added, cautiously, "you have to keep them from taking out the important stuff, like character."

I didn't know Eleanor had cancer. When she died in March of 1981 I sent her family a note of condolence. Her daughter wrote back with something that surprised me: that her mother had spoken of me, and that she had my review of *Blue Pages* thumb tacked above her desk, and it was there the day she died.

I was never able to sell *Townies* for the very reasons Eleanor had warned me about. Of course, I dedicated it to her. When the third prospective producer told me to add more sex, change it to a happy ending, and make the characters less complex, I was almost relieved that Eleanor Perry, who inspired me, didn't have to face what Hollywood had become after she was no longer around to be seduced by it.

⬧

"I'll have a double scotch, no ice, water on the side, the way O'Toole does it," said actor Robert Shaw, preparing to face the press luncheon for *Young Winston*. Shaw played Lord Randolph Churchill in Sir Richard Attenborough's biopic of the British Bulldog, but—in 1972, when we went drinking together—he was more readily known for writing plays (*The Man in the Glass Booth*), novels, and for beating the snot out of Sean Connery's 007 in *From Russia With Love*.

"Acting is a monstrous profession," Shaw declared between drinks. "You never work unless someone asks you to, you speak other people's words, and you take orders from a director. That's why the ego, and why so many actors have drinking problems." He ordered another round: he had double scotches, I nursed single bourbons. (I still had to write the story). This, Shaw said, was why he turned increasingly to writing and was acting less and less, except for the occasional remarkable foray into filmed Harold Pinter screenplays such as *The Birthday Party*, *The Caretaker*, and *The Go-Between*.

"Let's see," he mulled, "*Winston* was made over a year ago and I finished doing *Old Times* just this Spring, so I guess I haven't been working." *Jaws* wouldn't come for another three years, after which neither Shaw nor motion pictures would ever be the same. At the time we drank, he was living with his wife and nine children in Ireland—"In the Republic!" he quickly added—"on one side is O'Toole, and the other is John Huston."

Shaw finished his third double scotch and walked out of the bar as if he had been drinking water. I barely made it to my desk to read what were barely coherent notes and to write what I remembered of our encounter (most of which you've just read). Shaw died in 1978 at the age of 51 after filming *Force 10 from Navarone*. Ten years later, I interviewed one of his co-stars in that film, actor Carl Weathers, for Weathers' then-current release, *Action Jackson*. Both of us realized without saying so that *Action Jackson* was a job of work and the less said about it the better. Once that was done, I closed my note pad and said, "You worked with Robert Shaw!" Instantly Weathers—who was impressive too—warmed up, and we spent the rest of our time talking about a man who wasn't there.

When Dom DeLuise died, the world lost one of its finest comic actors and I lost a good friend. Dom and I had grown close in his declining years when various infirmities sapped his strength but not his spirit. Often he would phone me in the morning and ask, "What are you doing for lunch?" This was an invitation to an afternoon of food and laughter. It was Dom who taught me how to cook sausages, onions, and peppers in the Italian way; his sister Antoinette, visiting from Brooklyn one week, tutored me on constructing a proper lasagna; and I reciprocated with a pulled pork meal that had Dom wiping the plate. Dom's wife, Carol (a Broadway musical star under the name Carol Arthur), who also became a dear friend, told tales of acting on the stage with Noel Coward and Beatrice Lillie; sons Michael and David showed how they inherited their parents' talent (firstborn Peter was in Canada directing TV shows); and a parade of celebrities and civilians was always stopping by.

Self-deprecating is the word that says the most about Dom. In a town full of egos, he never threw his around. He remains one of the very few people I've ever met in Hollywood who asked others about themselves because he wanted to know the answers, not to score off of them. True, some of those questions were, "Tell me about the first time you got laid," but they were also, "What did your father do for a living?" and "What was your favorite subject in school?"

Toward the end, he was not a well man. Hip replacement, diabetes, high blood pressure, anemia, prostate cancer, cholesterol, muscle atrophy, overweight, wheelchair-bound, you name it. But he held on heroically and comically. In March of 2009 I arrived for lunch to find a copy of the supermarket tabloid *Globe* tacked up in the foyer. Its headline screamed "Funnyman Dom DeLuise Given Two Weeks to Live." At the time, Dom was in the kitchen chopping onions to add to the huge pan of sausages simmering on the stove. Even though he was in a wheelchair, he was fully present and in charge of a staff that included his longtime assistant Elizabeth Adams, handyman Jesus Reyes, housekeeper Betty Topete, and a succession of medical caretakers such as Jayce Venditti who doubled as prep chefs. Karen, the mail lady, had just made her delivery; contractor Mike Dayem may have just been there with an estimate on the floors; filmmaker Deren Abram was completing the video portrait *According to Dom*, and, who knows, an appliance guy had probably tweaked the Frigidaire and been handed a freshly baked, foil-wrapped muffin on the way out.

Amidst all that, Charlie—Dom's beloved green and orange parrot—was perched on his master's shoulder grooming his haircut and dropping the occasional poop down the back of his apron. I entered, we hugged, and I asked him about the tabloid headline.

"Somebody who used to work here musta sold 'em a story," he said in sadness more than anger. "There's always people like that hanging around out front asking questions. If the news is slow they call and see if I'm still alive. You can't stop 'em."

He was, no doubt, remembering the time when he'd been hospitalized and one of the scream sheets bribed a nurse for access to Dom's hospital room, broke in, and stole a photo of him in bed. I asked if those invasions of privacy bothered him and he said that it didn't upset him as much as it made him concerned that his family and friends would worry. Then he set me to work slicing celery. I asked if he wanted me to freshen them first in water. "Don't give me a hard time," he said, his twinkling eyes pretending to frown, "remember, I got two weeks to live."

Sadly, Dom had five weeks to live. He died on May 4, 2009.

I still use his pizza recipe. I miss him more than words can say.

John de Lancie, Leonard Nimoy, and Ethan Phillips perform *The First Men in the Moon* at the Variety Arts Theatre in Los Angeles on November 2, 1997. It was the first live TV/Internet simulcast courtesy of the SciFi Channel.

John de Lancie, William Shatner, and Leonard Nimoy perform *The First Men in the Moon* at the Variety Arts Theatre in Los Angeles on November 2, 1997. It was the first live TV/Internet simulcast courtesy of the SciFi Channel.

The Author, Leonard Nimoy, and John de Lancie
at our first Alien Voices taping in 1995.

Big and Little Downey. Robert Downey, Sr. (a prince) was a huge
influence on today's ribald comedies, but few who benefit from
his legacy show him gratitude. Photo by Dale Robinette

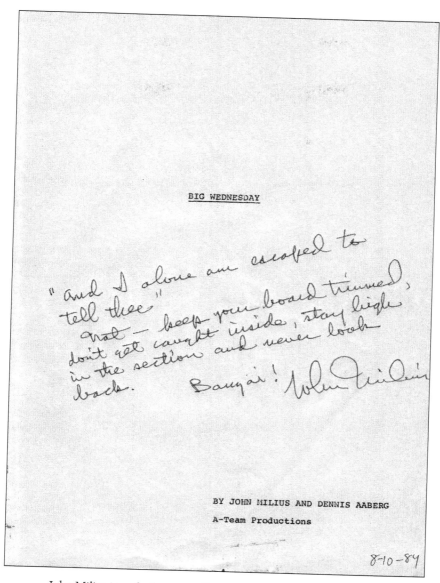

John Milius inscribed a copy of his and Dennis Aaberg's screenplay for *Big Wednesday* to me. It reads, "'And I alone am escaped to tell thee' – Nat, keep your board trimmed, don't get caught inside, stay high in the section, and never look back. Banzai!"

Charles Bronson goofs off with Dino DeLaurentiis. Bronson
is probably the only man who could get away with it.

Brooke Shields at the *Blue Lagoon* press junket. The photo looks like a
paste-up, but it isn't. Not only was she charming and unassuming, she is
the first actress I met who proved that the camera loves some
people (she) while others have a face made for radio (me).

Edward Asner,
my Hollywood Godfather.

My accidental screen debut in *The Friends of Eddie Coyle*. I showed up
to interview director Peter Yates for *Boston After Dark* and he thought I was
a scruffy extra sent over for the scene, so he put me into it. I didn't get paid
as an extra, but I got my story. L-R Peter Boyle, Bill-whose-last-name-I-forgot,
yours truly, and Peter Yates. No, we did not know at the time that the film would
become a classic, only that it would be very good. (Photo by Muky)

Gregory Hines graciously got back into microphone for me so I could ask him about *The Cotton Club*. (Photo by Paul Schumach)

Harvey Appell (R), my first boss in the movie business; his sales manager, Harold Levin (L); and the bright young man (C) who had just made *Take the Money and Run* for their company, American International Pictures.

Christopher Connelly, Gino Conforti, and James Hampton in *Hawmps!*.
"This camel is sick," said Gino, "notice the swelling on top."

Producer Irwin Allen (foreground, right, in toupee) at the Hartford,
Connecticut Showcase Cinema studio sneak of *The Towering Inferno*
in 1974. The author and his sideburns are in the background. Publicity
Director David Forbes sent this photo to me with the note, "Now you've
had your picture taken with I.A." (Photo by Edmund A. Lescoe, Jr.)

Writer-director James Bridges, a gentle man with a powerful talent.

Joanna Cassidy, one of the rare actresses sent on the road to do publicity. I was given orders to protect her; instead, I developed a crush.

John Houseman in his signature role, Professor Kingsfield in *The Paper Chase*.

Jon Voight came to town to promote *Conrack* in what became an adventure in discretion.

Joseph E. Levine. No comment.

Cliff Robertson directs Geraldine Page in *J.W. Coop* as script supervisor Margaret Tary looks on. Cliff was an incorruptible man in a highly corrupt business. We were friends.

Lan O'Kun, Dom DeLuise, Barbara O'Kun. I wish I knew what I did in a previous life to be blessed with their friendship in this one. (Photo by the Author)

Nina van Pallandt and Elliott Gould in *The Long Goodbye*. Robert Altman's film was an instant classic but only a few of us knew it at the time.

Leonard Nimoy and William Shatner after our audio taping session of
The First Men in the Moon for Alien Voices on July 26, 1998.
I believe that this was the last time these two friends and icons
acted together. (photo by the Author.)

Michael Caine, the most dazzlingly
charming actor I ever met.

Otto Preminger (no comment).

Carol Burnett and Martin Ritt rehearsing *Pete 'n' Tillie,* a challenging film that
had a remarkable sneak preview adventure.

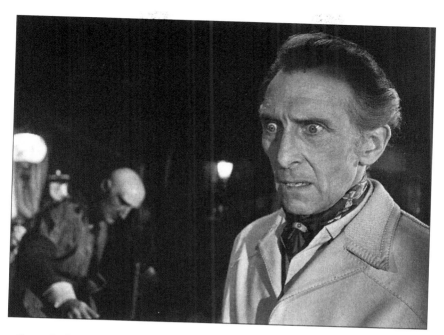

Peter Cushing in a screen pose completely opposite to the real personality of this lovely, polite, unassuming (and terribly depressed) man.

Jessica Tandy and Hume Cronyn. Royalty.

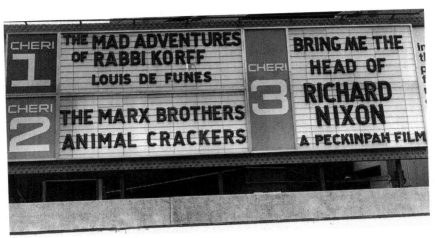

Marquee of the Cheri Theatre in Boston after unnamed vandals rearranged the letters to make a political statement in hopes of getting publicity. Wonder who did it.

Marquee Politics

Boston, Sept. 12—Passers by the Cheri, which is showing "Bring Me The Head Of Alfredo Garcia" and the "Mad Adventures Of 'Rabbi' Jacob," did a double take the other a.m., when the marquee spelled out: "Bring Me The Head Of Richard Nixon," and "The Mad Adventures Of Rabbi Korff." Nat Segaloff, Sack theatres press agent, said they didn't know who the marquee-changing prankster was, but he was sure it was not Donald Segretti.

NAT—
JUST IN CASE YOU
MISSED THIS IN DAILY
VARIETY'S FRI SEPT 13
EDITION.
—DAL LAMAGNA

Trade item reporting the Cheri anagram when Boston's papers wouldn't
(courtesy of Dal LaMagna)

Old-fashioned Hollywood "One happy family" photo of *The Towering Inferno* cast.
This picture was ordered pulled from presskit for unspecified reasons
(perhaps silliness?).

Director Martin Ritt (seated) and producer Robert Radnitz (standing, in tennis
duds). I worked with them separately and I'll never understand how they ever got
along together, but out of their partnership came *Sounder* and *Cross Creek*.

Joseph E. Levin and Ben Sack grip-and-grin on Levine's arrival to promote
The Night Porter and to bury the hatchet with his old Boston buddy....

... Lord knows what they were each thinking. Fay Foto by Harry Selig.

Steve McQueen dodges crowds at the Boston premiere of *The Thomas Crown Affair*. UA advertising VP Al Fisher is to the star's right.

Steve McQueen holds a press luncheon for the Boston critics at Locke-Ober's. Left to right: Virginia Lucier (*South Middlesex News*), McQueen, George McKinnon (*Boston Globe*), Nora Taylor (*Christian Science Monitor*) and, back of head, Alta Maloney (*Boston Herald*).

Pi Alley theatre manager Doug Kelly and I stand in front of the marquee for *Pete, Pearl, and the Pole*. Doug had nothing to do with the scam.

Ben Sack. Photo by Michael Dobo
©Michael Dobo/Dobophoto.com

Sack Theatres management team, 1974. Left to right: A. Alan Friedberg, VP; Bill Glazer, operations; Ken Gore, concessions; Ben Sack; Nat Segaloff, publicity director; David Traister, VP. Guess who looks out of place.

Variety coverage of Ben Sack's ouster from his own theatre chain. Note the date: December 25, 1974. Maybe I left the company a month too soon.

EXECUTIVE OFFICES
539 WASHINGTON STREET
BOSTON, MASS. 02111

Sack *theatres*

December 18, 1973   PERSONAL AND CONFIDENTIAL

Memo to: Alan Friedberg

From: Nat Segaloff

Subject: repercussions from Monday's press luncheon

Please know that the following conversation, in approximation,
transpired this evening (Tuesday) just past 6 PM between Mr.
Sack and myself:

S: Who's this?
N: Nat.
S: Anyone else there?
N: No, just me; I'm doing some work.
S: Did you ever find out what happened to Alta yesterday?
N: Yes; it seems that when they tried to call her from the paper
   she was out trying to start her car. There were power lines
   down all around her house and she was afraid to go out. I saw
   her this afternoon and that's what she told me.
S: Were there any newspapers of any consequence that didn't show
   up yesterday?
N: Well, the suburbs...
S: They're not important...
N: Then except for the Herald, no one. There aren't that many
   papers left.
S: We're not going to throw any more luncheons. They'll have to
   stand on their heads before we throw them any more fuckin'luncheons.
   You hear about any more luncheons, you let me know, okay?
N: Yes, sir, I'll get to you first on luncheons.
S: All right; good bye.

I can corroborate my half of this dialogue because, as it happens,
I was on a business call on another line at the time and had both
lines open.

Just didn't want this to hit you cold first thing in the morning.

Thank you.

NS/rw

My CYA memo to my boss after Ben Sack called me to complain about the press.
Keep in mind that not only didn't Sack pay for press luncheons,
he made side money from them.

The Worst of
Both Worlds

THE MOGULS who created the American movie industry were pricks. Some of them had taste, some of them had morals, but on the whole they were pricks. They had to be. It was the only way they could survive, not just in the mercantile eel pit of Hollywood but in the Eastern European world they fled to come there.[1] The merchant mentality built the studio system, and businessmen like Samuel Goldwyn, Louis B. Mayer, Adolph Zukor, Jesse Lasky, Harry Cohn, Jack L. Warner, and William Fox skillfully wielded it to forge their empires.[2]

Those who inherited their realms in the late 1950s had a lot to live up to but, like most second generations, they didn't always have matching mettle. While some fancied that better manners would get them further than their vulgarian predecessors, it turned out that corporate acumen would have been more helpful. Dore Schary was a polished, erudite man when he succeeded

---

1   A notable exception was Darryl F. Zanuck, a Protestant from Wahoo, Nebraska, who suffered discrimination because his name sounded Jewish to California's entrenched WASP society. The experience sensitized him and he became the most progressive, though not politically liberal, first generation studio boss. He was also one of the very few executives who could actually make a movie himself.

2   A famous wisecrack tells it all: Goldwyn was making a point to Mayer by jabbing him in the chest and Mayer shot back, "Don't point that finger at me. I knew it when it still had a thimble on it."

Louis B. Mayer at MGM in 1951. He lasted five years. Carl Laemmle, Jr. took over for his father "Uncle Carl" at Universal in 1928 and was deposed by creditors in 1936. Jack Warner sold Warner Bros. to the corporate TV firm Seven Arts in 1967 and the rest is more about Wall Street than Hollywood. Paramount's Lasky and Zukor were hit hard when they were forced to sell off the studio's lucrative theatre chain in 1948 and, after that, the company wandered through numerous leaders and owners, the most colorful of whom have been Charles Bludhorn (Gulf + Western Industries) and Sumner Redstone (Viacom), both of whom reserved their considerable mettle for boardrooms. When Harry Cohn died in 1958, the Columbia Pictures Board promoted corporate officers Sam Briskin, Leo Jaffe, and Abe Schneider to run the company. All three were no match for one King Cohn.

Modern producers fancy themselves in the mogul mold. Joel Silver and his former assistant Scott Rudin are savvy hit makers, but they're also supposedly screamers, and only their remarkable box office successes preserve their power. Harvey Weinstein of The Weinstein Company has both taste and nerve but often draws more publicity for himself than for his pictures. Perhaps the most consistently successful producers at this writing are Brian Grazer (Imagine Films), Frank Marshall and Kathleen Kennedy (Amblin' Entertainment), Jerry Bruckheimer, Tyler Perry, and George Lucas. But there are many others whose track records distinguish them such as Roger Corman, Mark Johnson, Robert Evans, Edward Pressman, Arnon Milchan, Arnold Kopelson, Dino De Laurentiis, Peter Guber, Don Simpson, and Jon Peters. Some ran studios—most famously and controversially Guber and Peters—but most are essentially businessmen who produce whatever they can raise the money to produce rather than running brick-and-mortar studios with weekly payrolls and the need to churn out twenty titles a year.

The grand studio days, of course, are gone forever, and so are the men (yes, they were all men) responsible for them. In a bizarre twist of fate, I encountered two of the last of the breed—neither of them named Cohn or Mayer or Warner, but both cut from the same *shmata*: Joseph E. Levine and Ben Sack.

Sack has already appeared in these pages: the former junk man (okay, wartime butcher and semi-precious metal smelting magnate) who ran the major theatre chain in Boston during the critical years of the 1960s and 70s when every other exhibitor migrated to the suburbs. He was gruff, racist, foul-mouthed, and lucky to have bright people working under him. He blew down the door and the college graduates would seal the deal. Yes, he smoked the requisite cigar. No, he was not colorful, he was just gruff.

Joe Levine was a latter-day Real Thing. Born in hard luck in Boston, stumbling into the movie business the way Ben Sack had done it by making an investment that paid off in glamour as well as profits, he variously produced, bankrolled, and/or distributed upwards of 500 pictures by 1974 when he picked up the rights to *The Night Porter* and Ben Sack agreed to book it.

It was not an easy decision for either man, and not for any reason that had to do with the film. *The Night Porter* concerns a concentration camp survivor (Charlotte Rampling) who meets her old tormentor (Dirk Bogarde) thirteen years after the end of World War Two when he is working as a night porter in a hotel. For reasons it would take a psychiatrist to explain, they fall back into the S&M relationship they had while she had been a prisoner. Sack saw the film at a trade screening and knew its blend of beauty, Holocaust, and sex would ring box office bells. The only problem was that Joe Levine was distributing it.

Levine and Sack had a blood feud running back to 1965 when Sack played Levine's picture, *Darling*, at one of his best theatres. Despite glowing reviews, the John Schlesinger film with Julie Christie (who would win the Oscar® for her performance) as a jet-setting, ennui-filled woman, did no business. Sack wanted to pull the film despite having signed a contract for an extended engagement. Levine protested, knowing that the Boston booking was crucial to the success of the film's national release. In anger, Sack told Levine, "People wouldn't come to see this picture if I gave it away for free!" Levine dared him, and the next day Sack threw *Darling* open to the public at no charge. (Just to show how much *chutzpah* people can have, some patrons even complained when they couldn't get free popcorn and soft drinks). Levine was furious, but when Sack put the ticket prices back in place the next day, attendance once again dropped to nothing. Levine swore he would never allow Sack to play another picture. But when the old man agreed to ante a $50,000 advance against box office receipts for *Night Porter*, Levine agreed.

To ensure that *The Night Porter*, which carried a hard R rating, would garner maximum press attention, I was ordered to pull out all the stops for the "duel of the titans." My one caveat was that I couldn't mention the *Darling* imbroglio, so all that the press had to go on was that two old Boston film guys were doing business again. I arranged for Sack's personal limo to meet Joe Levine on the tarmac of Logan Airport (in those pre-911 days such things were still possible), had photographers handy to rush their grip-and-grin photo to the papers, and rode with them to the hotel.

They did not speak with each other the whole trip.

I told them they were going to be doing dual interviews all that afternoon and the next day, including taping the premiere of a show that Boston's acclaimed WCVB-TV was kicking off. At the time, WCVB was being called the best local station in the country.

The print interviews went well but, when we arrived at a night club location for the TV taping, everything stopped. Bruce Marson, the station's executive producer and a seasoned show runner, apologized for the technical delays getting the location set up. Cramped at a round cafe table, sipping soda water, Ben and Joe were forced to make small talk.

"How's your sex life?" Sack asked.

"What sex life?" Levine growled back. "I been without sex so long, all I got down there now is a hole."

It went like that for two hours. I am not easily offended, but Levine's conversation was littered with such creative obscenity that I began to wonder if he had invented a new language. I have never had occasion to use half the words I learned that day, and I've worked for Westinghouse. Eventually both Levine and Sack managed to agree on something: "Let's get the hell out of here."

I don't know if the show ever got on the air, but I do know that Levine left town the next day, *The Night Porter* opened a week later and did little business. Predictably, Levine refused to amend Sack's deal, and the two men never exchanged another word.

I, however, exchanged words with Levine several years later when I had become a critic and his 1978 production of *Magic* was about to be released. Based on William Goldman's novel and screenplay about a ventriloquist, Anthony Hopkins, who was dominated by his dummy, it was uncomfortably close to the 1962 *Twilight Zone* episode "The Dummy" written by Lee Polk and Rod Serling. At a private lunch with Levine at the Ritz, I asked him about the resemblance and he deflected the question by remarking how brilliantly Goldman wove a love story into the concept. He rightly sensed that I didn't care for the film, which was directed by Richard Attenborough, so he allowed our conversation to wander throughout his career—with the odd exception of his early days in Boston. No, he said, he preferred to think about the future, to his next production (which turned out to be *Tatoo*, in 1981, which was even less well realized than *Magic*).

"Talent is nerve," Levine stated resolutely. "A great director needs the nerve to do things differently. Take Mike Nichols. He made *The Graduate* (1967) for me. Then he made *Carnal Knowledge* (1971) for me. Then he did *The Day of the Dolphin* (1973). It died. George C. Scott ruined *Day of the Dolphin*. He was so busy trying to get to make his own movie (*The Savage is Loose*, 1974) that he didn't care about my movie. I'll never work with George C. Scott again."

"What about Mike Nichols?"

"I'll do any picture Mike wants to make."

"Then why have Mike Nichols' last few films been so bland?"

"He lost his nerve."

Joe Levine died in 1987. Ben Sack died in 2004. The film business they loved died somewhere in between. It lost its nerve.

Virgins

IN THE old studio days, stars were manufactured, not born. Each of the big seven film factories—RKO, MGM, Columbia, Paramount, Twentieth Century-Fox, Universal, and Warner Bros.—kept dozens of performers under contract while they taught them acting, movement, singing, and how to deflect reporters' questions. Despite the confining, moralistic control that the moguls exercised over their talent stables, by the time the performers blossomed, if they ever did, they had become expert at their job, which was seduction—otherwise known as entertainment.

When the studio system clicked, the results were nothing short of astonishing. One afternoon I was scheduled to do a fifteen-minute phone interview with Debbie Reynolds to run in the newspaper ahead of the arrival of her one-woman show in town. We had never met, but as soon as we'd exchanged hellos she gave snappy answers to my questions, none longer than one or two sentences, and by the end of our call I had a full and complete feature story with no leftover quotes. A week later, Reynolds had to pull out of the show for personal reasons and Donald O'Connor stepped in. So back on the phone I go with O'Connor, whom I had likewise never met, and in fifteen minutes I had another fat-free feature story as if we had been friends since Louis B. Mayer was stalking the earth. God bless MGM and Howard Strickling (MGM's crack publicity director). They truly don't make 'em like that anymore, and it's a marvel that they ever did.

Those days ended during the 1960s when the existing studios were sold to conglomerates who had neither the expertise nor the patience to nurture anyone, let alone actors, and canceled much of the training regimen except what was necessary to populate the TV series that were replacing features on company balance sheets. But that didn't mean that the film companies stopped believing in publicity, for they continued to send actors, actresses, and others on the road to hype their product. The old-timers took it in stride, but the kids making their first couple of pictures were shoved in front of press and public with little or no preparation. It fell to the first press agent they met on the road to teach the tyro how to survive.

"One thing you have to learn," I told Debbie Turner, "is never sign autographs the way you sign checks or contracts because, in a crowd, when someone shoves a piece of paper at you, you never know what you're signing." Debbie had played one of the singing von Trapp children in *The Sound of Music* in 1965 and, nine years later, was being sent ill-prepared with her mother on a multi-city publicity tour to talk up its re-release. She had not acted since that blockbuster and had precious few memories to share with politely inquiring reporters. Having moved on from acting, and being blessed with two normal, loving parents (actually named Ken and Barbie), Debbie learned quickly. She spoke in phrases that journalists could copy down easily, she shared a few funny stories about her juvenile co-stars, admitted that none of them knew the film would ever be such a hit while they were shooting it, remembered the names of the people who interviewed her. And here's the capper: she sent thank-you notes.

Unlike Debbie Turner, Jeannie Berlin didn't want to be on press tour even though her film, *The Heartbreak Kid*, and her performance in it, were being acclaimed. Berlin is the daughter of Elaine May, the celebrated writer/director/actress. Berlin was sent on tour by the studio accompanied by a boyfriend and an attitude that everyone was out to cheat or exploit her. It's hard to say she was wrong, but, after she canceled one appearance after another, insisting she was ill, the studio called off her whole publicity tour rather than have her tarnish the film's possibilities. Since then, she has matured into one of the craft's most highly regarded acting teachers. One wonders whether this fine actress might have been offered more roles had she been willing to discuss her early ones.

Brian De Palma, in the days before he became the stylish auteur, was an independent New York filmmaker scraping for success. Having made two ultra low-budget satires on the military draft and the porn industry in the late 1960s (*Greetings* and *Hi Mom*), he was offered a studio deal by Warner Bros. for his quirky story of a tap-dancing magician, *Get to Know Your Rabbit*. It starred Tommy Smothers and, depending whom you believe, De Palma was either fired from the film before he finished it or Smothers took it over and ruined it. Either way, De Palma bounced back with the independent thriller *Sisters*, starring Margot Kidder as conjoined twins separated at birth, one of whom is a murderess. Eager to discuss his work with the press, he arrived armed with storyboards, production notes, and film theory—in other words, expecting the critics to be interested in learning something about the filmmaking process. The director quickly discovered that all they wanted to hear about was working with Orson Welles on *Rabbit*.

"Orson is a whore," De Palma declared, accommodating them. "What I mean is, he takes acting jobs for the money to make his own films. Trouble is, he's lazy. He doesn't want to memorize his lines. So what you have to do is keep on doing take after take until he can't help but learn them. It was a game we played."

Before Pauline Kael discovered what the underground press had known for years and beatified De Palma in *The New Yorker*, most mainstream critics didn't "get" his dark, playful jokes. Even the skillful tension he generated in *Sisters* was edged with humor.

"I wanted to start my film with silence," he said. "A blind girl enters a locker room and takes off her clothes. She is watched by a man standing there who she can't see. It's both funny and uncomfortable. I showed the cut of the film to the composer, Bernard Herrmann. Bernie said, 'What is this?'

"I told him I wanted people to get to know the characters before anything happened to them. He asked how long I expected the audience to wait for this. I said, 'In *Psycho*, you and Hitchcock kept the audience waiting forty minutes.' Bernie said, 'That's Hitchcock. For Hitchcock, they'll wait. For you, they won't wait. You need music.'

"So he composed ninety seconds of title music and we made a montage of a fertilized egg splitting in the womb. I listened to it and it scared the hell out of me. After that, nothing happens for half an hour, but you stay there waiting for it. So Bernie was right."

One might say that De Palma began his romance with Hitchcock, and his cynicism toward the press, with that film. Over time he became a master at directing his interviews, too, but, at the beginning, he was burned by the dismissive attitudes of others. "Review the film that I made," he challenged, "not the film you wanted to see." That was a good point, when I became a critic, I tried to follow it.

⁕

I've already stated my rule of not holding an interview subject accountable for anything he says while drunk. The same holds true for what he says when angry. The actor son of a famous actor was having a tiff with his father when we spoke, and he spent most of our time together telling how his father cheated on his mother. It was great dish but could only cause anger and pain if I printed it. I called the kid back to tell him that he really shouldn't be trashing anyone in the media because it could only blow back on him. He took the advice as it was intended, and I constructed my story out of the ten percent of our conversation that was usable. He's still acting and now directing, and he's good at both.

At the time that the Disney people sent Kurt Russell on a multi-city promotional tour, all that the strapping young man wanted to do was ditch acting and become a professional baseball player. Too young to be jaded, too polite to be glib, and too smart to go against the studio, he was ingratiating and earnest, if bland. That was in 1973 when he was in *Charley and the*

Angel. Seven years later he was the lead in *Used Cars*, a raucous comedy from Bob Gale and Robert Zemeckis; was married to actress Season Hubley; and had jettisoned the Disney yoke forever. Brash, personable, and boisterous, he practically grew up in front of the public. His work since then has shown the emergence of a mature talent.

If anyone grew up in front of the public, it was Liza Minnelli. Mindful of what the publicity machine did to her mother, when Liza came into her own in 1969's *The Sterile Cuckoo*, she had the good sense to have her director, the beloved Alan J. Pakula, accompany her on a tour of college film classes. As Pookie Adams, the lovable but fragile heroine of the romantic drama, she won the public's and the press's hearts. As a visitor to the Boston University film school, she won over an entire room of cynical young filmmakers (including this one) with an impromptu performance.

It was then the custom for filmmakers to speak at colleges while they were visiting cities on their publicity tour. Pakula and Minnelli showed up at the basement screening room at B.U. where Professor Robert Steele introduced them (in malapropistic seriousness) as "Alan Palooka" and "Lisa McNulty."

A highlight of *The Sterile Cuckoo* was an intense telephone conversation between Liza and her co-star, Wendell Burton. She believes in fantasy, he holds to reality, and it is at this point that she realizes that their relationship is doomed. As they described doing "the telephone scene" in the movie, Pakula stayed in one of the room's canvas director's chairs while Liza got up and sat in a window seat. Pakula began reciting Burton's dialogue and Liza slipped into character. The performance was subtle and without contrivance, and the whole class fell in love with this gamine. In the next few years, *Cabaret, Arthur,* and *New York, New York* would prove her acting chops over and over. Having been raised wise to the ways of show business, Minnelli (who had already appeared on Broadway and in concerts) knew how to work a crowd and protect herself at the same time. Of all the novices I met who learned their lessons on the road, she was the one who was ahead of the game just by entering the room.

Publicity Stunts

TOO OFTEN, the best publicity stunts are devised for the worst movies; after all, a publicist's job is to get a good opening, anything beyond that is up to the filmmaker. In the old days, movie publicity departments would engage in such "ballyhoo" as dressing people in costumes, walking wild animals through town, planting fake newspaper stories, and any number of harmless gimmicks that would draw attention to a new movie. The press, usually let in on the stunt, would dutifully include the film title in their human interest coverage.

Sometime the stunts got out of hand. For the 1967 all-star "*Casino Royale*"—very loosely based on the only Ian Fleming James Bond novel that Cubby Broccoli didn't own at the time—John Markle, the New England Field Representative for Columbia Pictures, implemented a publicity stunt that came to be known everywhere as the "*Casino Royale* Riot."

His collaborator was the then-major exhibitor in Boston, Sack Theatres, whose intown Savoy Theatre was slated to open the picture in late May. Markle and Sack's Vice President, A. Alan Friedberg, decided to hold a midnight promotional screening a week before the premiere. Since 007 was a secret agent, they announced that anybody who showed up dressed as a spy would get in for free. The stunt was trumpeted by an upstart entertainment tabloid called *Boston After Dark*, which later became the hugely successful *Boston Phoenix* before succumbing to Internet euthanasia in 2013. Everybody was thrilled to go along with the gag.

In hindsight, one needs to remember that, in 1967, midnight showings had not yet become a cult tradition. Another thing nobody figured on was that the stunt was scheduled for the middle of college reading period, a whole week in which approximately 100,000 Boston-area students had nothing to do and lots of time to do it in. Consequently, 10,000 of them arrived at midnight at the 2,800-seat Savoy Theatre expecting to see a free movie. All were variously costumed in trench coats, dark glasses, Army boots, wigs, and fake moustaches. The doors had closed hours earlier when the theatre had filled to capacity, but nobody knew how to pass the word along to the people who were shut outside. Throngs began rushing the doors. The ushers got so scared, their faces cleared up. Then the Boston Police were called out to disperse the crowds, which they did with absolutely no violence. (In May of 1967 Vietnam anti-war protests hadn't become a regular occurrence in New England.)

The Hub's bus and subway system had closed at midnight so, by three AM, there were 7,200 unemployed spies ambling back to their dormitories or queuing up at a single forlorn Dunkin' Donuts on Boylston Street in Back Bay. Twenty-four hour drugstores hadn't been invented yet (for that matter, drugs hadn't permeated the youth culture yet, either, so it was a curious event to see a fully populated city with nothing open).

Meanwhile, the 2,800 lucky patrons who had been admitted to the theatre had no idea that anything unusual had been going on outside until they read the morning papers. The front pages carried news of the "riot" from Tokyo to Times Square. Not long afterwards, the Boston Mayor's Office advised exhibitors to admit promotional audiences by advance physical ticket only, not just by throwing doors open. *Casino Royale*, of course, died the quiet box office death it deserved, but not because nobody had ever heard of it. When the rights to the property were reclaimed by Danjaq, the company founded by the late Cubby Broccoli to produce the authentic James Bond films, it was remade into a superb 2006 action drama that rekindled the 007 franchise.

Nothing says that a publicity stunt has to be classy, it just has to work. When the feisty Hallmark Releasing company in New England bought a cheaply made 1970 German horror film with the catchy title *Hexen bis aufs Blut gequält*, they had the good sense to rename it *Mark of the Devil* (its direct translation is *Witches Tortured to Death*). Nominally it's a period piece about two witch-hunters (Udo Kier and his mentor, Herbert Lom) who discover the errors of their ways but are apprehended before they can spread the Word; Lom escapes but Kier is tortured to death. It's bloody, it's noisy, and it's gross, but that wasn't enough to assure Hallmark of box office success. They needed a gimmick, like in the old William Castle days of floating skeletons and tingling theatre seats. They stumbled on it during a preview screening of the picture when they heard audiences gag at a scene where a woman's tongue was torn out of her mouth in full view. Their response was to print tens of thousands of *Mark of the Devil* airline sickness bags and give one to every ticket buyer in case he or she needed it during the show. The gimmick was playfully perverse but it did the trick and won tons of press coverage to boot. Not only was the picture a hit, but the original barf bags have been known to sell for $100 at collectors' shows. And that's nothing to throw up at.

Humor also helped sell a soft-hearted 1974 romance called *The Girl from Petrovka* which starred Goldie Hawn and Hal Holbrook. Universal Pictures hadn't a clue how to draw attention to it, but one theatre seized on the heart-shaped tattoo that Hawn's character had on her cheek and made a slew of promotional T-shirts for their poor ushers to wear. The T-shirt said, *I Have a Heart On for The Girl from Petrovka*. It didn't help.

A good publicity stunt is clever enough for the press to play along with, but not too clever for its own good. The most important rule is not to try to fool the press, since you need them to cover it. I confess to breaking all the rules at the same time with a game of anagrams using the letters on a theatre marquee.

In late 1974 America was in political and social turmoil. Richard Nixon was up to his ass in Watergate, he was defended by, of all people, a right-wing rabbi named Baruch Korff, and Massachusetts' progressives were seething with frustration. Against this background the three-screen Sack Cheri Cinema complex in downtown Boston was running a trio of films that were doing poor business: Sam Peckinpah's muddled *Bring Me the Head of Alfredo Garcia*, an unfunny French farce (that sounds redundant, doesn't it?) called *The Mad Adventures of 'Rabbi' Jacob*, and The Marx Brothers in *Animal Crackers* (which, though finally being freed of a rights embargo, alas, died quickly because it was playing in the wrong theatre).

With the whispered consent of Sack's Vice President, A. Alan Friedberg, Cheri assistant manager Doug Kelley and I donned dark clothes, took the ladder out of storage, and went to work on the marquee as soon as the lights were turned off after the last show. It took us a couple of hours, but we finally rearranged the letters to read: *The Mad Adventures of Rabbi Korff* and *Bring Me the Head of Richard Nixon*.

At 6 AM the next day I phoned the newspapers from home (this was before Caller ID) pretending to be an irate citizen who had driven past the Cheri and was offended by what I saw. By the time I got to the Sack office, I had phone calls from both the *Globe* and *Herald*. As the Sack Theatres publicity director, I expressed alarm that somebody had dared change the letters around and, of course, we would investigate which of our employees may have done it. Instead, the sales managers of both papers called back to assure me that they were killing the story because we were such valuable advertisers that they didn't want to embarrass us. The lesson we learn from this is that, if Richard Nixon had bought more advertising linage in *The Washington Post*, he wouldn't have had to resign the Presidency.

I Spent the Night with
James Bond, Napoleon
Solo, and Ed Norton

I<small>N</small> *TARGETS*, Peter Bogdanovich's remarkable 1968 directing debut, there's a galvanizing moment of pure cinema: A sniper, Bobby Thompson (Tim O'Kelly), has hidden behind the screen of a drive-in movie theatre and is picking people off in their cars using a rifle with a telescopic sight. This happens to be the same night that Byron Orlok (Boris Karloff), the star of the horror movie being shown there, is making a publicity appearance. Police capture Bobby and, as they drag him past Orlok, he looks at the actor, then up at his huge image on the screen, then back again, his face torn in haunting confusion between fantasy and reality.

Targets (which I screened for the Boston critics in 16mm in my apartment after the distributor had abandoned it) is one of only a handful of films that deal with the movies as a medium of dreams rather than with Hollywood as the place where dreams are shattered. *September 30, 1955* is another such work, a 1977 semi-autobiographical film by writer/director James Bridges that follows what happens to a small group of Arkansas teenagers on the day that James Dean dies. A brilliant merger of images, themes, and music from *East of Eden* and *Rebel Without a Cause*, the Bridges film (also titled

9/30/55) is fueled by a bravely alienating performance by Richard Thomas in which his character forgets where reality ends and the screen begins.

The power of film is also its danger: at the same time that it transports, it deludes; it effortlessly presents lies as truths; it manipulates emotions and implants images as vividly as if they were actual experience. When I was working in the New York publicity department of United Artists, which released the James Bond movies, one of our duties was sorting through the fan mail and forwarding any that were legitimate while disposing of the requests for autographed photos and hair samples. The most heart-rending were those that were sent to "James Bond 007" by people who were in crisis and sought the British secret agent's help. These were neither fakes nor jokes, but clearly well-meaning pleas from people who believed that Ian Fleming's invention was real.

I sampled a taste of that delusion, albeit more benignly, in 1996 when I formed a short-lived science fiction production company called Alien Voices® with John de Lancie and Leonard Nimoy, two actors who were known for their work in *Star Trek*. One of the first things Leonard advised me after we signed papers was, "Be sure to make your phone number unlisted. I once got a call from a Guam radio station at 3 AM. I'll never know how they got my number, but they did, and they wanted an interview."

I followed his wise advice.

True Trekkers know that Leonard Nimoy isn't really Mr. Spock and that William Shatner isn't really Captain Kirk and that John de Lancie really isn't Q. They are respectful of the difference between private and public. At the same time, they have constructed a separate reality in which Spock, Kirk, Scottie, McCoy, Uhura, Chekhov, Sulu, Q and the others actually exist. The difference between "Trekker" and "Trekkie" was once explained to me thus: a Trekker likes *Star Trek.* while a Trekkie has a set of the Spock ears.

Fans have always had trouble keeping actors apart from their screen image. Basil Rathbone used to get hissed in restaurants as the villain before he became Sherlock Holmes, after which he started getting detective offers. People sought insults from Groucho Marx and wore them as combat badges.

Show-offs were always trying to pick fights with John Wayne. Don Ameche didn't really invent the telephone. Peter Graves would often find tape recorders placed in front of him at restaurants as if he really was "Mr. Phelps" from *Mission: Impossible*. And restaurateur Dave Chasen was right on the money when he said, "The trouble with Humphrey Bogart is that, after three drinks, he thinks he's Humphrey Bogart."

When I sat beside Art Carney as he demonstrated a napkin-folding trick at dinner,[1] adding the elaborate hand fakes that drove Ralph Kramden nuts on *The Honeymooners*, I had the urge to bark, "Cut it out, Norton!" I had my own Tim O'Kelly moment when I walked actress Susannah York into a screening of Robert Altman's *Images*, in which she plays a dual role, and, as we emerged, the theatre manager said, "My God, now there are *three* of you." I also confess to interviewing a young Brooke Shields and being mesmerized by the difference between the sweet and slightly gawky teenage girl sitting two feet away from me in person and the sultry, violet-eyed minx whose image appeared on the video monitor. It was the first time I had actually seen proof of the adage, "There are some people whom the camera loves."

Growing up bedeviled by movies, and then working on the side of the demons, I should have learned objectivity. Robert Vaughn erased any vestige of it for me. Any teenager living in America in the 1960s had his choice of secret agents. Ian Fleming's James Bond, of course, was the king, but he only made movies every two years. Harry Palmer, in the form of Michael Caine, was Len Deighton's "thinking man's" counterpart to 007. Dean Martin spoofed his way through Matt Helm, as did James Coburn's *Our Man Flint*. There was even a "female James Bond" in the form of Monica Vitti as *Modesty Blaise*. But the only one I took seriously was *The Man from U.N.C.L.E.* starring Robert Vaughn as American-born secret agent Napoleon Solo and David McCallum as his friendly Russian counterpart, Illya Kuryakin. *The Man from*

---

1   He turned it into a brassiere—ta-DAAA! When properly motivated, I have been known to perform the trick myself (in Art's honor).

U.N.C.L.E topped the ratings from 1964 to 1968 with its blend of fantasy elements like hand-held communicators ("Open channel D, please"), headquarters hidden in the back of a dry cleaning establishment, and plotlines that carried a continuing subtext of Cold War paranoia.

Vaughn was as suave, playful, and bright as his TV character. He was also as intense, as I discovered when we were stranded in Buffalo, New York while plugging *The Towering Inferno* in the winter of 1974. Ensconced at the airport hotel after a day's gathering snowfall, the only thing to do was eat the bland food and drink from an unexpectedly ambitious wine list (on studio expense, natch). Vaughn selected a reasonable *Pouilly-Fuissé* for which he signaled an encore before we were halfway through the first bottle, and we followed the meal by deeply denting a fifth of cognac.

Vaughn was political, not just in word, but in deed. His doctoral thesis on show business blacklisting, *Only Victims*, was published in book form in 1972 as one of the first serious studies of this American disgrace, even though the Blacklist had supposedly ended a decade earlier. Naturally, we discussed politics and, when he realized I had come from Massachusetts, he leaned forward—the Muzak was too loud—and opened Channel D on his voice.

"Let me tell you something you won't have heard anywhere else," he began. "In the weeks after the Warren Commission Report came out pinning the assassination of President Kennedy on Lee Harvey Oswald —" the waiter returned to replenish our waters, and Vaughn backed off until he'd gone—"Jacqueline Kennedy's doubts about its truthfulness led her to act. She hired a private detective, a very good one, I won't name him, to investigate the things she had been hearing from the Secret Service and the growing conspiracy movement. She paid him well and he worked for weeks, reporting that he was making headway. Then, one night, at home, her private telephone line rang. This was a number known only to Mrs. Kennedy, her family, and the Secret Service. She answered it, and a voice at the other end warned her that, if she did not call off her investigation, she and her children would be at great risk."

He drained his snifter and set it down sharply to make the point. I couldn't move. Not only was the revelation itself shocking, but it was being told to me in the most dramatic way not by Robert Vaughn, a mere actor I was handling for publicity appearances, but by Napoleon Solo, the Man from U.N.C.L.E. Several years later I found a pristine copy of *Only Victims* and asked him to inscribe it. He wrote, "To Nat with all good wishes that 'it' can't happen again." Anyone reading it might assume he's talking about the Blacklist. But Napoleon Solo and I know better.

Roger Moore was quite another secret agent—oops, an actor who had played one. Unfailingly charming and relaxed, he had given up his license to kill and, in 1991, was acting in (and producing sans credit) a gentle comedy-thriller called *Bed and Breakfast*. His co-stars were Talia Shire (wife of line producer Jack Schwartzman), Nina Siemaszko, Jamie Walters, and Ford Rainey. I was assigned by my newspaper to trek to Maine, on whose rockbound coast the production was being shot, to interview Moore, but I was also eager to speak to his co-star, the great actress Colleen Dewhurst, who was also in the cast. By the time I arrived, the New England climate had decided to take over. A night shoot was scheduled for the climax in which Moore, a good-bad scoundrel, saves a houseful of women from a hoard of attacking miscreants. The rain couldn't make up its mind whether or not to fall and, since there were no other scenes left to shoot, director Robert Ellis Miller and his company had no alternative but to do everything both dry and wet, and whichever version wrapped first would be the one that went into the film.

Dewhurst was relaxing in her trailer between set-ups when the gentlemanly Miller asked me to look in on her. "She probably won't give you an interview," he said, "and, for God's sake, don't bring up her divorce from George C. Scott! But keep her occupied."

A steely, sad-eyed woman with downturned mouth and a bourbon voice earned with real bourbon, Dewhurst was a formidable actress who emitted a no-nonsense aura. Although film and television seldom used her talent to advantage, her stage work was electric, winning her two Tony awards out of eight nominations in such now-classics as *A Moon for the Misbegotten*, *Ballad of the Sad Cafe*, *Who's Afraid of Virginia Woolf?* and *All the Way Home*. Miller was right about the interview; Dewhurst declined it politely, but asked me to stay. We sat together for half an hour chatting about absolutely nothing. I tried the technique of not talking about her in an effort to get her to talk about herself. She preferred to talk about her co-stars and how nice they were, and there were long silences that I got the feeling she didn't want me to fill in. When the assistant director fetched her for her next scene, she asked for a minute alone to get herself ready, and I departed.

"What did you talk about?" Miller asked.

"Nothing," I had to tell him. "I guess she just wanted to be with someone who didn't want anything."

Miller shook his head in modest bewilderment and continued preparing the scene. What neither of us knew at the time was that Dewhurst had been diagnosed with the cancer that would take her a few months later.

After the shot was made and Moore was back in his trailer drying off from the misty rain, he beckoned me in. "I hate actors who talk about acting," he said as soon as we sat down, "it sounds so artsy-crafty. Say the lines and hit the marks. Or, as Lee Marvin said to me, 'Say the marks and hit the lines.'"

On the subject of the accouterments of fame, Moore was dismissive. "I don't stay in hotels," he said. "I have houses where I work—in England, France, Switzerland and Los Angeles. It saves me traveling with all those suitcases. More than that, if one lives in a place, one is accepted there and doesn't draw attention. I become like a banker or businessman and not a film actor, and nobody pays me any attention. On the other hand, if people don't recognize you, then you've done something wrong in your profession."

"Is there anything that scares you?"

"Apart from a third world war coming, nothing, really. Do you mean if someone might take a pot shot at me? No, I don't have bodyguards. When there was a question of kidnapping, I had some for my kids. Now I can't get anybody to take them away." We both laughed.

Then it was Moore's turn to respond to the assistant director's knock at the door. He took his place in front of the camera for the "dry" shot and Miller called "Action."

I looked at my notes and realized that we had spoken for twenty pages and not once mentioned James Bond. I took that as an achievement. My editor did not, and reminded me of how I'd let Jimmy Olsen get away, too. Unlike those fans who wrote to James Bond thinking he was a real person, my editor knew the difference. And so did Roger Moore.

Alien Voices®

I SELDOM WATCHED *Star Trek®* when it was new. My idea of science fiction at the time was Jules Verne, H.G. Wells, Ray Bradbury, Harlan Ellison, and the unsettling anthology TV series, *The Twilight Zone.* Whenever I happened to catch *Star Trek* during its initial NBC run, all I saw were the cheap sets, the tacky monster suits, and the gimmickry (I missed the episode that Harlan Ellison had written, "City on the Edge of Forever"). It was only when John de Lancie dragged me into the *Trek* universe thirty years later that I realized the power and pull of those 79 seminal episodes and the people behind them. I have a deep respect for the fans who not only kept the show going but have kept the show's hopeful, positive ethics alive for over half a century.

My relationship with *Star Trek* is tangential, but intense. As I noted earlier, I was a founding partner with John de Lancie and Leonard Nimoy of Alien Voices, a production company originally devoted to audiobook dramatizations of classic science fiction stories as acted by *Star Trek* performers. We had a deal with Simon & Schuster Audio, published five titles and did one TV special, and then dissolved for reasons that had nothing to do with either us or the product.

My introduction to *Trek* began in 1993 when Ed Asner, whom I call my Hollywood godfather, encouraged LA Theatre Works to produce *The Waldorf Conference,* a comedy-drama about the secret 1947 meeting of movie moguls that began the Hollywood Blacklist. Ed played MGM President Louis

B. Mayer, and John de Lancie directed an all-star cast that included Charles Durning, John Schuck, John Randolph, Shelley Berman, Bill Macy, William Schallert, John Kapelos, Richard Masur, George Murdock, Ron Rifkin, and David Ellenstein. LA Theatre Works, founded and run by the dynamic Susan Loewenberg, produced audio dramatizations that aired on various NPR (and later, Pacifica) radio stations. LATW has been called the only profit-making non-profit theatre troupe in America but, at least in those days, they gave important exposure to tyro playwrights, and *The Waldorf Conference* — co-written by Arnie Reisman, Dan Kimmel, and me — was just such a creature. We enjoyed a live broadcast on KCRW-FM under the auspices of the gutsy Ruth Seymour and had four sold-out live performances, setting a record.

When I visited LATW's Venice, California offices after *Waldorf* had been contracted, I was informed that John de Lancie would direct it. "Who is he?" I asked.

"He plays the character called 'Q' on *Star Trek: The Next Generation*," I was told.

"How is he to work with?" I asked suspiciously.

"He's a little regal," they said.

"We'll see about that," I muttered, and went about my business.

John called within a few days and offered to drive to where I was living in the Fairfax neighborhood of Los Angeles. A director and TV star offering to visit a writer? An unusual (and appreciated) move. Within five minutes we were friends. He respected the text, he said, and his goal in working with me (although my partners, still in Boston, had to approve) was to track the characters, make the motivations clear, and sharpen the drama of the scenes. As he was leaving, he said something that I have used ever since: "We are inevitably going to disagree at some time in the rehearsal process," he said evenly. "My only request is that we not disagree in front of the actors."

As it happened, we didn't have any disagreements, but with a cast of veterans like that, there were bound to be some adventures.. John Randolph, who had been blacklisted, was astonished by the information we uncovered in the play. "We were having a Screen Actors Guild board meeting at the same time," he said, "and if we'd known that the Waldorf meeting was going on, we might have been able to fight it from the beginning."

Shelley Berman, whose comedy album "Inside Shelley Berman" was the first I had ever heard (yes, he autographed it for me), recalled an experience he had on stage of San Francisco's hungry i night club. It was essential for the stage to go black at a specific point in his monologue for full dramatic effect. When, one night, it didn't, Berman lost his temper at the man who operated the lights. "You put me through hell up there," he said, "you left me hanging on stage." The spotlight operator then told him, calmly, "you don't know what hell is." He was Alvah Bessie, the blacklisted screenwriter who had gone to prison as one of the Hollywood Ten. When he got out, the only job he could get was running the spotlight at the hungry i.

There were lighter moments. The cast performed while standing at floor mics in the manner of old-time radio shows. Ed Asner and Charles Durning were both heavy men, and John de Lancie first had them sharing a single microphone. The first time we had the play on its feet, we saw—and the giggles started — that Ed and Charlie had such large guts that only one at a time could get close enough to the microphone to pick up. They were moved.

The Waldorf Conference was a success. People came up from the audience afterward to confide that they were "members of the tribe" (meaning children of blacklistees) and that they appreciated learning the background that led to their families' ordeals. The day after the live broadcast, we even got a message to call a development person at Icon Productions, Mel Gibson's company. They were interested in the screen rights. We called back. All these years later I am still waiting for them to return their own phone call. My guess is that their development person wanted to show his boss how alert he was by being able to say, "why yes, I have a call in to the authors now," never intending to pursue it. Welcome to Hollywood.

Waldorf became an adventure that led us to a purchase by Warner Bros. Television, their unfortunate inability to sell it to a cable TV network, and a gambit with a conscientious producer named Stephen Israel and a scoundrel of a producer (whom my lawyer says I can't name) who tried to steal our project. But it led, the next year, to John de Lancie asking me if I wanted to work with him on a new production of the Howard Koch-Orson Welles radio drama *Invasion From Mars* based on H.G. Wells's *War of the Worlds*. The gimmick, John said, was that it would have an all-*Star Trek* cast headed by Leonard Nimoy in the Orson Welles role. We'd talk about it over dinner, he said.

I arrived at the de Lancie home for dinner and was told by his wife, Marnie Mosiman, that John would be delayed, but that I should relax with a guest who was already there while she finished preparing dinner (the de Lancies and I have had countless dinners since this one). The guest, Robert Egan, was Producing Artistic Director of the Mark Taper Forum, a major theatrical venue in Los Angeles, and I learned from Marnie that it was John's clever but devious plan to have me pitch the buttonholed Egan on presenting *Waldorf* at the Taper. The timing could not have been worse. Bob, at the time, had just come through a brutal divorce from actress Kate Mulgrew, and not only was he in no mood to be pitched, he was in no shape for it. He and a bottle of *Pouilly-Fumé* had been getting acquainted before I got there, and by the time he and I were introduced, the only thing he wanted to talk about was the details of his late marriage. It was, as I described it to him years later in sobriety, a Stephen Sondheim musical comedy without the music or the comedy. (I also got to know Kate and was duly impressed.)

When John arrived, he told me his plan. *Invasion from Mars* only ran an hour and he and LA Theatre Works needed something to fill out the program. What about writing a sequel? He said that he had already spoken with Howard Koch about extending his 1938 radio play but that the then-92-year-old writer was, thus far, unable to offer anything more than, "We go to Mars and continue the encounter." When it became clear that Howard (we had met some years before) was going to be unable to deliver, John asked me to take over.

Under Writers Guild rules it is mandatory for a writer who takes over from another writer to inform the first writer of the change. Otherwise you are what's called "writing behind" the first writer, something that was so confusing, unfair, and yet common during the pre-Guild era that it became a major requirement when the WGA was formed. But LA Theatre Works was not a Guild signatory, and I was not doing Guild work, and so I had the dubious but legitimate honor of writing behind the man who had co-written *Casablanca*.[1]

John and I decided on a concept of pretending that we were still on the air after performing the Koch script with the actors assuming their real names, congratulating each other in the green room, and preparing to disperse when word comes in that Martians are actually landing in Santa Monica, California. The broadcast then cuts back and forth among them as they try to get home, braving a roiling Santa Monica Bay and dodging death rays. They try to get word out that it's the end of the world for real, but everyone they call is so distrustful of the media that nobody believes them. This was right after the O.J. Simpson trial, so the credibility of the mass media—and, in particular, its obsession with garbage news—was a major concern. At the end, Leonard Nimoy wrapped up the broadcast by repeating Cassius's famous admonition from Shakespeare's *Julius Caesar*: "Men, at times, are masters of their own fate. The fault, dear Brutus, is not in our stars, but in ourselves."

While we were in the green room waiting to go on, the actors ate a light meal and talked of anything except the play we were about to do. As these were all *Star Trek* folk, the conversation quickly turned to the latest memoir by William Shatner. Apparently Shatner had spoken with a number of those present about their experiences on the various series but had not, according to them, disclosed that he was going to use their recollections in his book. The outrage grew until everyone noticed that Leonard was quietly eating a piece of cheesecake and keeping his own counsel. The room grew silent and Leonard could feel everyone's eyes staring at him. Finally he said, softly

---

1   Howard Koch died on August 17, 1995.

and flatly, without looking up, "I'm writing a book too." After a beat, everyone laughed and the tension was broken. *I Am Spock* was published in 1996. Leonard told me that he was at a party just after it came out and another Hollywood celebrity congratulated him and asked him who wrote it. "I did," he said.

"No," said the celebrity, "I mean who really wrote it?"

"I did," Leonard insisted. Somehow the other person couldn't accept the fact that, in Hollywood, some people are actually capable of writing their own autobiographies.

John and I named our *Invasion from Mars* sequel *When Welles Collide*, a twist on the well-known 1933 science fiction novel by Philip Wylie and Edwin Balmer, *When Worlds Collide*, and a comment on the opposing themes that, in 1938, the invasion was fake but everybody believed the media, and, in 1994, the invasion was real but nobody believed the media any more. Our cast included, in addition to Leonard and John, Ethan Phillips, Gates McFadden, Dwight Schultz, Armin Shimerman, Brent Spiner, Wil Wheaton, Megan Fay, Jerry Hardin, and Tom Virtue. The audiences for the 1994 production, which included not a few *Star Trek* fans, had a ball. For reasons still unknown, when it was broadcast over KCRW, LA Theatre Works cut out most of Megan Fay's role as a bag lady and have refused to issue the sequel on audio as they do all their other productions. (I happen to have the only existing complete digital dub.)

The adventure was so much fun that John, Leonard, and I decided to keep it going. We set up Alien Voices® the next year and, through the efforts of agent Andy Zack, almost immediately landed a deal with Simon & Schuster Audio to produce a series of multi-voice dramatized versions of classic science fiction stories featuring *Star Trek* actors. Our eventual titles were *The Time Machine* (H.G. Wells), *A Journey to the Center of the Earth* (Jules Verne), *The Invisible Man* (Wells), *The Lost World* (Arthur Conan Doyle), and *First Men in the Moon* (Wells). We insisted on remaining as faithful to the source material as possible, although we fudged *The Invisible*

Man by inserting a romantic subplot. (Strangely, nobody said anything about our having made an audio version of a story about a character nobody could see, when nobody can see *anyone* in an audio version.) All were done in a studio save *The Lost World,* which was recorded at a *Star Trek* convention in Pasadena, California under the guidance of Creation Entertainment, the people who stage such events. Additionally, we produced *The First Men in the Moon* as the first-ever live television/streaming Internet presentation with the Sci-Fi Channel, directed by Jack Fletcher and executive produced by Brian Gadinsky and Matthew Papish. Jeff Howell produced and John Chominsky edited the bulk of them for audio, and Peter Erskine—the brilliant jazz drummer—composed a series of remarkable scores.

Those are the broad strokes. The details are more memorable, if not revealing.

John, Leonard, and I settled on a process with our first production, *The Time Machine.* I would break down the book and write the adaptation and, once I got a first draft, John and I would rewrite it together. Finally, Leonard would bring his clout and expertise to bear. Leonard was pretty much retired by this point so he had the time to spend. I was responsible for the day-to-day functioning of Alien Voices including sending cease-and-desist letters, clearing the rights, and negotiating production contracts.

I quickly learned that, while actors can be a little strange, stars are extremely so. John was pragmatic and usually agreeable, but Leonard was more cautious; a lifetime of being taken advantage of had heightened his reluctance to make any sudden decisions. And, when he did, things had to be done his way. More often than not, this meant that I would line up business prospects and he would have the final word, which was usually "No." I learned that he and William Shatner had decided, early on in shooting *Star Trek,* to keep each other abreast of what Desilu Productions, NBC, or Gene Roddenberry had said to them about the other so they could not be played against each other in a negotiation. The remarkable thing about Leonard was that, despite the ongoing Hollywood chicanery, he remained an honorable and stalwart man.

As a writer dealing with actors, however, I did learn that, when an actor says, "I want to study the script so I can make the words my own," the result is generally that he thinks he actually wrote it. Fortunately, Jules Verne, H.G. Wells, and Arthur Conan Doyle were always there to back me up.

Hanging out at Leonard and Susan Nimoy's home in Bel Air was a privilege. There were a few dinner parties, but what I enjoyed most was the informality (not as much as the de Lancies', but most welcome) and Susan's warm presence. Leonard often seemed on the curmudgeonly side, but only because he was in work mode and totally focused on the task-at-hand. I made it a point never to bring up *Star Trek*. I did it once in pursuit of what I thought was an appropriate question but was met with a stare from Leonard as if as he was thinking, "Oh, god, not another one." (No, he didn't raise an eyebrow as Spock would have.) Apparently the rule was that, if anyone was to mention the series, it had to be him. At the script conference, we came to the part where the Time Traveler in Wells's story ponders, "What if, in my time travels, I stop and rematerialize in a solid structure somewhere in the past or future?" At this, Leonard said, "Funny, but that's something Gene Roddenberry and I talked about before the show went on. What if we happen to beam down onto a planet and we hit a rock or an existing structure?" I listened as closely as I could, but inside my head I'm thinking, "Holy shit, I'm listening to Mr. Spock telling me about the technology of beaming down!" I can't recall the rest of Leonard's story, but it was as close to being a Trekkie as I have ever come.

At one point, John and Leonard were about to embark on a tape called *Spock vs. Q* with which I was not involved. I was, however, concerned as an Alien Voices partner that Paramount, which owned both characters, might launch a complaint. When I voiced this, Leonard said matter-of-factly, "I defy Paramount to call me to the witness stand and ask if I have ever played Spock."

We had disappointments. I adapted both *The Mysterious Island* and *Lost Horizon* for us to produce. For the first, I could never lick Jules Verne's amorphous novel as long as I held true to his padded story, and our ethic was not to depart from it. As for the second, Leonard wanted very much to play Conway, the romantic visionary in James Hilton's popular novel about Shangri-La. I managed to clear the audio rights with Columbia Pictures and the Hilton estate, and went ahead with what I think is my best script adaptation. But we could never get Simon & Schuster to give us an answer or, to the best of my knowledge, even read it.

Indeed, Simon & Schuster Audio was a disappointment. We finally figured that they only signed us so the executives could have bragging rights at cocktail parties. Although their editorial department was supportive, the sales department was a disgrace. We only learned, after signing, that S&S, despite being owned by Paramount and having held the rights to *Star Trek* novels for decades, had never allowed *Star Trek* products to be sold at *Star Trek* conventions. It was their way of protecting their brick-and-mortar bookstore customers. Instead, independent vendors had to acquire *Star Trek* merchandise from a sub-distributor such as Ingram, set up a card table, and pray for business. To say the least, this unforgivable short-sightedness (particularly with the rise of online book and tape sales) cut into business. I am still waiting for reviews.

Alien Voices was a superb gambit. I left the company when it became clear to me that its future, or at least mine, was limited. When John and Leonard mounted a live tour of cut-down versions of *The Lost World* and *Invasion from Mars* years later, they paid me royalties even though they were under no obligation to do so. The three years I gave to it allowed me the pleasure of working with good and talented people, many of whom I still count among my friends, especially John de Lancie. As for Leonard Nimoy, we spoke just a few weeks before his February 27, 2015 death when I interviewed him for my book on Harlan Ellison. I was fortunate to know him away from *Star Trek*, outside of the Spock cult, and beyond the immense pressures of fame. We were just two Boston guys talking about outer space.

The Blacklist and Me

*T*HE WALDORF *Conference* was a galvanizing experience, not only from what Dan and Arnie and I learned while researching it but also from the people I met in California who had been caught in the Blacklist's evil vortex. In addition to John Randolph, I got to know, to varying degrees, Ring Lardner, Jr. (known as the friendliest of the "Unfriendly Ten"), Marsha Hunt, Bernard Gordon, Jean Butler, Norma Barzman, Joan Scott, Paul Jarrico, Walter Bernstein, Jean Porter Dmytryk, Robert Lees, and, in many cases, members of their families such as Chris Trumbo, Becca Wilson, Billy Jarrico, and Tony Kahn (whom I had known in Boston).

The energy thrown off by these folks and others like Ed Rampell, Helen Colton, Larry Ceplair, and Pat McGilligan, who were also part of "the tribe," was intoxicating and led me, in 2003, to produce a revival reading of *Waldorf* in partnership with the Writers Guild Foundation and the Hollywood chapter of the American Civil Liberties Union of Southern California. Four years earlier, in 1999, as a board member of the ACLU of Southern California, I had produced a tribute to the Hollywood Ten at our annual Bill of Rights Dinner at which Ring Lardner, Jr. accepted our honors on behalf of the Ten. By then, Ring was bent over and stone deaf, but he gamely made the trip from New York to LA to thank us and announce that it would be his last public appearance. The ovation and affection he got from the capacity audience was validating.

This *Waldorf* was again directed by John de Lancie, who also played Eric

Johnston, the head of the Motion Picture Association of America who, on November 24 and 25, 1947, wrangled all the studio moguls into one room. Other cast members included Ed Asner, again playing Louis B. Mayer; James Cromwell, Paul Mazursky, Harlan Ellison, Ethan Phillips, Jacob Snyder, Alan Toy, Kenny Morse, Lawrence Pressman, Robert Picardo, and Michael Laskin. Ramona Ripston, Executive Director of the ACLU/SC, and Del Reisman, Director of the WGA's Blacklist Credits Restoration Program, made moving introductions. Adam Huss was our liaison with the Guild.

This time, rehearsals were less playful and more, well, I don't know the word for it. We had three days to get the show into shape before the single benefit performance on November 24, 2003 (the fifty-sixth anniversary of the Waldorf meeting). The first person to limp into rehearsal was Jamie Cromwell, who had fractured his leg skiing a few days earlier but insisted on keeping his commitment to us. He hobbled in on crutches. Ed Asner's knees were giving him a hard time (he eventually had replacement surgery). Harlan Ellison was only recently out of heart bypass surgery and his doctor had cautioned him not to sit down for too long, so every half hour or so he would leap out of his seat and do laps around our rehearsal table. Finally, there was Alan Toy, who uses a wheelchair. John de Lancie, mindful of his ringmaster's experience with the 1993 production, was wise enough to let these capers play themselves out.

With so many actors incapacitated, watching the cast climb onto the stage was a performance in itself. Once there, they gave me a playful hard time when I announced proudly to the audience that they had all agreed to forgo their fees. Instead of the audience applauding, however, they laughed as Mazursky started leading everybody off the stage in mock revolt at working for free.

We had invited as many blacklistees and their families to the performance as we could track down, and genially apologized for "naming their names" as we recognized them for applause. As before, the play struck home and we also made money for both the ACLU and the WGF.

Four years later I produced another Blacklist event for the ACLU, this time in partnership with PEN West, the writers' organization. I had become friends with Marsha Hunt, the actress who starred to fine notices in *None Shall Escape, Smash-Up: The Story of a Woman,* and *The Happy Time,* among other films, before being blacklisted. Marsha's late husband, Robert Presnell, Jr., had written, with Norman Corwin and Millard Lampell, the scripts for *Hollywood Fights Back. Hollywood Fights Back* was a two program series that aired on ABC radio while the 1947 HUAC hearings were still going on. Featuring appearances by scores of Hollywood and Broadway stars who opposed HUAC's inquisition, they are credited with helping turn American opinion against the Committee, which went into recess early. (Little good did it do anyone, however.)

It was my idea to re-create the broadcasts and add new material to reflect the USA Patriot Act and other government abridgements of the Bill of Rights in the wake of 9/11. We titled it *Hollywood Fights Back. . .Again* and assembled a remarkable cast: Ed Asner (of course), writer Norma Barzman (blacklisted 1951-1976), actor Catherine Dent, writer Larry Gelbart, professor Isabelle Gunning, playwright Christopher Hampton, filmmaker Tiana Silliphant, writer Christopher Trumbo (his father, Dalton Trumbo, blacklisted 1947-1960), actor James Whitmore, and Becca Wilson (her father, Michael Wilson, blacklisted 1952-1965). Actress Lee Grant (blacklisted 1950-1967) and writers Ray Bradbury and Norman Corwin sent letters for us to read.

But the star of the event was unquestionably Marsha Hunt, who had appeared in the original 1947 broadcast and had journeyed to Washington, DC to protest the hearings as a member of the Committee for the First Amendment, a decision that contributed to her being blacklisted from 1949 to 1957.

We obtained permission from Marsha as well as Norman Corwin to perform and amend the original script, but I failed to coordinate dates with Norman, a mistake that resulted in his being unable to attend the October 26, 2007 event at LA's Skirball Cultural Center. As it happened, Corwin – then age ninety-seven – was having a new play of his own performed across town.

The fun started in the green room when James Whitmore, then eighty-six, entered and saw Marsha, then ninety, and said, "Jesus Christ, I thought both of us were dead!" (Sadly, sixteen months later, he would be.)

Our format was elegant. Whenever one of our cast was to speak, he or she announced whom he was reading for in the original broadcast. For example, when playwright Christopher Hampton (*Dangerous Liaisons, Appomattox*) stepped forward, he would say, "This is Christopher Hampton and I'm speaking for Humphrey Bogart," or Catherine Dent (*The Mentalist, The Shield*) would say, "This is Catherine Dent and I'm speaking for Judy Garland," and so forth. When it came time for Marsha Hunt to repeat the words she had said in 1947, she stepped forward and said, "This is Marsha Hunt and I am speaking for myself." It was a "Mrs. Norman Maine" moment and the audience joyously applauded her. That is the moment at which I felt validated – not for myself, but seeing Marsha, Norma, and the other survivors vindicated in a wash of love and respect. Filmmaker Roger C. Memos, whose documentary *Marsha Hunt's Sweet Adversity* tells this dynamic woman's story, caught it all on video.

Later in the performance Christopher Trumbo read his father's famous "Only Victims" speech. Becca Wilson honored her late father, Michael, and described how he had been denied credit for *Lawrence of Arabia, Bridge on the River Kwai*, and other films. Norma Barzman gave a first-hand account of being blacklisted. Paul Jarrico's widow, Sylvia, and their son, Bill, made comments. Alvah Bessie's son, Dan, sent a letter of solidarity. It was, as someone said, probably the last time that so many survivors of the Blacklist would be thus assembled.

In preparation for the event I held a dinner at my apartment for a steering committee that included Norma Barzman, Marsha Hunt, Ed Rampell, and a number of other survivors and friends. By coincidence, that same evening I received an eviction notice from my landlord, who needed my first-floor unit for his elderly mother who had become infirm. I was friends with my landlord (still am) and his mother (since passed) and, in fact, had been tipped off by my friend Ami Lahmani that the letter would be coming. Nevertheless, it was still a shock to see it slipped through my mail slot. My dinner guests asked what it was. "An eviction notice," I said in a tone that begged sympathy. I got none. Instead, Norma Barzman said, with her customary exuberance, "Oh, that's nothing. We all got eviction notices when we were named. Welcome to the club!"

Not all Blacklist-related social interaction was as cordial. People who were named sought the companionship of others like themselves. Those who named names lost friends, and the friends they gained were not necessarily to their liking. I once asked screenwriter Bernard Gordon (*The Day of the Triffids*) how one should react when one meets someone who named names. Bernie said, "Hate them." That happened to me twice, and neither time did I take his advice. The first was at William Friedkin's house when he hosted a dinner for composer David Raksin followed by a screening of *The Bad and the Beautiful*, which Raksin had scored. Raksin had capitulated to HUAC years earlier and, while he had since apologized, he still bore the guilt. Under such circumstances it would have been an insult to my host to bring it up, so I was polite, if chilly.

On another occasion I was the guest of Jean Dmytryk at a motion picture Academy event when a small old man approached us. She introduced him as Dick Collins. I froze. Richard Collins, a writer, was perhaps the most notorious namer of names. The husband of actress Dorothy Comingore, he had been a member of the Communist Party who, like Elia Kazan, quit and testified against his fellow members, lots and lots of them. Jean was my friend. Her late husband, Edward Dmytryk, who was one of the Hollywood Ten, had served jail time for Contempt of Congress. He also, on his release from prison, named names (Jean preferred the term "cleared his name") so he could work again. Jean is a dynamic and attractive woman and former actress, whose insights into the Blacklist era were invaluable to me and richly personified people like her and Eddie (she said I could call him Eddie) who were first vilified by the right, then hated by the left, and finally had to make a whole new set of friends. It was through Jean that I gained a deep understanding of both sides of the Blacklist. So when she told Collins that I was a Blacklist scholar, Collins almost defensively launched into a personal apologia about how, after naming so many people, he had then tried to get them work through fronts. At first I was outraged at his self-justification, but then my blood cooled and I saw a frightened, flawed old man who had been used by the Committee, thrown away, and lived the rest of his life as a moral demimonde. He died in 2013.

People constantly ask if the Blacklist could happen again. My answer is always Yes, but in a different way. The government may be prohibited by the First Amendment from asking us about our personal beliefs and associations, but with the erosion of the Fourth Amendment and the invasions of privacy that the Bush and Obama Administrations launched and the U.S. Supreme Court affirmed, Uncle Sam no longer has to ask. All he has to do is electronically eavesdrop with neither supervision nor recourse. The "Great Fear," as David Caute called it, is now so subtly woven into our daily lives that we joke about the NSA monitoring our e-mails, phone calls, locations, tax returns, travel, and snail mail as if it's the new norm in a free society. As the parable goes, if you toss a frog into boiling water, he jumps right out, but if you lay him gently in cold water and raise the heat gradually, he is first lulled into going to sleep, and then he dies. Right now the water is pretty warm, and I may well have sealed my own fate with the words you have just read.

Travels with Charly

CLIFF ROBERTSON was one of the most moral people in Hollywood—not in a smug religious way but out of honesty and decency, and it scared the crap out of people. He didn't try to be, he just was; all he had to do was walk in the room and people felt they were being held accountable for something they'd done, only they didn't know what it was.

In early 1977, Robertson received a notice from the IRS asking him to account for a $10,000 discrepancy in his previous year's earnings from Columbia Pictures. What made Robertson pause was that he hadn't worked for Columbia that year, nor had he received any royalty checks from them which, even if he had, would never have been for such an even dollar amount. He asked his business manager to look into it. Eventually the Los Angeles Police Department looked into it, too, and it turned out that David Begelman, the President of Columbia Pictures Corporation, had forged Robertson's name on a $10,000 Columbia check, cashed it, and reported it as income paid to the actor. Begelman also forged checks for director Martin Ritt and restaurateur Pierre Groleau for a total of $65,000. At the time, his own salary was over $1 million.

Why would such a successful, powerful, and well-paid man like Begelman do such a stupid, easily uncovered thing? As the questions circulated, it emerged that, years earlier, when he had been an agent, he had been accused of improper management of funds, including those of his client, Judy Garland.

And yet Begelman was beloved in Hollywood. Soon the town closed ranks around him and blamed not Begelman, but Robertson.

Where Robertson screwed up, Hollywood-wise, was in questioning malfeasance before he knew who committed it. By the time he learned it was Begelman, it was too late to protect himself. Or perhaps he would have done it anyway. Either way, he did nothing wrong. Let me repeat that: he didn't do anything wrong. Would Robertson have kept quiet if he had known Begelman was the culprit? That's what Groleau and Ritt did (Marty and I never discussed it but, as a gambler as well as a Blacklist survivor, he surely weighed the odds). Robertson spoke up, not to ensnare Begelman, but because the IRS was dunning him for taxes on money he knew he hadn't received.

Hollywood insiders were nonplused; to them it was business as usual. Even publicly traded Columbia Pictures—led by Allan Hirschfield and abetted by investor Herbert Allen—refused to take disciplinary action because Begelman made money for the company. In October of '77, however, the continuing press coverage finally forced them to suspend him. Two months later, however, they brought him back, albeit without his title or stock options. When the press outrage didn't stop covering the scandal by February of 1978, Begelman was finally forced out completely, fined $5,000, and sentenced to make an anti-drug TV commercial as community service. Then, because he was so valued as a deal-maker, in 1979 he was hired to run MGM.

Meanwhile, the guiltless Robertson was blackballed out of movies. The exile lasted three years (three of his prime acting years) until 1981 when he was hired by director Douglas Trumbull to co-star in his science fiction film, *Brainstorm*. Robertson's troubles were not over, though; as cruel fate would have it, *Brainstorm* was being made by MGM which was headed by Begelman. Worse, it was the film that Natalie Wood was shooting when she drowned on November 29, 1981.

"Poor Natalie," Robertson said when he called me in mid-June of 1982 to vent. "She was wonderful to work with and really felt that this was going to be one of her best performances. We all took it very, very hard." Then he changed his tone of voice and said, "It looks like the chickens are coming home to roost. Now MGM is looking into David's behavior too."

"Has he embezzled again?" I asked.

"No," Cliff said, "but he's trying to kill *Brainstorm*. He's been insisting that Natalie didn't finish her scenes and that the film has to be scrapped. I don't even think he's seen it and he wants to cash it in for the insurance."

"How much of that is because he wants to cash in on you?"

"I don't think that has anything to do with it," Cliff said. "When he came over to MGM he knew I was in the film and didn't say anything about replacing me. No, I think he just wants the money back for a film he doesn't believe in."

"How much of it still has to be shot?"

"That's the thing. We finished principal photography. Maybe some cutaways left to do, but we wrapped. The rest is the special effects and looping, and everyone knew they would take a long time to do."

Douglas Trumbull subsequently confirmed that, where Wood's on-set dialogue was inaudible and she obviously couldn't re-record it, the audio engineers devised ways of filtering out the background noises. Consequently Wood's final screen performance is, ironically, the one that she actually gave on the set rather than one that was reconstructed, like those of her co-stars, in post-production.

Begelman persisted in trying to pull the plug on *Brainstorm* until Trumbull and his legal representatives made it clear that the film was complete and that the long post-production period was not because it was in editing limbo but because of its complex special effects. Nevertheless, by the time the picture was released in September of 1983, it was barely supported by the financially strapped studio. Begelman had resigned in 1982 with three years to go on his contract. He entered independent production by forming Gladden Entertainment in 1986 and, true to form, cheated a number of actors, writers and directors out of $4.1 million before declaring bankruptcy and bringing down a federal probe in 1994.

On August 7, 1995, after disappearing for several days, he surfaced long enough to check into a Los Angeles hotel where he shot himself to death.

Cliff and I first met in 1971 during one of his Boston visits to promote *J.W. Coop*. We stayed in touch over the years as both our careers went through ups and downs, he because of Begelman and I because of advertiser pressure on the newspaper I was writing for. Sometimes we exchanged letters, sometimes we swapped phone calls. He even put me in touch with one of Ralph Nader's "Nader's Raiders" who was investigating corruption in the movie business. During the whole ordeal, Robertson, who was married to actress (and Post Cereal heiress) Dina Merrill, stayed in the public eye. He traveled extensively ("I practically live on American Airlines," he said) and became spokesman for AT&T long distance after focus groups revealed that he was one of the most trusted men in America. Hollywood, however, kept its distance. By the mid-1980s he was in his sixties, no longer leading man material in an age of youth-market films, but too young and handsome to play character roles.

He was always, let's face it, a maverick. In *PT 109* (1963) he played President John F. Kennedy as a war hero. In *The Best Man* (1964) he played a demagogic politician that was a cross between Bobby Kennedy and Richard Nixon. He flew his own plane and made a film about it (*The Pilot*, 1980), developed a fascination with rodeo clowns and directed a film set in their world (*J. W. Coop*, 1971), and tenaciously worked his way to an Oscar® in 1968 playing a retarded man in *Charly*.

"That was just self-preservation," he explained. "Back when I was doing live TV, I appeared in JP Miller's drama, 'The Days of Wine and Roses' (1958). I campaigned to be in the movie version but Jack Lemmon bought the rights and did it. So when I did 'The Two Worlds of Charlie Gordon' on *The U.S. Steel Hour*, I made sure I had the film rights to Daniel Keyes' short story, 'Flowers for Algernon.'" It took two screenwriters—William Goldman, whose work wasn't used, and Stirling Silliphant's, whose was—to get a script Cliff liked well enough to ask TV veteran Ralph Nelson to direct it. The picture was a hit, and so was Robertson, winning the Oscar® for Best Actor as the mentally retarded Charly.

Born and raised a Calvinist, Robertson was never able to shake that religion's severe, humorless image. Its ethics were reflected in his devotion to public service. In 1968 he traveled to famine-ravaged Biafra to draw world attention to that tragedy. Later he made the same kind of pilgrimage to Ethiopia to report on the famine there. His film roles became sporadic, but in 2002 he spoke to a new audience when he played Uncle Ben Parker in *Spider-Man*. It was his onscreen murder that inspired his young nephew, Peter Parker, to fight criminals as the web-throwing wonder and live up to the challenge, "With great power comes great responsibility." The irony is that the quiet but intense Cliff Robertson had been fighting that fight all his life, only for real. When he died on September 10, 2011 the world lost an actor and I lost a role model.

Mike Weiss

MIKE WEISS was the most joyously corrupt man I ever met in the film business. Not big corruption, just an awe-inspiring array of little ones. He should have been running a studio accounting department. Mike taught me everything I know about how to steal from film companies. Since film companies know everything about how to steal from film *makers*, you can see where my admiration for Mike comes from. Like all legends, Mike's reputation preceded him. This was due in large measure to his older brother, Harry, who was the Boston-based New England field publicity rep for Twentieth Century-Fox. Mike handled those same chores for Universal Pictures' middle-Atlantic region. He was based in Philadelphia.

The Weiss brothers were a team. Where Harry was tall, bombastic, and confrontational, Mike was diminutive, stocky, and charming. I can't speak for Harry, but Mike, like John Dillinger, only stole from companies, not people. He didn't even really break the rules, he just found the loopholes. He survived by never stealing anything big, and by either keeping his bosses safely in the dark (in the words of Fox Vice President Johnny Friedkin, "Please give me the courtesy of deceit") or cutting them in.

Mike had a way of saying hello that made you feel he came to town just to see you. He would spread his arms apart, palms up, and smile as warmly as a summer day, cocking his head slightly to one side, and grasping your hand with both of his. Then he'd get down to business.

"Here's an old press agent's trick," Mike would say. "You go into a bar and you tell the bartender, 'I bet you ten dollars you can't run me a receipt that says fifty dollars.' The bartender takes out his receipt book and writes 'paid $50' and hands it to you. You say, 'I lose' and you hand him ten dollars. Then you put the $50 receipt on your expense account and you're $40 ahead." Mike went on to explain how he and other press agents used to work each other's companies in the reimbursement game. "You're staying in a hotel, so you go into its coffee shop and you sit near the cash register. You make nice with the waitress. Then," he stressed in a softer, more confidential voice, "when she steps away, you swipe a blank order pad and pull out three pages—top, middle, and bottom—so the numbers aren't continuous. You expense them that you had breakfast, lunch, and dinner with three newspaper people. And if you're *really* on the ball," he added with relish born of experience, "you lift the whole order book and you send a bunch of pages to every press agent you know. But you gotta make sure they work for different companies so nobody's accounting department gets wise." Traveling press agents did this all the time, he assured me, as if that made it okay.

Some traveling press agents didn't even travel. "Say you're supposed to fly from Philadelphia to Washington every two weeks," Mike said. "But why do you need to go to Washington every two weeks? You know everybody there, right? So here's what you do. You buy your airline ticket on your credit card and put the receipt in for reimbursement on expenses. Then you cancel the ticket and get your money back from both the airline *and* the film company. Instead of traveling to Washington, you phone everyone and mail them the material you were supposed to hand them. You don't waste their time and you make a little money. But you have to actually make the trip every now and then so they know what you look like."

This was called "traveling on paper." It ended when the airlines changed their refund policies and the film companies started issuing air travel credit cards instead of having their field employees carry the expenses on their own credit cards. Mike assured me that a man could net thousands of extra dollars a year, and it was untaxed because it was reimbursement, not income.

Harry was different from Mike. I'm not even sure he liked me. With Harry, it was hard to tell; even his whispers came out loud. I encountered him when I was a college freshman begging for those 16mm TV commercials that I would run as previews for the films I played at the campus theatre. Some of the publicity reps, like Warner Bros.' Floyd Fitzsimmons, Arnold Van Leer at United Artists, Karl Fasick at MGM, John Markle at Columbia, and Paul Levi at Paramount were visionary enough to grasp my purpose, but Harry Weiss resisted. I made one last pilgrimage to his office to make my case.

"Yeah?" he bellowed from inside the frosted glass door, and I entered. It was a one-room office dominated by his paper-filled desk. I said hello and he stood up, putting on his jacket as if getting ready to leave for an appointment. I made my pitch.

"I'll have to see," he said. "We don't usually do things like that. What if a local theatre found out you were running them? I have to protect my theatres."

"First, Mr. Weiss, we won't run them until we book the films ourselves two years down the line." There was a two year window on Fox films, unlike today's short video window. "Or, second, we can run them as cross-plugs to promote your first run engagements." This intrigued him.

"You mean advertise on campus for the intown theatres?"

"Yes."

"Is that your idea?" he said dismissively, as in, "Is that why you're bothering me?"

"Well, yes."

"Hmm," he said. "You're in college, right?"

"Yes, sir."

"What do you want to be? I guess you want to be in the picture business, right? Okay, what part of it?"

I couldn't tell if he was making an offer or a challenge. He stared at me through tinted glasses. This was 1966 when film schools were opening up in colleges across the country to milk the fast-growing "film generation" that had cut its teeth on Super-8 cameras in high school. In truth, these schools offered neither assurance nor access, only a 2-S draft deferment from Vietnam. Since I had already decided (foolishly) that the best way to get to Hollywood was to enter a union and, from there, get onto a crew and into a creative office (also foolish), I revealed my grand scheme to Harry.

"Well, first I need to get into a union. The best way to do that would be to become a projectionist, because projectionists are. . ."

That was as far as I got. Harry went ballistic.

"A projectionist? A goddamned *projectionist*? *That's* what you want to do? *That's* what you're going to college for?" he bellowed.

"I thought that if I started there. . ."

"*Anybody* can be a projectionist," he interrupted again, even more outraged. "*I* could be a projectionist. Only I don't want to be. What do you *really* want to be? What job do you *really* want?"

When he paused for air, I figured the 16mm TV spots were a lost cause and I had nothing to lose. I looked into his eyes through his tinted glasses and said, "How about field representative for Twentieth Century-Fox?"

If this had been a movie, he would have smiled, laughed, offered his hand, and said, "You're okay, kid. Have a seat." But life isn't a movie, and movie life is the farthest thing from being a movie. Instead he barked, "get the hell out of my office!" It wasn't a scream, but the timbre of his voice made the glass door shiver as I frantically opened it to flee. Not only did I eventually get 16mm commercials for Fox films from a Boston TV station when they were finished with them, I also (and it didn't hit me until right now as I type these words) became field representative for Twentieth Century-Fox when I went to work with Nico Jacobellis eight years later. By then, Harry was long gone (no doubt from high blood pressure).

Mike idolized him, so I never said anything to him about Harry except that I knew and respected him. Besides, Mike had other plans for us.

"Here's what we'll do," Mike said. "Do you know any printers?" Of course I did. By then I was running the publicity department for Sack Theatres and

Mike had left Universal (the circumstances were vague) and taken up with the new National General Pictures. National General boasted such films as *The Boys in the Band*, *Little Big Man* and *The Reivers*. The gem that Mike had to tub-thump for, however, was a dubbed period Italian gangster film called *Pete, Pearl, and the Pole*. It had been booked as a favor into one of the chain's lesser screens.

Mike called an antique auto club and got one of their members to don a Borsalino and drive his 1930s-era car with a running board over to the theatre and to pose against its front bumper. That was our gangster. We papered the town with thousands of free tickets hoping to get at least 200 people to show up so we could photograph a line waiting to get in. As for the printer, Mike needed him to produce hundreds of stickers the size of business cards that we would post on every street light, stop sign, and bus stop in the city with the film's title and opening date. Forget the printer. Instead, we ran a few sheets of Avery labels on a Xerox machine for $10 and sent a bill to National General for $150, splitting $75 apiece (Mike sprung for the initial ten-spot). Chump change, to be sure, but I went along with it, like the kid who takes his first slug of whiskey out of his big brother's flask. It wasn't like I was the FBI agent who stood by while Whitey Bulger killed people, but I was "in."

Despite our efforts—or perhaps because of the limited promotional budget (the rest of which we actually spent)—*Pete, Pearl, and the Pole* didn't draw enough people to even half-fill the first show, and those who did come didn't last to the end. Neither did we. We paid an honorarium to the antique car guy, rushed to the office to put our expense accounts through before the grosses came in, and agreed to meet the next morning for breakfast.

Mike was late entering the main dining room of the Copley-Plaza where he was staying. He liked the hotel, which was patterned after New York's Plaza. He knew the reservations manager and boasted that she could always find accommodations for him or a touring celebrity even when the place was full. I was nursing coffee when Mike stormed in, seething.

"Can you believe that?" he said. "I got out of the cab to pay the driver, I had a twenty in my hand, I was leaning over to pay him, and a guy runs past me, grabs the twenty, and takes off down the street. What's this city coming to?"

He calmed down by the time the waiter brought our breakfasts, which included an order of toast that arrived in a silver caddy. Mike couldn't take his eyes off it.

"I take pride in my profession," he said. "Okay, so I look out for myself and Blanche (his wife). We live in a nice place, I work my ass off, and I always do what's right for the pictures. I never hurt a picture. Gee, isn't that a nice thing?"

"What thing?" I asked.

"That thing they brought the toast in."

"It's a toast caddy. Yeah. Now tell me, Mike, how far would you go with your schemes and still not hurt a picture?"

"Harry and I always talked about this. Did you know Harry?"

"Um, he once gave me some career advice."

"Look, Nat, these people know when they're handling shit. They know if a picture is gonna perform or not perform. That's why they give it a budget. Or not. Our job is to make their job look good. Hand me that thing."

"What thing?"

"The whaddayacallit. The toast caddy." I did. "Like I said, I've worked hard and I provide for my family. I could write a check right now for $300,000. What do you think of that?"

"Very nice," I said. I didn't know what else to say, or what he was getting at.

"Sure I do a little angling here and there. That's part of the game. They expect you to. They don't pay you enough, so they expect you to steal. As long as I don't make them look like a crook. The big guys, they take care of each other. But us, nobody takes care of us except us. Is anybody looking?"

Before I could answer, Mike took his linen napkin, wrapped it around the silver toast caddy, and stuffed it inside his brown tweed jacket. He quickly signed the check and, seeing my expression, said, "close your mouth and walk out with me like nothing happened."

We hit the lobby and he headed toward the elevators.

"I'll put this in my suitcase and what are you staring at?" he said. "C'mon, they have lots of these. They're a hotel." He got into the elevator, pressed his floor, and smiled at me. "See you next trip." Then, as the door closed, he pulled the napkin out of his jacket and tossed it to me.

Pilfering was the rule in Mike's world; his métier was fake receipts, kickbacks, sweetheart deals, and eyewash. But more than the scams, he sold confidence. Having taken $75, I was no longer a virgin, but neither was I a fully credentialed grifter. Others in the business pulled off schemes that I wouldn't have believed if I hadn't seen them myself yet been powerless to stop.

(Here is where my lawyers tell me I can't use proper nouns:) I once came upon actual evidence that an exhibitor was routinely defrauding film companies through an advertising scam involving blank billing heads. I approached the Motion Picture Association of America whose lawyer told me point-blank that she had no interest in seeing any evidence or pursuing the matter. Later an assistant Attorney General for the Commonwealth of Massachusetts told me the same thing, explaining that, if the aggrieved film companies declined to press charges, there was nothing the State could do. I lost count of the number of other people, especially independent exhibitors and producers, who came to me, when I was a reporter, asking me to write about some injustice they felt was being perpetrated against them. I always told them that I would be happy to cover the trial if they would go to the authorities and bring charges. No one ever did.

Everyone has heard about Hollywood's bizarre, if not duplicitous, accounting practices. Most people who work on profit participation in the movie business have been cheated by them. So far neither the SEC, the Justice Department, Congress, nor the MPAA has sought to make any substantive changes. Hollywood donates too much money to both political parties for them to rock any boats.

Unable to make even the slightest dent, I did the next best thing: when I started teaching college I told all my students about these scams. I felt that I was merely passing along the advice of Mike Weiss and the others who trained me. Many of my students went on to make pictures and TV shows, and I wonder if any of them uses the tips. Life goes on. Or, put another way, what goes around, comes around.

I did, however, have a confrontation with one miscreant. I once left a job and stopped into my boss's office to say goodbye. I had enjoyed working for him and admired his business acumen. After we shook hands, he said, "Nat, you've learned a lot about how we do business while you've worked here. I like to think you will keep this knowledge to yourself as you move on." I said that I respected his wishes and would indeed keep such knowledge to myself as long as he never used those practices against me. He smiled up at me, lowered his pipe, and said a cordial, "Fuck you."

Buccaneers

T HEY SAY the reason the American film industry settled in Hollywood and not San Francisco, Chicago, or New Jersey (where it started) is that Southern California, aside from having sunny weather and a widely varied terrain, is only a couple of hours away from the Mexican border. In the early days of film when Thomas Edison's Motion Picture Patents Company, a trust formed in 1908, controlled all the equipment and charged a royalty per foot of film shot, anyone who used unlicensed cameras risked being sued by Edison. Or worse, like being shot at and having their machines destroyed by the thugs hired by the Trust to thwart competition. Once the Trust was busted in 1915, the movie business truly flourished, but the mindset remained of dancing on the edge of the law.

Everyone has heard about "Hollywood bookkeeping" but few know what it really means. Here's what it means in one sentence: no matter how much money a movie makes, it will never show a profit. That doesn't mean that nobody gets rich off it. It just means that anybody who was foolish or weak enough to accept "net profits" will never see any. (That's why they're called "nyet profits.") According to a phenomenon called "rolling breaks," everyone will keep dipping into the revenue stream until there is barely a trickle left to pay off the film's profit participants. The film companies use this time-honored accounting method (based on seminal contracts that the Loeb & Loeb law firm devised in the 1920s) to make sure that the shareholders get money but no one else does. This explains why films cost so much money: those who can demand large up-front salaries or a percentage of the gross do so, inflating the budgets and making it take longer for films to recoup their investments.

Wags have said, "It's not a business, it's a racket" and have described it as a system "where even the books have books." When the Northridge earthquake struck Los Angeles in 1994, the joke went around that the U.S. Geologic Survey said it was an 8.2 on the Richter scale but Paramount's accounting department insisted it was only a 4.1.

In my experience, I've seen a few scams that were colorful and memorable, but because the principals as well as the principles are still around, I can't use real names here, either.

The most inventive was a theatre company that went into the distribution business on the side, only not with its own movies. They discovered an obscure film that was owned by a small distribution company; let's call it Embassy Pictures. The theatre company rented a number of prints of Embassy's movie for a flat rate of $50 a week and promised to place them in their theatres. Nobody else was interested in the film, so Embassy consented to the low-cost booking. Instead of running the picture on their own screens, however, the theatre chain spliced a new title onto the old film and rented it to other theatres on a percentage basis, collecting far more revenue than the flat $50 per copy they paid Embassy. And Embassy didn't catch on because the title was different.

The practice of bicycling is another scam that's as old as Hollywood, though digital film delivery means it isn't used any more. It also occurred before theatres installed platters that whole prints were mounted on as one continuous loop. With bicycling, a theatre rented a movie and showed it at 10, 12, 2, 4, 6, and 8 PM. Because the film is provided in twenty minute reels, they have an usher standing by on a bicycle to run the print to a second theatre across town that shows the movie at 11, 1, 3, 5, 7 and 9 PM. Back and forth the kid rides his bicycle carrying the reels to and fro, sharing one print between two theatres, and the exhibitor only reports ticket sales from one house. Nowadays the process has been streamlined when one multi-screen complex punches more than one button on the digital projection system. Most multi-screen bookings are legal and licensed, but the term "bicycling" remains as a vestige of the days when movies were movies, not ones and zeros.

The most elaborate scam I ever heard go down involved a theatre owner who discovered that the distribution rights to the 1972 X-rated film *Deep Throat* had not yet been sold in Canada. He managed to borrow a 35mm print of the film from its local U.S. distributor and shipped it to a contact in Canada to test the waters. His Canadian contact consulted his lawyer and learned in a millisecond that he would be charged with pornography, so he returned the print to his American exhibitor friend. That's where the story would have ended except the print was seized at the border by U.S. Customs officials. *Deep Throat* was still deemed to be obscene in America. The exhibitor to whom the return shipment was addressed feigned ignorance; who on earth would be shipping him a print of *Deep Throat*? At this point, the film's local U.S. distributor called the theatre owner and said, "Where's my print?" The exhibitor had to say that it had been stolen (not that he sent it to Canada). The distributor, for reasons known only to him, replaced the print and never followed up on the obvious irregularity. I suppose there's still an unclaimed print of *Deep Throat* picking up dust in a storage room on the US-Canada border.

At about this same time, the theatre chain I was working for in Boston, Sack Theatres, looked into opening *Deep Throat*. The company was interested in attracting the carriage trade as the World Theatre had done in New York City under the color of "porn chic." No fools, the Sack people also submitted the film to Boston District Court for a declaratory judgment, essentially asking, "If we open *Deep Throat*, what will happen to us?" The judges on the court viewed the film alone in one of our better theatres and responded with a startling lack of uncertainty, "You will be arrested." The Sack folks thereby decided against opening *Throat*. But wait. That isn't the funny part. The funny part was that the judges had to watch the film three times in order to make their determination.

Not all Hollywood scams come from within the film industry. Because the public thinks everyone connected with movies has deep pockets, frivolous lawsuits are filed on a regular basis seeking, if not damages, then harassment settlements. When I was handling publicity for Sack Theatres in December of 1973, I became a defendant in a criminal complaint filed by one Rita Warren of Brockton, Massachusetts for "obscenity, blasphemy, and corrupting the morals of a minor." The reason? Warren had taken her underage daughter to see *The Exorcist* in one of our theatres and the girl was affected by it. Not that it matters, but so were hundreds of thousands of other people. I mean, it was *The Exorcist*.

When the papers were served, I phoned the California office of William Friedkin, the director of *The Exorcist*, who was slated to visit Worcester, Massachusetts on a college lecture tour. I was concerned that he would be hit with a subpoena should he set foot in the Bay State. Within hours, Friedkin returned my call. I was paged out of a meeting to take it. You can imagine the jaws that dropped all over the Sack executive offices when Jackie, the receptionist, announced that the Oscar-winning director of *The French Connection* and the biggest hit in the country was calling me.

Billy was supportive and passionate. He said, "You have to stop these people" and insisted that he was going to come to Massachusetts anyway because the controversy would help the picture. He did indeed visit Worcester—nothing happened except standing-room-only crowds at three colleges—and it kicked off an enduring friendship that led to my first book, *Hurricane Billy*, in 1990.

As for Rita Warren, her case was tossed out of court several weeks later. As it happened, the Court's decision was handed down on the first day of Lent. My press announcement gleefully reported, "In a blow for freedom of speech, Massachusetts District Court gave up Rita Warren for Lent." Years later I learned that someone named Rita Warren was running a religious lobbying group in Washington, DC. Their activities included picketing the Capitol building in support of putting prayers back in public schools. Could she be the same Rita Warren? Perhaps; after all, she is legion.

Good Deeds

THERE'S A joke they pin on whatever male happens to be Hollywood's current power broker: A gorgeous starlet sidles up to him and, in a sultry voice, offers to have sex with him. "Just a minute," he asks, suspicious, "what's in it for me?"

Hollywood functions on favors, back-scratching, log-rolling, quid-pro-quo, and one hand washing the other. Whether it's old-time moguls swapping the services of contract players or agents forcing producers to hire an up-and-coming talent if they want access to a star, it's all part of the business of show.

Sometimes, though, people do things because it's right. This confuses everybody. I submit that, as a whole, the entertainment industry does more public service than any other profession. There are countless instances of actors, singers, dancers, writers, musicians, and other creative people donating their talents to charities, social causes, fundraisers, community events, and assorted good deeds. Often they bear their own travel and production expenses. And yet entertainers are the first to be criticized as overpaid, for speaking their opinions, or choosing to support one cause or another. Good deeds don't make headlines, only bad behavior does. That's why you used to hear about Frank Sinatra calling his biographers "whores" but not about the way he would secretly pay destitute friends' hospital bills. Producer Joel Silver yells and screams at his staffers, but, on the side, he buys and restores Frank Lloyd Wright homes, preserving the architect's legacy.

Why should it seem odd that famous people act unselfishly? Brad Pitt and Angelina Jolie bring attention to world hunger. Sean Penn put his career on hold to help Haiti recover from flood damage. Madonna adopts children when "people of Faith" do nothing. And how many performers have traveled to war zones of the decades to entertain the troops?

Loyalty runs deep with some people. When Art Carney was touring for *Harry & Tonto*, Paul Mazursky's lovely 1974 film about a 72-year-old man and his cat, he placed a phone call to Anthony LaCamera, the former TV critic for the *Boston Record-American*. When he was reminded that LaCamera had retired and that it might be better to phone the current critic, Carney said, "No, Tony was very supportive of me when I was on TV and I just want to say hi to him, see how he's doing."

Boston movie publicist Karl Fasick had a similar habit. He would keep unemployed critics on his movie screening list when other film company reps would take them off the instant they lost their bylines. When they found work again, as most good writers do, they remembered that Karl had remembered them. Karl didn't do it because he was calculating, but because he was decent.

People in the entertainment business give back in numerous ways. Ventriloquist Paul Winchell invented a component for a valve that is used in heart surgery. Actress Hedy Lamarr invented the frequency-shifting technology that makes cell phones possible. Walt Disney had his artists create thousands of emblems and insignia for the military in World War Two. After he won the Academy Award for designing the special makeup for *Planet of the Apes*, John Chambers could have named his price in Hollywood. Instead, he went into the business of sculpting foam latex facial appliances—noses, ears, cheekbones, etc.—for people who'd had disfiguring accidents or diseases so they could venture confidently back into public. His technique allowed for makeup to be applied as if the latex was real skin, and he supplied replacements at cost. This story never made the papers, but he improved countless lives without publicity.

The Disney people may be notorious for treating their own employees coldly, but they regard their fans as sacred. For a time, when they released a new animated feature, the Disney publicists would send costumed characters on a multi-city advance publicity tour. These are the characters with the grotesquely large heads worn by overheated dancers and mime artists who are not allowed to speak for fear that their voices will destroy the illusion. When they appear at the theme parks, the oversized puppets of Mickey, Donald, and Pluto always work in teams so that, if one of them is endangered by a mob of onrushing children, he signals the others with coded hand gestures and they race to his rescue, using flanking techniques to peel the young fans away. When they silently tour to promote new films, they are usually accompanied by a human character who serves as interlocutor.

Head characters are notoriously difficult for a press agent to book. I mean, who cares? They don't do anything except jump around and you know the people inside them are uncomfortable (rules say 20-minute shifts, max). Even more grotesquely, when kids come up and look them in the "eyes," the height differential means that they're really talking to the performer's crotch.

When I was working for Paul Levi, we were asked to book one of these hydrocephalic troupes onto various local kiddie shows (they still had them in those days before cartoons took over). "And then when they're finished doing TV," Arlene Ludwig, the ultra-bright Disney head of publicity said, "We'd like you to take them to Children's Hospital. See if you can set up a show or have them visit the wards."

"Great!" I said. "It'll be a good photo-op."

"Oh, no," Ludwig countered. "No reporters or photographers. These kids are our audience but we don't want to exploit them. Since they're sick and can't get out, we feel we owe them the courtesy of entertainment."

She meant it. Never mind that the Disney folks go around suing schools, hospitals, and day care centers that paint Donald, Mickey, Pluto, Goofy and other Disney favorites on the walls without permission. When it came to actual contact with fans, for one solid hour these emissaries from the Magic

Kingdom turned a hospital children's ward into the happiest place on earth. Several years ago, Arlene herself was sidelined by a freak accident. Perhaps her recovery was speeded by a visit from some of her ambassadors.

I'm not sure if this is a good deed, but it certainly is a creepy one. It involves Rosalyn Bruyere, a healer from California whom Universal Pictures sent around to answer questions about *Resurrection*, the powerful spiritual drama starring Ellen Burstyn and Eva Le Gallienne. I liked the film and had enjoyed an unusually intimate radio interview with Bruyere. This was in September of 1980. At the time, the Shah of Iran had just died in exile following his overthrow by the Ayatollah Khomeini and his student partisans. But before that, he had been ill with lymphoma and the thought suddenly occurred to me, during our taping, to ask Bruyere if she was ever worried about being kidnapped and forced to heal someone like the Shah. The question threw her for a moment and then she dismissed it being as of no concern.

Half an hour after she left the studio, I was editing the tape and, when I got to the Shah question, I felt uneasy. Not uneasy like I'd get in trouble or uneasy that it might give somebody ideas, just uneasy. I cut it out and tossed away the piece of tape. No sooner had the tape hit the trash can than the phone rang. It was Bruyere saying that she was uncomfortable about the Shah question and wondered if I might remove it. The timing was frightening, and the reasons even more so. I not only cut the tape, I took the trash can out of the room and dumped its contents in the incinerator.

Good deeds come in all forms in Hollywood. As a member of the Board of Directors of the ACLU of Southern California, I have the privilege of writing and announcing our fundraising events at which we give awards to people whose work on behalf of civil liberties has strengthened the Bill of Rights for all people. In researching and writing some of the speeches, I am often rendered speechless by our recipients' accomplishments, whether it's Cindi Lauper's support of the True Colors Fund and other LGBT causes; composer Hans Zimmer backing Amnesty International, International Medical

Corps, Alliance for Climate Protection, and many other causes; MTV's Amy Doyle green-lighting a telethon to benefit Haiti; NPR's Jarl Mohn wielding his family's philanthropic fund in support of human rights; manager Troy Carter co-founding the Born This Way Foundation; multi-talented artist Usher giving and working on behalf of the Red Cross, Keep a Child Alive, childhood diabetes, and a dozen other charities; manager Scooter Braun underwriting building plans for schools as Pencils for Progress; and countless other donations, services, and endorsements that the general press never covers. If this isn't charity, then Webster has it wrong.

On the Road

DESPITE ITS decades of public service, the moment there's a juicy Tinseltown scandal, all bets are off. The conflict between artistry and morality did not, of course, start with Hollywood. Socrates probably got it on with students of both genders behind the Parthenon; Picasso was a beast with women; Oscar Wilde did time in Reading Gaol; Charles "Lewis Carroll" Dodgson liked little girls; Michelangelo liked boys; and Dr. Samuel Johnson didn't like anybody. Move on.

Does an artist create his own moral universe? Should society forgive an artist's indiscretions because of his creative achievements? No one is above the law, but Hollywood gets more attention than any other profession (even politics) when one of its celebrities crosses the line. The press has a lot to do with fanning the flames even though they may not have ignited them. Movie stars sell papers and attract eyes. In the 1920s there were headlines about silent screen personalities Mabel Normand, Roscoe "Fatty" Arbuckle, Mary Miles Minter, Thomas Ince, William Desmond Taylor, Wallace Reid, Charles Chaplin, and Rudolph Valentino. In the sound era Ingrid Bergman, Robert Mitchum, Busby Berkeley, Marilyn Monroe, Lucille Ball, Mary Astor, Errol Flynn, Woody Allen, Hugh Grant, Michael Jackson, Russell Crowe, Robert Downey, Jr., Christian Slater, Mel Gibson, Eddie Murphy, and the ever-popular Lindsay Lohan were tabloid fodder. And that's not even counting Roman Polanski or a limitless supply of Kardashians.

Whether Hollywood corrupts people or attracts people who are already corrupt has never been determined, although (and this is a personal note) any kid who's ever been snubbed in high school by the handsome quarterback or rejected by the beautiful prom queen knows that life is different for those people whom society favors. Talent and fame don't necessarily breed class. The founding moguls may have gone "from Poland to polo in one generation" but it didn't earn them entry into Los Angeles's restricted country clubs or WASPy neighborhoods. Instead, they built their own community and used it to create images and ideas that shaped world popular culture.

Like any closed industry, Hollywood protects its own–up to a point. For decades, the town even had its own police force, namely the all-seeing, all-bribing studio publicity and security machines that worked hand-in-hand with the Los Angeles Police Department and the press corps to keep their bad investments (i.e., naughty stars) out of the headlines. Many studios maintained in-house security forces that spied on their own employees. If that failed, some reporters and columnists were kept on the take and could be counted on to kill unfavorable stories unless the police reports were unavoidable, in which case key police authorities were on the take to expunge records. The practice continues with today's supermarket tabloids who can often be bribed, not with money or advertising, but by providing them with stars for exclusive interviews in exchange for having the publisher kill scandalous pieces.

In the world of Hollywood triage, lesser stars were expendable. Lee Tracy, for example, was fired from *Viva Villa!* after he urinated off his hotel balcony onto the Mexican Army while on location, and his scenes were re-shot with someone else. Major stars, however, like Lucille Ball, had both CBS and her sponsor Philip Morris go to bat for her when the redhead was accused of being a pinko in the 1950s. When both Gene Kelly and his wife, Betsy Blair, were smeared with Red during the Blacklist era, Kelly was cleansed by MGM while Blair, a lesser star, was cut loose. Similarly, Larry Parks was forced to crawl through the mud by HUAC while his wife, Betty Garrett, kept her stardom. The elegant actress Marsha Hunt wasn't even given the courtesy of being allowed to clear her name; one day she simply found herself blacklisted with no recourse (or, for that matter, evidence).

Once they step outside of Hollywood, celebrities are at greater risk. Studio field men—regional publicists in the employ of the film companies (there were no women in the years I served as one)—routinely quashed stories and leaned on authorities to go easy on visiting celebrities. The price was sometimes cold cash, but it could just as easily be free passes, promotional T-shirts, or invitations to premieres. The newspaper's advertising department was often involved. Even a jaded and presumably incorruptible press can be reasoned with. As a press agent, I once killed photographs that were taken of my male client leaving a hotel room with a female news reporter who wasn't his wife, then went back and had the hotel manager change the registration on the room. Another time I pretended that a visiting director's mistress was my date when we all walked into a TV studio where we happened to run into a married couple who knew the director's wife. Later the director told me that, of the married couple, the husband also fooled around.

Being a beard was small potatoes. A colleague of mine once had to make his studio pay for the damage done to the Ritz-Carlton by members of The Who who decided to party there. Actor Rex Harrison was so stingy that he ran up a huge bill at that same august hotel, then left without giving anyone a tip. He was asked never to return, and a twenty percent gratuity was added onto his tab. Yul Brynner, scheduled to play Boston in *The King and I*, sent a list of requirements ahead of his arrival, including the demand that his room be painted black and a special chef hired for his meals. He was politely informed that he would be welcome without his stipulations and was reminded that he was not the real King of Siam, only an actor playing him.

Buford Pusser posed a different problem. The former sheriff of McNairy County, Tennessee, Pusser was the real-life law officer on whom the movie *Walking Tall* was based. It told of how he fought corruption and raised so many local hackles that, one night in 1967, assailants blew a shotgun into his and his wife's faces while they were driving on a moon-lit back road. His wife was killed and Pusser had his jaw blown off. In 1973, when he came to town to promote the film, Pusser—by then repaired with plastic surgery—insisted on wearing a firearm and showing it to anyone who doubted that he was still concerned about his safety. He also carried a pocket full of medical photos of his dead wife and his splattered face to show to all his interviewers. After our press luncheon, he was gentleman enough to say, "I wanted to wait for the ladies to leave" before whipping them out for the curious male journalists who stayed behind. Being film critics and not crime reporters, they were not used to seeing something that wasn't special effects. I don't want to go into details about what Pusser's face looked like before doctors reconstructed the lower part of it, but it put me off steak tartar for years.

"Tell me something, Sheriff," I asked while we were riding between interviews. "Do y'all have a drug problem down in McNairy County?"

"Oh, a little here and there," he said in his casual Southern drawl. "But I tell you what I do. IffinI come across some kid usin' that stuff, I don't run 'em in. That don't do no good. Instead, I ask him to come with me out back of the Sheriff's office and we have a little discussion, and after that he don't do it no more."

Pusser died in 1974 after being thrown from his custom-built Corvette which, according to reports, crashed into an embankment while traveling at an undue speed on the Tennessee back roads he supposedly knew so well. Several years later I had occasion to visit that beautiful region to do a TV show and, hoping to ingratiate myself to the people I met there, mentioned how impressed I was with their late Sheriff.

"Buford was an asshole," each of them proclaimed. "We have types like him all over the South, and, unfortunately, he's what the rest of the country thinks we're all like down here. We're sorry he's dead, but he was a thug and we voted him out of office as soon as we could."

Crews shooting movies on location are strangers in a strange land. Because of the expense involved, out-of-town productions work six days a week instead of five, unlike when they're home in Los Angeles. This means that, on the seventh day, cast and crew either rest or blow off steam. The former is of no interest, but the latter can raise eyebrows. Actor Brad Davis kept to himself during the Boston scenes of 1980's little-seen *A Small Circle of Friends* but, when he vacated his Copley-Plaza Hotel suite, the cleaning crew found dozens of cans of flat ReddiWip® dessert topping under his bed. Davis had used the nitrous oxide propellant—laughing gas—to entertain himself. While the eccentric actress Tammy Grimes was doing *Mr. North* in Newport, Rhode Island, in 1987, she indulged herself by assembling a rock collection in her motel room. When she left, she took the rocks with her for a stone wall she was building. And the night crew of the Ritz-Carlton still has memories of Rock Hudson hosting a late night dinner party in his suite where, instead of oil and vinegar, he and his young male guests produced their own salad dressing.

Crew members are less visible than actors; no one asks them to pose for snapshots or gives them free meals in restaurants. Sometimes they use this to their advantage. A stunt driver once came clean and warned me to never book a rental car for a Monday pick-up. The reason, he explained with conspiratorial glee, was that, when a stunt driver has to perform a car gag on a Monday, he will rent the same make and model over the weekend and practice in an empty parking lot till he gets it right. He will speed, skid, slalom, brake, and leave tire patches with the rental car, then return it first thing Monday and head out to the set while he still has muscle memory. I could never figure out why picking up a rental car on a Monday was worse than picking one up on a Tuesday, but I took his advice.

Angelinos and New Yorkers are jaded, but the rest of America loves to watch movies being made. The joy pales quickly. Screenwriter William Goldman has said that the most exciting day of your life is your first day on a movie set and the most boring day of your life is your second day on a movie set. Although a movie set looks like a hundred people sitting around doing nothing, the fact is that everyone has a specific job to do; they just don't all do it at the same time.

Assistant Directors are the workhorses of the movie business. Contrary to their title, they don't tell the stars what to do, they keep the production moving by dealing with traffic, crowds, and extras. Inevitably they deal with the public, who will approach them to ask, "Hey, what movie are you filming?"

"When they hear the title, of course they've never heard of it," a top Assistant Director explained. "That's because it isn't released yet. So, lately, I've been telling them it's whatever just opened in theatres. I'll say, 'We're making *Iron Man*' and they go, 'Oh, wow, that's a good movie!' and walk away smiling. It probably hits them a block later."

Before *Love Story* opened in Boston in 1970, Paramount Pictures held a private screening for all the Harvard people who had helped during its charmed production at the college. *Love Story* became the first modern blockbuster when its $2.2 million budget grossed over $100 million and saved the studio. It also validated the marriage of the film's champion, production VP Robert Evans, and the film's star, Ali MacGraw. At the time, however, nobody knew that it would capture the affection of America's dating crowd and make the meaningless catch-phrase, "Love means never having to say you're sorry" part of the vernacular. At the invitational screening at the Cleveland Circle Theatre in Brookline, Massachusetts, Robert Evans—who had flown into Boston to host it—made his welcoming announcements standing beside the man who owned the theatre and would soon own Paramount Pictures itself, Sumner Redstone. Evans spouted the usual pleasantries and then Redstone, a former magistrate and a fearless businessman, proceeded to not only congratulate Evans but vocally twist his arm in front of 800 people by leaning on him to award him Paramount's spring release, *Plaza Suite*. Evans squirmed—not something he generally did—and tried to get off Redstone's hook, but the exhibitor was relentless.

At last the show started. When the blue screen lights didn't go down fast enough for Evans, he went ballistic. "Turn down those lights!" he screamed from the back of the house. "Get those lights off the screen! You're ruining my movie! What makes you think I'll give you *Plaza Suite* when you can't even show *Love Story* right?"

But Evans' tantrum was quickly drowned out by the sound of 800 pairs of hands clapping while the film was still on its opening titles, which was a montage of scenic Harvard and the surrounding city of Cambridge, Massachusetts. Critic Arnie Reisman wrote of the screening, "It's the only movie where they applaud the buildings." Evans relaxed, and *Plaza Suite* opened at the Cleveland Circle Theatre five months later on May 12, 1971.

Class Consciousness

"WHAT THE hell do you people do, investigate my tax records?" Stanley Kramer barked at the fifty or so film majors who crammed into the seminar room at the Film School at the Orson Welles Cinema complex. "What the hell business is it of yours how much I make?"

Kramer was the brush-cut grey-haired producer-director behind the socially conscious hits *Inherit the Wind, Guess Who's Coming to Dinner* and *Judgment at Nuremberg*. But those days were gone and now he was on the road, preceded by a forty-minute "greatest hits" clip reel to remind the younger generation who he was. His latest effort was *Bless the Beasts & Children* (ampersand mandatory) about a group of kids who try to stem the slaughter of a buffalo herd. Like several of Kramer's most earnest efforts, it was important but klunky and, minus the presence of the stars who drew attention to his earlier hits (Spencer Tracy, Katharine Hepburn, Fredric March, Montgomery Clift, Maximilian Schell, Frank Sinatra, Cary Grant, Judy Garland, etc.), it needed all the help it could get. In a grotesque way, Kramer had outlived his influence as Hollywood's conscience.

One of the first independent producers and an unapologetic liberal, he was skillful in wrapping his social messages in compelling, often controversial plots. Yet as the "movie brats" started making their inroads into Hollywood with sex, drugs, rock 'n' roll, and hand-held cameras, Kramer's fastidious work seemed archaic. His one attempt at radicalism—a campus protest polemic called *R.P.M.* (**Revolutions Per Minute*) (asterisk mandatory)—seemed as out of place as a fifty-seven-year-old hipster, which is what he was when it was released in 1972.

He was defensive as he fielded questions about *Bless the Beasts & Children*, especially those reflecting the film students' desire to be independent of Hollywood.

"I've always been independent," he said. "What makes you think I'm part of the Hollywood system just because that's where I make my films? I've always put my own projects together. I've never worked for a studio. Sure, I go to them for financing. But I keep final cut." Slowly he won over the young filmmakers. He relaxed his craggy face and took on the role of the tough but respected professor.

"Does anybody here know a scoundrel named Harry Cohn?"

No one did. Kramer smiled at the memory. "Harry Cohn was the SOB who ran Columbia Pictures," he began. "Ran it? He built it with his own two hands." Kramer then described the way he would have shot his story as a movie. "We start with the camera tilting up over Harry Cohn's tombstone. Back when I was just a producer—before I started directing too—I had an agreement with him. It was with Columbia, but Harry's handshake was more reliable than a contract. I was producing a picture called *The Sniper* for Columbia to release. At the same time, I was editing my last picture across town over at United Artists.

"Harry heard about the UA picture and wanted to see it. Wanted? He demanded. I said, 'It's not your picture, Harry. You can't see it.' He said, 'You're making a picture for me. What the hell makes you think you can do another picture for yourself?' We went back and forth and he used language I can't tell you even here.

"Okay, so I go home for the weekend, and I come in on Monday morning to work on the UA picture. As I drive through the gate the guard says that Harry Cohn sent his car Friday night to pick up the picture but, don't worry, he brought it back in time. I lost it. I completely lost it. I raced over to Columbia and stormed into Harry's office and screamed, 'You sonofabitch!

You tsetse fly! How dare you steal my movie just because you wanted to see it? Of all the nerve! I oughta —' 'Relax, kid,' Harry says. 'Sure, I ran the picture. So what? You can keep it for all the good it'll do you. It isn't gonna make a dime. It stinks!'

"Now we flash to the next year's Academy Awards. My picture wins the Oscar. It was *High Noon*."

The students applauded. Film students can be insecure, arrogant, curious, and intolerant all at the same time. Hollywood filmmakers courting them do so at their own risk. Unlike those who are allowed into the American Film Institute in Los Angeles, whose hallowed halls keep their secrets from the public except when it's time for the annual AFI Life Achievement [fundraising] Award, filmmakers venturing into the provinces become almost evangelical.

"We're making the first Hollywood film to deal with the Blacklist," Director Sydney Pollack promised when he visited Boston University's basement screening room. He was promoting *They Shoot Horses, Don't They?* but he seemed more excited about a film he was developing, *The Way We Were*. *Horses* had been well received and the frank, charismatic Pollack had the students in the palm of his hand. As a desperate woman who begs for release from the Depression—America's and her own—in a grueling dance marathon, Jane Fonda was riveting in a role that denied her the distraction of her beauty and star bearing. The film was raw, and so was she. At the end of the film she breaks down and begs her partner, Michael Sarrazin, to kill her, and he does, explaining his deed with the film's title. Said Pollack, "When someone goes insane it's seldom because of one traumatic experience. That's something you can usually deal with it. No, what pushes most people over the edge is something small. Something that becomes the last straw, like a broken fingernail or a run in your stocking. That's why Jane was so terrific."

As for his Blacklist film, *The Way We Were* was about mismatched lovers—Katie Morosky and Hubbell Gardner (eventually played by Barbra Streisand and Robert Redford)—who make different moral decisions when the Red Scare strikes. Hubbell names names in order to clear his own; Katie refuses and loses her career. By the time the film was released, however, most of the Blacklist subplot of Arthur Laurents' meticulous script had been removed, rendering the denouement emotionally incoherent. "It just didn't test well with preview audiences," he would later lament, so it was cut. (The excised scenes were later offered as DVD special features.) Pollack went on to become one of the most beloved and celebrated directors of his era. But he never again attempted anything overtly political without being careful to wrap the politics in the trappings disguise of a thriller, notably with *Three Days of the Condor.*

One of the most tireless college lecture guests (as previously noted) is director William Friedkin. As youthful as anybody in the room, "Billy"— that's what everybody calls him—works the crowd as skillfully as he manipulates millions of moviegoers with *The French Connection, The Exorcist, To Live and Die in LA, Killer Joe,* and his other intense films.

"If people leave the theatre talking about what something in the movie means," he told an audience at MIT at a time when he was Hollywood's "boy wonder" and was challenging the studio status quo by taking filmmaking to the streets, "you've got yourself a hit. For example, the black slab in *2001.* That's why I put the gun shot at the end of *The French Connection.*" In that *policier,* in which two New York detectives, played by Gene Hackman and Roy Scheider, pursue a French heroin smuggler, played by Fernando Rey, the tense climax is played out in an abandoned warehouse. Jimmy "Popeye" Doyle (Hackman) has his gun pulled and is stalking the dealer. He thinks he sees him but, by accident, he shoots an FBI agent. A little later the screen goes dark and more shots are fired, but never explained.

"It simply means that the movie ends with a bang," Friedkin told the students with a twinkle in his eyes. "That's all. It wasn't in the script. I did it in the dubbing room on our last day. I did it as a joke. I said, 'let's put in a gunshot.' So we did, and a number of studio executives said, 'What the hell does it mean?' I made up all kinds of stuff: Doyle has gone crazy, he's firing at shadows, his partner put a bullet in the FBI guy to take the onus off of him. I ad-libbed three or four possible reasons, none of which had anything to do with the shot." Since then, Friedkin has become known for putting images and sounds after the credits at the end of his films: a growling truck engine tagging *Sorcerer*, a shot of a killed cop in *To Live and Die in LA*, an airplane on a mission in *The C.A.T. Squad*, and other references that are symbolic, playful, or both.

Arthur Penn may have been one of the most thoughtful campus guests. Educated at the legendary Black Mountain College in North Carolina—by which to say he educated himself with the help of others—he offered particularly articulate views at Dartmouth College in 1968, a year after his *Bonnie and Clyde* changed the trajectory of American cinema. Admitting that "I went to films very seldom as a child" after being frightened by a horror movie at the age of seven, he set his sights on theatre and wound up becoming a top director in television's Golden Age and on Broadway.

"Then I was invited to make a film at Warner Bros., and I made one, and I was bewildered by what I encountered. Those things that bewildered me in film would continue to bewilder me and continue, in a certain sense, to describe the character of American film. I was very startled that the people in Hollywood referred to motion pictures as an industry and to the films themselves as product." He cited the hierarchy of relationships in Hollywood based on salary rather than talent, as if the former was the only criterion anybody could recognize.

"They used to say, 'Send me a writer.' I recall hearing the story from Clifford Odets that, during one of the temporary crises on a movie set, the word went out, 'send me a writer' and a young man arrived and the producer said, 'How much do you make?' and the young man said, 'seventeen-fifty' and the producer shouted, 'I told 'em to send me a writer,' meaning that if he didn't make thirty-five hundred a week, he wasn't a *writer*."

When television and foreign films began arriving, Hollywood initially ignored both, Penn said. While the studios had their heads in the sand, independent filmmakers gained the creative edge. "Now we are at a different crossroad and a different kind of film will emerge," he opined, "but I think that crossroad is a crossroad of our culture as a nation and part of the world. A confrontation of whether or not we will be mobilized into a kind of impersonal unity or allow ourselves the privilege of disparate and individual choices is a profound one in all forms of art, but, most peculiarly, that form of art which is the motion picture because it involves ever so many people and so expensive a medium."

Penn's vision came true for only a short period in the early 1970s. After that—in the summer of 1975, precisely, which is when *Jaws* proved that a movie could make huge amounts of money in a short amount of time—the studios began a relentless program of market-driven films. Fortunately, *Jaws* was a brilliant work of cinema that also happened to be a commercial phenomenon; few such hits that followed have been both. No longer would movies be made that reflected the view of individual filmmakers. Now movies would be made that fit a marketing formula. Instead of drawing audiences to fit movies, movies would be drawn to fit audiences. With 5,000 prints opening day and date across the country, it became less important to sway critics or send filmmakers around the country discussing their work. Now a press junket can draw a hundred reporters to a single location for a weekend, or a satellite press conference could do the same job in an hour. It has become easier to spend $40 million advertising a film, beg the stars to do five minutes on a network chat show, and keep the machine oiled than to give each film the courtesy of its own campaign. The machine has become efficient but the movies are all the same. The system now recycles rather than creates, and chokes on originality. It feeds on its own waste. Worse, the fun is gone.

Feeding the Brontosaurus

JOHN HOUSEMAN came to prominence in the 1930s as the man who created the Mercury Theatre with Orson Welles, dominated Broadway, changed radio, and then moved to Hollywood to take on movies. Like Welles, Houseman had suffered ups and downs, but he survived by virtue of his imperious bearing and orderly mind. He blossomed as a studio-based producer, first with Welles at RKO and then at MGM with a succession of brilliant collaborators. He headed the Voice of America during World War II, produced theatre, and founded The Acting Company at Juilliard in New York. But it was when his writing-directing protégé James Bridges asked him to play Harvard Law Professor Charles W. Kingsfield, Jr. in *The Paper Chase* in 1973 that Houseman moved from backstage to the spotlight. He won an Oscar at age seventy-three for that film and continued to travel between Hollywood and his New York home enjoying his late-in-life fame and leveraging it to bring attention to Juilliard and the young performers he was shaping there.

He traveled to Boston for the world premiere of *The Paper Chase* where we met for the first time. Typically, he took the opportunity to mix pleasure and business. One of his *Paper Chase* co-stars, Regina Baff, was appearing in *Veronica's Room* in pre-Broadway previews, and he arranged tickets for his wife, Joan, and himself.

"The problem with being who I am," he said matter-of-factly in the car on the way to the theatre, "is that, through no fault of my own, I intimidate people."

"You have to admit that being Professor Kingsfield has its advantages," a companion offered. He countered regally, "Yes, but only when one wants to make a point. It wasn't that much of a stretch for me to play him, but now everybody thinks I'm aloof and indomitable. In truth, I am neither."

"Are you going backstage after the play?"

"That's another thing," he said. "The actors are all going to look through the peephole to see how I react. I'm going to either sit perfectly still, or I'll have to pretend I'm enjoying myself even if I'm not. They won't have merely the critics to worry about, they'll have me. And I'm on their side."

"What will you do if the play isn't any good?"

"Oh, I'll lie, of course. There's not much else you can do. They'll see through it, naturally, so we'll both play the game. Anyway, I hope it won't come to that."

But it did. As the Housemans got back into the car after curtain, he said, quietly but deliberately, "Please, back to the hotel." Once we were safely en route, he let out a sigh and said, "Oh, it was just dreadful. But I had to go backstage. What can one say to them? They all knew how awful it was. All one could do was offer support and tell them how wonderful it was to watch them perform." The rest of the ride was spent in silence.

Houseman was a survivor, not only of life, but of Hollywood. Movies were his second career, acting became either his fourth or fifth—it's hard to keep track—but writing definitely became his sixth when he published his best-selling memoir trilogy *Run-Through*, *Front and Center*, and *Final Dress*. We reconnected on the second of these in 1979 and compared notes on how movies and TV had changed in the six years since *The Paper Chase*.

"Very simple," he said, pacing his hotel room. "In the old days, they used to *help* a producer make a movie. Now they *dare* him."

He described how the TV adaptation of *The Paper Chase* had won critical plaudits but poor ratings, and how the producers had urged the public to write letters to CBS asking them to renew the show.

"The network must have received ten thousand letters," Houseman said, "but they just pissed all over them." Despite this, Showtime Networks stepped in and bought the series, producing it through 1983 and bringing Houseman along. It also survived briefly on PBS. The experience drove home how the business had changed, not just in six years, but in sixty.

"The studios were always interested in making money," he lectured. Actually, he didn't lecture, but when John Houseman talked, it sounded like a lecture. "But every now and then they'd do something for the artistry of it. Irving Thalberg and, later, Dore Schary (each headed MGM) used to say that a prestige picture is good for the industry."

At the time we spoke, the average studio picture cost just under $5 million with another $4 million needed for prints and advertising. By 1990 it was almost $27 million with marketing costs half again as much. By then Hollywood was well into the blockbuster era, in which mass-appeal films would open on thousands of screens at once, with the first weekend deciding a film's commercial fate. There was still room for more specialized fare to roll out city by city, gradually expanding its run as word-of-mouth built audiences, but the grosses for those, if they came at all, came slowly and took a lot of work. In any other artistic endeavor, this would be called creativity. But to film companies that were desperate to appear fiscally responsible to the conglomerates that were buying and selling them throughout the 70s and 80s, it became a path to nowhere. By the start of the twenty-first century it would cost $150 million or more to make a "tent pole" film—a franchise (pre-sold or not) that defines a studio's profitability for the season. By then the marketing costs had risen to between $40 and $50 million for TV and newspaper ads and other media buys—whatever it took to draw audiences and neutralize the Twittersphere.

Why does it cost so much? I call it "feeding the brontosaurus." The brontosaurus, in this case, is the studio system. In order to run efficiently, a studio with a physical plant (Paramount, Disney, Universal, Fox, Warners, Sony) has to have a film moving through each stage of its organization—development, legal affairs, budgeting, set construction, costuming, transportation, production, lab, editing, mixing, marketing, distribution, accounting, etc.—at all times to justify its immense operating expense. The salaries of each department are billed to the budget of the film as it wends its way along and must be earned back from sales. If there is no film at a given department, the cost of running that department is ascribed to studio overhead. This affects the stockholders' dividends.

Attaching expenses to a film's budget can reach bizarre lengths. While I was working briefly at Twentieth Century-Fox in 1975, the studio's only successful releases were *Young Frankenstein* and *The Towering Inferno*. There were also plenty of less successful films: *11 Harrowhouse, S*P*Y*S, The Four Musketeers*, etc., and we were instructed to attach no expenses to them because they could never be earned back. Thus every long distance phone call, lunch, postage stamp, taxi ride, messenger service, or paper clip had "YF" or "TI" written beside it to signify that the expense was to be added to the distribution costs of that picture and not studio overhead. And it isn't always piddly stuff like phone calls. One Monday I arrived at the Fox office in Boston to find that, over the weekend, the place had been covered with ugly florescent lime green wall-to-wall carpeting. It was so garish it made you squint walking on it. Come mid-November and the first screening of *The Towering Inferno*, I understood why: the main set of the burning skyscraper in the film was outfitted in the same carpet. The studio had simply ordered extra and billed it to producer Irwin Allen's account.

Unlike a studio, independent producers need only rent what they need when they need it. They don't have to shoulder the weight of a whole film factory, so their budgets can be lower. Often they will seek the distribution facilities of a big film company, in which case the resultant expenses (and probably a lot more) will be billed to their earnings. If independent films are cheaper, you may ask, why aren't all movies independent movies? Because the studio films get preferential access to theatres, leverage in collecting ticket money, and clout for attracting stars and filmmakers. They have assets and equity. A studio film is more likely to get theatrical release than to go straight to video.

The brontosaurus survives because it takes up a lot of space, but it's a long way from its mouth to its tail and it costs a lot to keep it alive.

Studios have a way of covering up their mistakes the way doctors bury theirs. Columbia Pictures threw a junket in 1980 to publicize their upcoming slate: *The Blue Lagoon, The Competition, Used Cars*, and the studio's soon-to-start-shooting *Annie*. The press recognized Robert Zemeckis and Bob Gale, the makers of *Used Cars*, as innovative young filmmakers; they interviewed the cast (Brooke Shields and Christopher Atkins) and director (Randall Kleiser) of *The Blue Lagoon* as earnest craftsmen; and appreciated the people behind *The Competition*, about a piano recital contest, as dedicated, if self-absorbed. But it was Garrison True, the casting director of *Annie*, who made the assembled reporters gasp. In announcing that he would be scouring the country for a perky redhead to play Little Orphan Annie for the studio's $50 million musical, he handed out Little Orphan Annie dolls. They had curly red hair, a cute smile, Annie's distinctive red dress, and blue eyes. What's that, you say? Blue eyes? Harold Gray's adorable Depression-era comic strip character was famous for having tiny circles for eyes. No color. No pupils, even. The murmuring of the press as they discovered this gaffe was lost on True and his studio brethren, but to everyone else it was unmistakable: the people making *Annie* didn't have a clue what they were doing. In the end, the public agreed; it grossed $57.1 million, less than half of what it needed to just break even. Director John Huston was thoroughly out of his element making a lumbering musical, which wound up being little more than *Oliver* in drag. It was no secret that the man who'd made *The African Queen, The Asphalt Jungle* and *The Maltese Falcon* took *Annie* strictly for the payday, and it showed. He didn't even care when everybody and his brother-in-law, including producer Ray Stark, interfered with the production. Years later, Huston was quoted as saying, "They want it bad? We can make it bad. It'll cost more, but we can make it bad." And he did.

I was a guest on that fateful junket representing, not a Boston media outlet, but a television station in tiny Rhode Island, so I didn't complain when I was shown minimal courtesy by the studio's cadre of harried publicists. I understood their position and accepted mine. Instead, I used the trip as a chance to catch up with Los Angeles friends, one of whom was writer/director James Bridges, whose friendship I had secured by working with him and John Houseman on the Boston world premiere of *The Paper Chase*. Once my junket duties were over, Jim and I met in the coffee shop of the Beverly Hilton Hotel where Columbia had placed me. Midway through our breakfast, the entire Columbia Pictures publicity department entered and took a large table behind us. They smiled forgetfully at me, but then, one by one, they recognized Jim and grew defensively silent. Because, the year before, James Bridges had written and directed *The China Syndrome*, the picture that saved Columbia's financial ass and all their jobs.

Jim leaned forward. "Those people look familiar," he said. "Who are they?"

I leaned forward too. "They're the Columbia publicity department. They handled your picture last year."

"How did they treat you?" he asked.

"Okay," I said flatly.

"As bad as that?"

"Rhode Island is hardly a king-making state," I averred, quoting Gore Vidal.

"Nevertheless," Jim said, his warm eyes twinkling with mischief, "let's have some fun."

We stood up to go, and he embraced me with a smile as big as his Arkansas roots. Then he took my arm and led me over to the publicists who, by now, were passing their coffee through their noses. Jim spoke only to the Vice President.

"I hope you took good care of Nat this weekend," he said evenly. "He's an old friend of mine and treats our pictures fairly."

The Vice President blanched. "As a matter of fact, we were just about to start a follow-up. Are you okay with everything you got on the junket, Nat?"

"No problems," I said. "Jim and I just wanted to stop over and say hello."

Jim turned to me and winked. "Come on. I'll take you to the airport. Bye fellas."

When we cleared the door I begged off on the ride to the airport; I was moving to a friend's couch to stretch my LA stay to research a book. But Jim's gambit worked. When I got back to Rhode Island, my show's producer asked, with some concern, "Did everything go okay in LA?"

"Sure," I answered. "Why?"

"Because the Vice President of Publicity of Columbia Pictures has been calling twice a day to ask if you have everything you need and could he send more material if you don't?"

I laughed and told her the story, then reached into my bag and handed her the blue-eyed Little Orphan Annie doll.

"Eeyeeeew," she winced. "She has eyes. What for?"

"Damned if I know," I said, shaking my head, "and I'll be damned if they do, either."

The Critics

W E DON'T really have film *critics* in America any more, except in cineaste journals. We have film *reviewers*. A reviewer is to a critic what Splenda is to sugar. A *reviewer* gives his reactions to a film where a *critic* gives not only his or her reactions but a skillful analysis that places the work in its artistic context. Reviewers are more like consumer reporters, whereas critics write for the ages (and, okay, occasionally their navels). Some say that reviewers write about *movies* and critics write about *films*. I think it was cartoonist Johnny Hart who said, "A film is a movie that you don't quite understand." But *film critic* sounds less pretentious than *film reviewer* when, in fact, it may be more so.

Nobody likes critics. I was one for twenty years and I don't even like myself. All the wisecracks you've heard about them are true: "A critic is someone who enters the battlefield after the war is over and shoots the wounded" (Murray Kempton); "Critics are like eunuchs in a harem; they know how it's done, they've seen it done every day, but they're unable to do it themselves" (Brendan Behan); "It is not the critic who counts . . . The credit belongs to the man who is actually in the arena" (Theodore Roosevelt); and so forth. Yet despite people insisting that they are never swayed by critics, they always seem to know whether the notices have been good or bad, and they consider them when deciding what to see or not see, usually the latter.

It's said that everyone has two professions: whatever they really do for a living, plus being a film critic. Oddly enough, professional critics today have been rendered virtually irrelevant, not by movie company advertising departments, but by audiences. A kid on Twitter can get word out about a new movie before the end credits have finished rolling. Websites such as Ain't-It-Cool-News, Rotten Tomatoes, Dark Horizons, and other open-access blogs make legitimate critics irrelevant. And yet do audiences even care? Ask most people what they think of a movie and they'll say only, "I liked it" or "It sucked." They seldom elaborate and rarely pontificate. Think about it: the fate of a $200 million film has gone from a 3,000-word analyses composed thoughtfully in *The New Yorker* to a sputtered, misspelled, acronym-laced wisecrack from a teenager sitting in the back of a mall multiplex. It isn't critics whom studios should be making irrelevant, it's the Twittersphere.

Film companies spend ridiculous amounts of money buying ads to compensate for the power that they also insist critics and bloggers don't have. Then, when a film gets good reviews, they spend even more money buying ads that quote the reviews that they said they would ignore.

As for audiences, filmmakers are forced to cater to a combination of immediate gratification, minimal attention span, and lack of knowledge of history and the human condition. Films have always been cut and recut based on preview audience reaction, but now audiences have come to regard themselves as filmmakers and give detailed instructions on preview cards. If a scene happens to be about character and not plot, and the audience coughs impatiently, it gets recut. Test audiences evince little patience for the orderly laying of a foundation that will pay off later, but they will complain that the ending doesn't make sense because it wasn't prepared for. Subtlety is allowed as long as it's obvious. This encourages stereotyping in order to establish a character quickly rather than be gradually revealed through a series of interactions with other characters. Depth has become shallow.

I've already made my point that the film critic has one of the most tenuous jobs in journalism, but I haven't said exactly what a critic is. Harold Ross, who founded *The New Yorker*, used to say that anybody could be a film critic as long as he hated films. He told Nunnally Johnson, who wanted to be one, that the job "was only for old ladies and fairies," and Johnson was neither. When I was teaching "Writing Film Reviews and Criticism" in the graduate program at Boston University, I reminded my students that a review is a standard argumentative theme that starts with a premise and attempts to persuade the reader with supporting examples. Although modern reviews include just enough plot summary to illustrate the work without spoiling it, strictly speaking, a critic writes for those who have already seen the film and want to explore its nuances. It sounds cut-and-dried, and that's the trap, because it takes flair to keep a reader interested. "Above all," I stressed to my students, "the one thing a critic owes the public is consistency." I forbade use of the word *flick* unless one was writing about de-feathering chickens. I eschewed the first person on the philosophy that the critic doesn't have to say "I think" because the byline affirms it. I allowed that no opinion was too weird as long as it could be supported.[1]

As enjoyable and scattered as our seminars generally were, I demanded that the criticism itself be taken seriously. A critic, after all, publicly appraises somebody's multi-million dollar risk. To drive this home, I would ask each student, at the beginning of the semester, what grade he or she wanted to receive. Invariably the student chose an "A." Thereafter, I would work that student up to an "A" level, handing back papers two, three, or sometimes four times for rewrites, even if additional papers were assigned in the meantime. It was a lot of work for all of us, but those who stuck with it came out with samples worthy of tacking on their resumes. They learned the most important lesson of all: writing is rewriting.

Critics on deadline seldom have that opportunity. Frequently, one is writing his review in the back of a cab between the theatre and the office. Nowadays one can file online and save the taxi fare, but time remains the enemy of thoughtful analysis. To help them cover films more conveniently,

---

1   I also levied a fine of one dollar if anyone, including myself, mentioned either Pauline Kael or Rex Reed during class. The money went into a beer fund.

critics are given advance screenings. These are usually held in private projection rooms or closed theatres under the best conditions. That's if the film company is proud of the film. If not, the picture won't be screened and critics will be forced to catch the first public showing. You might ask, "What's wrong with seeing a film with the public? You might learn something." The surprising answer is that, quite often, an audience is tougher on a movie than the critics, and paying patrons have no hesitation yelling their displeasure at the screen while the critic is sitting among them taking notes.

Before a screening begins, critics will usually ask the press agent the running time. This is because critics like to set their internal clocks to better judge the pace of a work they're reviewing. It is considered bad form for critics to talk during a movie, to use any kind of lighting instrument (if you can't take notes in the dark, don't be a critic), to eat food, or to use a cell phone. In Boston, where all the critics got along well enough, we had a tradition in which, if someone had to leave the auditorium to go to the bathroom, when he returned, he would ask, "What did I miss?" Without hesitation we would all say, "the car chase." This was particularly appreciated during Ingmar Bergman movies.

It is strictly forbidden for a publicist to ask a critic what he or she thinks of a film before the review is published. Likewise, critics who provide advance copies of their reviews to publicists so they can be quoted in advertising are whores. For a different reason, critics never discuss reviews in advance; why risk a colleague swiping a good wisecrack? In New York and Los Angeles, the two-block rule applies. This means that those leaving a screening or premiere keep their mouths shut for at least two blocks in case anyone connected with it is walking near them.

Some critics, unfortunately, praise everything, which, of course, doesn't make them a critic, it makes them a whore (see above). They couch this by saying that they "try to find something positive to say" about every film. This endears them to the advertising department but makes them a laughing-stock among their peers. As if they care. The fact that some such critics may actually *like* dreck ought to be grounds for banishment. One critic I know wrote his reviews so he could be quoted in the newspaper ads, always finding positive phrases that could be lifted from his notices even when the rest of the review was a pan. But he also managed to have it both ways because, when he shortened his reviews to capsule length for the paper's weekend entertainment guide, he finally wrote what he honestly felt. Thus the opening day fudge would be sent to the filmmakers, who came to love him, while the locals would see his honest opinion by the second day.

Consistency is not the same as predictability. *The New Yorker's* Pauline Kael, for example, seemed to have a personal stake in the films of Brian De Palma, Robert Altman, and a handful of other directors. Her acolytes, who called themselves Kaelites (but were derisively called Paulettes by everyone else), followed her taste so closely that, when one of them ventured a different opinion, the event was described in terms reserved for a religious schism. For years it was said that no major publication would hire a critic who had not been anointed by Kael, so pervasive was her power. The fact that Kael was wrong on most of the major films of her early career—as Renata Adler pointed out in well-researched and scathing 1980 article in *The New York Review of Books*—made little difference to those who venerated her.

Thanks to their television exposure in the 1980s and 90s, Roger Ebert and Gene Siskel became a mixed blessing. Both were highly credentialed yet, on television, they and their thumbs cheapened themselves as scholars even as they increased their power as personalities. Fortunately, their hearts were in the right place and they tirelessly fought to bring attention to little-seen titles that might otherwise have been overlooked. Their one blind spot, and it was a running joke to everybody but them, was that, as devoted Chicagoans, they almost invariably boosted any film that was shot in Chicago, was made by anybody who came from Chicago, or, who knows, mentioned Chicago.

Even the filmmaking process itself has fallen victim to self-analysis. In the 1990s a slew of "how to" screenwriting books began appearing by such writers as John Truby, Linda Seger, Robert McKee, and Blake Snyder. These people analyzed classic movies and discovered that all of them had the same structure: X happened on page 30, Y happened on page 66, and so forth. They concluded that there is a formula for screen success and that successful movies had to hit the same beats at the same place. Remarkably, their thinking came to pervade filmmaking, forcing writers to adhere to the McKee-Truby-Seger imperative. As many a distinctive filmmaker has pointed out, the problem is not that writers read these books, it's that production executives do. What is not formulaic is the knowledge of human behavior that enables a writer, director, producer, or actor to create a distinctive work, or (ahem) a critic who has a rich enough background to wisely place that work within the context of society. Critics see more movies, even bad movies, than normal people and, unlike paying audiences, they have to watch them all the way through. They are not allowed to be naive, and they really do go into each movie hoping that it will be the greatest they have ever seen. There is no feeling in the world like being able to call attention to an ignored masterpiece or rescue a fumbled one from the oblivion of bad distribution. On the other hand, critics—and I confess to this—become outraged, even angered, when someone abuses the medium, insults the audience, or fails to use his own gifts.

So, technically, we don't need critics. But without them we'd have only ourselves to blame.

Servicing the Press

I F EVER there was a more vulgar term than *servicing the press* for providing the media with publicity material, I have yet to hear it. In the small town that was Boston in the early 1970s, I was tasked by the gentlemanly Paul Levi with doing just that to the city's four major newspapers, *The Boston Globe, The Boston Herald-Traveler, The Boston Record-American* and the *Boston Sunday Advertiser.* We also "serviced" local suburban papers, but that could be done by mail. The Paul A. Levi Company represented Disney, Paramount, National General Pictures, Cinema Center Films, American International Pictures, and Showcase Cinemas, the flagship chain of Sumner Redstone's rapidly expanding National Amusements, Inc. All were demanding as clients, but none was crazy like you hear in some of the stories.

We were a placement agency. We did not create the advertising and publicity campaigns for our clients, we implemented them. The process began on Tuesdays, which was press agent day at Boston's papers. That's when I fell in love with journalism and journalists. In addition to the reporters of whom I wrote in "Otto the Terrible," there were editors, assistants, and foot soldiers who made the visits memorable. Although the ritual annoyed my fellow publicists who had office work to do (as Mr. Levi did), I cherished it. First I would visit *The Boston Globe* whose Arts & Entertainment Editor was Gregory Mcdonald. Soft-spoken, bright, and with a wit so dry you could strike a match on it, Greg formed a firewall between his staff and the paper's advertising department, who would have liked nothing better than slant the

Globe's arts coverage to favor their bigger advertisers. Greg became a friend and later gained fame and awards for writing the *Fletch* mystery novels. But he never stopped being a journalist. George McKinnon had more or less taken over film reviewing duties from Marjory Adams by the time I started calling at the *Globe*. George readily admitted to hating animated films, which irked me as a representative of Disney, but at least he was honest about it. Kevin Kelly was the paper's theatre critic but, when theatre openings were slow (largely because he was so nasty that play producers avoided Boston if they could), he reviewed film. After Greg left the paper, a new editor named Carole Surkin took over and promptly banned press agent visits, not just for movies but for theatre, music, fine art, dance, and other disciplines. Her staff secretly hated this decree because it meant that they had to leave the building to find out what was going on rather than have it brought to them. This may have been Surkin's idea, but it had the opposite effect of greatly reducing the amount of information her writers could meet and the venues they could cover. This happened while I was publicity director for Sack Theatres, and, as one of the paper's major advertisers, I simply ignored her and walked into the building by the back entrance to do my job. This went on for two weeks until George McKinnon tracked me down in the hallway to warn me that Surkin had armed guards waiting for me if I showed up on her floor. This marked my disenchantment with the *Boston Globe* and, as far as I am concerned, the *Globe's* disengagement from the arts community.

Aside from that bump, the routine was the same for every press agent who made the rounds at every paper. Often we would be stacked up outside an editor's office. This was not an inconvenience for us as much as for the writing staff who would have us looking over their shoulders spying on who was getting coverage in the next day's paper if it wasn't our clients. Once inside the editor's sanctum, I would hand over my press materials with a proper flourish. Each folder, or presskit, contained photographs, cast and credits, and press releases tailored by me toward the local engagements of our clients' films. The trick was to get as many of these into print as possible, so they had to be interesting. The editors took what they needed and handed back the rest. We would chat about who was coming to town for interviews, whom to call for phone interviews, and what films were expected to be popular.

My second stop was the *Boston Herald-Traveler* whose arts editor and theatre critic was Samuel Hirsch. Sam was an imposing man; goatee, rich voice, and years of experience. But his biggest claim to fame was that he was the arch-enemy of Kevin Kelly, the *Boston Globe's* theatre critic. To prevent the feud from blowing back on the shows they were reviewing, press agents diplomatically sat Sam and Kevin at opposite ends of the same row on opening nights. What made the whole thing silly was that, despite Kevin's and Sam's positions, Boston's leading theatre critic was the elegant and highly respected Elliot Norton, who reviewed for the *Record-American*. If Sam was tied up editing, I would go to the next office and visit Alta Maloney. Alta was an oasis of compassion for press agents, even though she was no pushover. Besides, she kept a box of Cadbury's chocolate bars in her top right-hand desk drawer and would hand them out to those of us who had to miss lunch while waiting for Sam.

When Alta retired she was replaced by Don Cragin, who became a good friend. Donald H. Cragin was old-line Boston Yankee and never let anyone forget it. Worldly and smart, deeply cynical, and acid-tongued, he gave me my best writing lesson: put a piece of paper in the typewriter and don't stop until it's full. (Think about it.) Don had a habit of insulting people both to their face and behind their backs. It did not make him liked. But that's not what he wanted. "If people hate me," he once said, "at least I know how they stand." He could never accept the fact that I liked him. Perhaps it was because I like honesty.

Don taught me more about being a press agent than I wanted to know. Early on, he asked me to hand him my entire stash of publicity photos, which I naively did. He put them in his lap and started flipping through them, removing those he wanted to run, but then I saw that he was taking out second copies. "You already have that," I said.

"I know," he replied, and kept going in silence. After it was obvious that he was removing more photos than the paper could ever run, I asked him what the idea was. He said, "I'm keeping the best photos so we can run them, and I'm taking out the extras so nobody else can." This led to a discussion of competition between papers, a subject that went back to the newspaper wars of the 1890s. "Let me tell you a few things," Don said (kindly handing me back the extra photos). "Look." He put two pictures on his desk: a vertical head shot and a horizontal two-shot. "If you give people the vertical photo, all you'll get out of it is a one-column cut. But if you give them only horizontal photos, the layout people will have to give you a two-column cut. Which will look better on the tearsheet you send your client?"

With my stash of photos restored, I would go to the *Boston Record-American* and *Sunday Advertiser,* two tabloids that shared an old building on Devonshire Street in Boston's financial district. Its old fashioned City Room dominated one end of the third floor and its reporters' desks were scattered around the rest of the real estate in what looked like a random burst. This was before computers, so every desk had a manual typewriter with pica type, and some even had pneumatic tubes that would carry completed copy down to typeset if no copy boy was available (yes, they still had copy boys, only they were called messengers).

My main stop was Maureen Taylor, the Sunday editor who held sway over all she surveyed, which was considerable. A stocky woman with a beautiful face, pulled-back greyish hair, lively eyes, and a hearty smoker's laugh, Maureen didn't take crap from anybody. As a woman in journalism, she had endured her share of knocks from men until they found out how skillful she was at pulling a good story out of a sea of typing. She was a hot ticket away from the paper, too; she once told me that she had been getting a series of rude phone calls at home. Tired of the nightly bother, the next time the breather called, she told him, "Hold on, if this is going to be an obscene phone call, let me get a cigarette." The man hung up and never called back. She also reported a conversation she'd had with a female clerk who was famous for wearing color-coordinated outfits. "I guess it's hard to find underwear to match your scarves," Maureen had said sarcastically. When the woman answered, "Yes, it is, especially the plaid," Maureen almost passed her coffee through her nose.

On Maureen's staff were Barbara Burtoff, the food editor whose cheesecake recipe I still use and who remained a friend for years; Michael Janusonis;[1] and Fran Weil. Fran was a dynamo. Unfailingly cheerful, with a cutting wit as sharp as Maureen's, Fran was the paper's chief interviewer. Her need for interview copy was so great that I would set up phoners (phone interviews) as often as possible to fill her column space. I became such a pest to the film company publicity executives that I wound up going over their heads and calling filmmakers directly in their offices. What's surprising is that they answered. This is how I wound up having impromptu phone conversations with directors Don Siegel, William Friedkin, Mark Rydell (whose *Cinderella Liberty* both Fran and I made a personal campaign), and John Milius, among other heavyweights. Since I always sent out thank-you letters to reporters, and I would have to do this two or three times a week for Fran, I mimeographed a fill-in-the-blank form for those I sent her.

The *Record-American* was a conservative paper in a liberal town (we used to call it "Boston's alternative newspaper"). In a city shaken by forced busing, town-and-gown rivalry, and the anti-war movement, the "Rekkid" was distinctly out of place, yet served a purpose. But it also had a darker side. If they ran a photo of a black person, it would only be a one-column cut unless the black person was accused of a crime, in which case it could go two or three columns. The advertising department would keep track of how many lines a client bought in the course of a year and would allow them only half as much free publicity space as they had bought in lineage. They also allowed a fair amount of chicanery when it came to advertising billing rates.

---

1   When *Love Story* went into its third or fourth month at the local theatre, Michael ran a photo from the movie with the caption, "Ryan O'Neal bids goodbye to Ali MacGraw in the ever-popular *Love Story*. Miss MacGraw still expires five times daily and Sunday on the big screen." He caught hell for it, but it was a great caption.

My only connection with this was when I was handed a list and told to give free movie passes to certain people at the *Record*, including the editor. They used the passes as tips and for favors; we used them as influence.

The *Record* had five editions a day. The first was a pre-date, which meant that, for example, Wednesday's morning paper came out at three o'clock on Tuesday afternoon. The news was current, but it gave advertisers a two-day exposure instead of one. That was the stated reason. The reason that everybody whispered about, though, was that the pre-date edition carried the Mafia's illegal betting payoff number if you know where on the sports page to look for it. Once the Massachusetts State Lottery started in March of 1972, the afternoon *Record* was no longer needed and quickly disappeared.

A city as large as Boston had many other papers, weekly and suburban, of course, and I've mentioned them. But it was the daily papers that grabbed my attention and won my heart. By the time I left publicity to become a journalist, the *Herald-Traveler* had folded (the result of a seminal legal decision involving cross-ownership of media), and Hearst had killed the *Sunday Advertiser*, acquired the *Herald-Traveler*, and rolled it into the *Record-American* to create *The Boston Herald*. Looking for work, I hit the *Boston Herald* first. Tabloid or not, also-ran to the *Globe* or not, and right-wing or not, they were, to me, the only newspaper in Boston that knew how to be a newspaper. And their reporters remain, for me, the quintessence of their profession.

Gang Bangs

I EARLIER wrote of the tradition of press junkets. Now's the time to go into more detail. Nobody likes them, except that they work. How else can you plant celebrity interviews in a hundred newspapers, fifty TV stations, and twenty magazines over the course of one weekend, even if it drives the filmmakers crazy and sets journalists at each others' throats? It would make a great reality show except, being Hollywood, it isn't real.

Press junkets are as old as movie publicity. In the days of profligate studio spending, they would fly hoards of writers to LA, house them in plush digs, and sign the hotel bill in the dark. Old-timers still tell (lament?) tales of powerful columnists and preferred writers charging cases of liquor, suits, dresses, and spa services, all of it paid for by a willing (and *quid pro quo*-savvy) studio. The only reason they didn't charge gigolos or hookers to the room was that those were supplied out of the ranks of contract players.

The pecking order among press could be brutal. Columnist Radie Harris, who wrote for *The Hollywood Reporter* for fifty years, was as demanding as her better-known counterparts Louella Parsons, Hedda Hopper, and Walter Winchell. She had lost her leg to a childhood accident and got around on a cane, which she poked at anyone who got between her and her story. Elizabeth Taylor once referred to her—out of earshot, of course—as "goody one-shoe." Coral Browne, seeing her in London surrounded by her retinue, remarked, "Look at poor Radie Harris with the whole world at her foot." (Browne later played a Harris-like character in 1968's Tinseltown melodrama, *The Legend of Lylah Clare*.)

Those days are over. Now only engineered photo ops and guarded interview access remain. In other words, boring professionalism reigns supreme as celebrities hop from table to table or from camera to camera praying for new questions and pretending that the old ones are fresh.

"Boy, I hope you're better than the last group!" Steve Martin said, smiling at twenty journalists as he took a seat at a speaker's table festooned with recording devices. He started pocketing them. "So far I've gotten three tape recorders out of this." And then he did something nobody expected. He stopped making jokes and held a seminar on comedy (he was there to talk about *Three Amigos!*), starting with whether he needed material or was innately funny.

"I hate the thought of that," he said. "If you have something to make funny, then you always have a feeling of confidence. Only lately have I started to consciously think about how funny a nuance can be. It always sort of came out naturally before. There's no explanation of where something comes from. But I love having substance. And, by substance, I mean material, something funny to go for, or something to save you. Of course, when I started my act, the whole key to it was that I had nothing, that I just *pretended* like I was going over." At that early stage, Martin was known for coming on stage wearing a trick arrow through his head, making balloon animals, and saying the catch-phrase, "Well excuuuuuuuse me!" It stuck, although Martin admits it was a happy accident. "You can't predict that," he says. "You look like an idiot and you come out there and you do it ten times and everybody goes, 'aw, not this again.' You're always constantly thinking, 'is this too silly?' But silly's a funny word because that's what comedy is: being silly. A lot. It's like when Lorne Michaels would say to me, 'oh, don't be silly,' and I'd say, 'don't ever say that to a comedian!'"

Jackie Gleason, Tom Hanks, and Garry Marshall teamed up on a press conference for *Nothing in Common* in which Hanks played an advertising man forced to make peace with his emotionally distant and dying father, played by the emotionally distant Gleason. Hanks is one of the most likable actors around, and Marshall played an ingratiating ringmaster, but Gleason sent out vibes that he was only at the press confab for the money. He seemed impatient when he wasn't asked questions, and even more impatient when he was.

"Why did it take so long for you to find the lost episodes of *The Honeymooners*?" someone asked.

"They weren't lost," the Great One corrected sharply. "They were in my basement. The only thing it took them a long time to find was the money."

Feeling Gleason's attitude, the room turned gladly to Hanks. "In the movie you did this thing where you threw a pencil at the ceiling and made it stick," he was asked. "Can you do that for us now?"

The room's hanging ceiling tiles beckoned.

"Sure," Hanks chirped. "Anybody got a pencil?

The room fell silent. Hanks and Marshall exchanged grins.

"A whole room full of journalists," Hanks chided, "And not one person has a pencil?"

Marshall rose to the rescue. "Maybe you could throw up a tape recorder," he said.

***

"A movie costs what a movie costs," pronounced John Landis. "Period." The filmmaker had successfully flown *Kentucky Fried Movie* and *Animal House* below Hollywood's radar, then hit it big with *The Blues Brothers*. By the time of *An American Werewolf in London,* he was tired of being called a budget-buster.

"The economic thing becomes a sore point with me. *An American Werewolf in London* is a small movie because it only has six people in it and that's not that expensive to do. If you're gonna make *Ben-Hur* it's gonna cost a lot of money. A movie costs what a movie costs and economics should never enter into whether you like it or not. If you look at a painting, you're not gonna go, 'I dunno, Rauschenberg had a pretty good canvas there, a pretty good quality canvas, I can't like it as much. Is that oil or acrylic?' When you look at a sculpture you can't think about how much the bronze costs. It costs what it costs. It's the work you have to judge by itself.

"I think the press has a basic ignorance of the realities of film production," he continued. "Hollywood, for a while, did, too. I think Hollywood was really shocked all of a sudden to turn around and have film costs go up four hundred percent. *Animal House* made hundreds and hundreds of millions of dollars and it only cost two-point-six, so their profit margin is enormous, whereas in a *Blues Brothers*, if it made the same amount of money, they have to make more money to recoup 'cause it's more expensive. You forget that *The Wizard of Oz* didn't make money until 1955 when it sold to television. *The Maltese Falcon* was a failure economically. I don't think economics are the issue whether you like a movie or not. A classic case for me was *2001* which got some of the worst reviews I ever read, and that's a seminal motion picture. Pauline Kael called it 'colossally unimaginative.' What movie was she watching?"

Producers catch a lot of grief. Some of them deserve it. "This is the producer," John Ford supposedly said when one appeared on his set. "Take a good look at him because it's the last time you'll be seeing him here." He also reported, according to his chronicler, Peter Bogdanovich, "There are three things you can point at—let me get the billing right—the producer, the privy, and the French pastry."

Joseph L. Mankiewicz, who was a producer at MGM before moving to Fox where he was allowed to write and direct as well, recalled that MGM's Louis B. Mayer once advised him to be a producer before he became a director, adding that "you have to crawl before you can walk." "Which struck me," recalled Mankiewicz, "as about the best description of a producer as I ever heard." Further on that subject, Mankiewicz repeated his instructive parable, "What does a producer do?" about a writer, a director and a producer scouting locations who find themselves lost in the Mojave Desert. At one point they decide to split up and search for a return route, each utilizing his individual talent to save the others. Immediately the writer comes upon a rock. Pushing it aside, he discovers an enormous can of tomato juice that has been chilled by being shielded from the sun.

"With his last bit of strength, he holds it up and says, 'I, the writer, have found the substance and the sustenance whereby we can exist. Come quickly!' The other two rush over.

"The director takes out his pocket knife, with his last remaining strength, and says, 'I, the director, will now open the can of tomato juice so that we can all drink from it and go on.' As the director is about to raise the tin to his mouth the producer says, 'Stop! First, I, the producer, must piss in it.'"

❦

Saul Zaentz was a producer that Mankiewicz would have adored because he let his directors make their movies. In doing so, he earned Oscars for *One Flew Over the Cuckoo's Nest* and *Amadeus,* both directed by Miloš Forman. "I don't think anyone understands what a producer does," he said at the time he was shepherding Ralph Bakshi's animated *The Lord of the Rings* to completion in 1978. "There are six or eight different kinds of producers, but there are also six or eight different kinds of directors. Some will go ahead and just direct anything, some will direct certain kinds of films, and some who are really, really good will bring a vision to it. Those are *real* directors. They may wind up losing everything, but there's also more reward. Independent productions have the most freedom. Studios only want the budget. Is it harder? Well, you always find independents managing to scrape together cash here or there to make pictures. Some pictures are good, some are really bad, whether they're made by independents or big companies. But it's still that vision that somebody has to start with."

❧

"Here's the difference between a producer and a director," said Irwin Winkler, who was one of the first before becoming one of the second. "It's all a matter of who has the power to control the budget. All during pre-production, the producer holds a gun on the director. Casting, sets, costumes, script, crew—they're all things that the producer makes sure the director pays attention to. Then, on the first day of production, the producer loses control. He hands the gun to the director, helps him aim it his head, and lets him keep it there until the film has wrapped."

❧

Occasionally, a press junket can get out of hand. Veterans still talk of the one that Orion Pictures threw for *Back to School*, a comedy about a rich but obnoxious businessman played by Rodney Dangerfield who decides to return for the education that his success prevented him from getting when he was young. Like *Caddyshack* and *Easy Money*, the film was just a life support system for Dangerfield's jokes. The junket, however, turned into a skiing trip for Dangerfield who would repeatedly disappear to the bathroom between tables and return with the sniffles. His interviews became incoherent and abusive. Afterward, several critics reported receiving phone calls from Orion begging them not to use the star's coked-up comments.

On the 1979 press junket for *Apocalypse Now*, on which the fortunes of both United Artists and Francis Ford Coppola were hanging, the national press was so baffled by the film and so hung up on star Marlon Brando's weight that they forgot to compliment Coppola on the brilliance of his achievement. Finally Coppola took the microphone and told the UA representatives standing at the back of the Warwick Hotel ballroom, "Guys, you better get me out of here." This turned the tide, and some of the younger reporters managed to break through to tell him how much the work was appreciated. In fact, when the main event was over, a number of them made their way to the front of the room and engaged Coppola in a dialogue about the future of the industry, during which the filmmaker described the digital revolution with frightening prescience.

Press junkets have today become mechanized. The publicists running them are no longer the tub-thumping showmen of the past, they are corporate image makers who demand that journalists sign agreements giving quote approval, name-and-likeness acknowledgments, and not to use the quotes in any story but the one they recorded them for. Access sometimes depends on whether the publication will guarantee a cover story and, in some cases, whether the writer is "acceptable." This is, in part, a reaction to the prevalence of stalkerazzi who hound celebrities and foment conflict in order to sell photos and stories. But it has also made it harder for legitimate coverage of the only art form to have been created in the twentieth century, even if its soul was stolen in the twenty-first.

Byline

THE THREAD running through all these stories has been the utter panic over how important everything seemed at the time but how little it all matters now. Deadlines? Movie Stars? Reviews? Press Tours? When time doesn't venerate the past, it dims it, especially for a commodity as ephemeral as entertainment. What makes the performing arts unique as a commercial endeavor is that audiences pay for them in advance, often in cash; they take away only the experience of having seen a show; and they can't get their money back if they didn't enjoy it. This is what made movies so attractive to the founding moguls, all of whom came from a mercantile background where the customer was always right and you always took advantage of them. In movies, theatre, dance, opera, cabaret, and other live venues, the River Styx is the door where they tear the tickets.

If possible, Hollywood treats itself worse than it treats the public. The only thing older than yesterday's movie is yesterday's movie maker. Films that dominate the box office one weekend turn up as a streaming freebie a month later. Names that drew crowds ten, twenty, thirty years ago become the answer to today's trivia questions. The average tenure of a studio executive is three years, and the average time it takes to get a movie made is five years; do the math and you see that the person responsible for making the right choice is seldom the one to win plaudits for it. Only the blame.

Most stars fade faster than an echo. It's a safe bet that nobody over forty watching an Oscar telecast can recognize any presenter under thirty. Feuds, scandals, innovations, and other events that once dominated the headlines now assume a sweet nostalgia. The only things that can be counted on to be with us forever are death, taxes, and *Star Trek* reruns.

Of all the people I met as a publicist, later as a critic, and finally as a producer, I keep in touch with perhaps a dozen. Interviewing someone or handling them on press tour does not constitute a friendship; at best it's only a passing acquaintanceship. When I set about writing and producing, I summoned the advice I'd gleaned from interview sessions with Robert Altman, William Friedkin, Paul Mazursky, Arthur Penn, Mark Rydell, Martin Ritt, James Bridges, Jack Larson, John Schlesinger, Norman Jewison, Eleanor Perry, Dustin Hoffman, Dom DeLuise, Leonard Nimoy, John de Lancie, John Milius, and the innumerable others I'd queried over the years. Talk about great teachers.

I apologize if, at various times in the preceding narrative, it was hard to know whether I was telling the story as a publicist or as a critic. To tell the truth, there were times I couldn't remember either. For example, the first time I met Gene Wilder, I was a junior publicist bringing him around town for *Willie Wonka and the Chocolate Factory*. The next time we met, I was a reporter questioning him and Dom DeLuise about *The World's Greatest Lover*. The third time, I was a producer interviewing him and his wife, Gilda Radner, about *The Woman in Red*. Good luck keeping those straight. Even more complicated was my friendship with Dom DeLuise who kept telling people that he and I had first met on a press junket for *Hot Stuff* on the Queen Mary in Long Beach, California. I've been in Long Beach, I've been on the Queen Mary (which is dry docked there), I've seen *Hot Stuff*, and I'd met Dom, but not all at the same time. But he was so sure of it that I went along with it. (If you're wondering what his advice was to me as a director, it was to always have protein such as turkey cold cuts for the actors to nibble in the afternoon when their energy flags.)

I now see my media meanderings as symbolic of the allure of entertainment itself. The reality of show business is to relieve the public of the burden of reality. Joseph L. Mankiewicz once said the origin of theatre was a caveman who passed the time between dinner and bedtime by sticking a feather up his ass and making like a chicken. The caveman got big laughs and kept doing it until his audience grew tired of his limited material. Watching reality shows on TV today, I'm not altogether sure we've come that far from prehistoric times, except, with reality TV, it's hard to tell who's the caveman and who's the feather.

But I sure wouldn't want to be the feather.

One last story that describes why I wrote this book. My appointment schedule for April 1, 1986 shows that I am to be at the Ritz-Carlton Cafe at the corner of Arlington and Newbury Streets in Back Bay, Boston at 3 PM to do an interview. It is not an April Fool's joke. The Ritz Cafe requires tie and jacket, and the 3 PM time slot means that I will not be enjoying lunch there. But I accept because the people with whom I am to have coffee and to interview are Hume Cronyn and Jessica Tandy.

The Cronyns had opened a few nights earlier in a play called *The Petition* about a staid British couple whose marriage is shaken when the wife signs an anti-nuclear appeal without consulting her husband. It was a two-hander written by Brian Clark and directed by Peter Hall, and it owed its production to Cronyn's wise manipulation of agent Sam Cohn, producer Robert Whitehead, and his own wife, who was looking for a follow-up to the couple's wildly successful *Gin Game* of eight years earlier.

"I thought it was a play of quality," Tandy began. "I thought it was about something, just for starters. I thought it was a brave play, and there aren't too many of those around."

I couldn't look away from this lady. Her eyes sparked, her voice was resolute, her poise was both relaxed and commanding, and yet there was nothing rehearsed about her. Similarly, Cronyn, though slumped in his chair (as opposed to the stiff-backed martinet he played on stage), exuded complete comfort without a dram of the superiority to which his credits and stardom entitled him.

They say that every actor should find a secret within each character that he plays and use it for resonance. Tandy and Cronyn were so comfortable in their skins that they didn't need secrets. In fact, I was the one who had the secret: the *Herald* was a staunchly blue collar newspaper and the only reason we were covering an elite stage play like *The Petition* was that the Cronyns had appeared in the hit movie *Cocoon* the year before.

"You don't see many stories about romance between people who are older than middle age," I began.

"It hasn't been discussed an awful lot," Tandy agreed, then deflected my question by adding, ". . . that and the nuclear issue."

"We lived through the McCarthy era," Cronyn jumped in, picking up on his wife's cue to talk about controversy rather than sex. "I was Vice President of the Screen Actor's Guild when Reagan was President of it," he offered, his set jaw making the connection between Reagan and the Red Scare. "I was blacklisted for a time, but I don't think it could get like that again unless— well, let's not talk about it."

What he delighted in talking about, though, was the filmmaker they'd both worked with at different times: she for *The Birds* and he for *Lifeboat* and *Shadow of a Doubt*.

"Hitchcock was a wonderful director," Cronyn began.

"He was certainly a genius with a camera," Tandy agreed. "He was a very good caster and he always got some pretty good actors. He knew what he wanted."

"After I acted for him, he let me do treatments for two films (*Rope* and *Under Capricorn*)," Cronyn continued, leaning forward. "Boy, what an education! But he had a habit which baffled me. He would be discussing a script. We would get into a passionate discussion and then Hitch would lean back and say, 'Do you know the story of the farmer's daughter and the traveling salesman . . . ?' He would keep doing this. It finally got to me—I didn't know him well then—and I said, 'Mr. Hitchcock, why do you do that? Every time we get going, you stop.' And he said, 'We're pressing. You'll never get it if you press.' And I realized he was right; you can't force a scene. It has to flow."

The waiter cleared the table of our empty cups. Cronyn used his hands to smooth the tablecloth, and his fingernail to sketch a pie shape on its soft surface.

"The other thing he taught me was this: we were sitting at a table and he drew a picture like this on a piece of paper. He said, 'If we're both trying to go in like this and pull the piece of the pie out, what would happen if we both went in from the other side?' I was confused by this and said, 'Do you mean that, if it's day, you shoot at night?' 'No,' Hitch said, 'it means that if you're playing the devil, look like the angel, and if you're playing the angel, look like the devil.'"

As Cronyn and I kept talking about Hitchcock, Tandy looked at her watch and announced that she had to leave for another appointment. Whether she really did or was just looking for an excuse to leave made me ask whether they ever took their stage characters home with them.

"No," both said simultaneously. Then Cronyn added, throwing his wife a loving smile, "I wouldn't attempt this play with anybody else, even if I could find somebody better."

Tandy returned his smile, then looked at me and whispered, "Just write down that I made no reply."

With that, she was gone.

And so am I.

Nat Segaloff Biography

Nat Segaloff always wanted to write and produce, but it took him several careers before he learned how to get paid for it. He was a journalist for *The Boston Herald* covering the motion picture business, but has also variously been a studio publicist (Fox, UA, Columbia), college teacher (Boston University, Boston College), on-air TV talent (Group W), entertainment critic (CBS radio) and author (fourteen books including *Arthur Penn: American Director* and *Hurricane Billy: The Stormy Life and Films of William Friedkin*). He has contributed career monographs on screenwriters Stirling Silliphant, Walon Green, Paul Mazursky and John Milius to the University of California Press's acclaimed *Backstory* series. His writing has appeared in such varied periodicals as *Film Comment, Written By, International Documentary, Animation Magazine, The Christian Science Monitor, Time Out* (US), *MacWorld,* and *American Movie Classics Magazine.* He was senior reviewer for AudiobookCafe.com. and now writes for the NPR word/game show, "Says You!" after appearing on it several times as a guest panelist.

As a TV writer-producer, Segaloff helped perfect the format and create episodes for A&E's flagship *Biography* series. His distinctive productions include *John Belushi: Funny You Should Ask; Shari Lewis & Lamb Chop; Larry King: Talk of Fame; Darryl F. Zanuck: Twentieth Century-Filmmaker* and *Stan Lee: The ComiX-MAN!* He wrote and co-produced the *Rock 'n' Roll Moments* music documentaries for The Learning Channel/Malcolm Leo Productions, and has written and/or produced programming for New World, Disney,

Turner and USA Networks. He is co-creator/co-producer of *Judgment Day* with Grosso-Jacobson Communications Corp. for HBO.

His extraterrestrial endeavors include the cheeky sequel to the Orson Welles *Invasion From Mars* radio hoax, *When Welles Collide*, which featured a *Star Trek* cast. It was produced by L.A. Theatre Works and has become a Halloween tradition on National Public Radio. In 1996 he formed the multi-media production company Alien Voices® with aActors John de Lancie and Leonard Nimoy and produced five best-selling, fully dramatized audio plays for Simon & Schuster: *The Time Machine, Journey to the Center of the Earth, The Lost World, The Invisible Man* and *The First Men in the Moon*, all of which feature *Star Trek* casts. Additionally, his teleplay for *The First Men in the Moon* was the first-ever TV/Internet simulcast and was presented live by The Sci-Fi Channel. He has written narrative concerts for the Los Angeles Philharmonic, celebrity events, is a script consultant, and was a contributing writer to *Moving Pictures* magazine.

Nat is the co-author of *The Waldorf Conference*, a comedy-drama about the secret meeting of studio moguls that began the Hollywood Blacklist. *The Waldorf Conference* had its all-star world premiere at L.A. Theatre Works. and was acquired for production by Warner Bros. Television. He produced a subsequent production to benefit the Hollywood ACLU and the Writers Guild Foundation, and has also produced such other celebrity events as a public reading of censored books and a recreation of the classic anti-HUAC broadcast, "Hollywood Fights Back."

Nat was staff producer for The Africa Channel, wrote and co-directed the dramatic short, *Devil's Run* (based on Tolstoy's "How Much Land Does a Man Need"). For BearManor Media he has written *Final Cuts: The Last Films of 50 Great Directors, Mr. Huston/Mr. North: Life, Death, and Making John Huston's Last Movie*, and expanded his Stirling Silliphant *Backstory* essay into the full-length biography *Stirling Silliphant: The Fingers of God*. His forthcoming book is the biography of famed speculative fiction writer Harlan Ellison. He also writes showbiz fiction for Nikki Finke's celebrated HollywoodDementia.com website.

Nat lives in Los Angeles and really tries to return phone calls.

Index